Operation Yellow Star

Black Thursday

TWO BOOKS BY

MAURICE RAJSFUS

Operation Yellow Star

TRANSLATED BY

Phyllis Aronoff and Mike Mitchell

Black Thursday

THE ROUNDUP OF JULY 16, 1942

TRANSLATED BY

Phyllis Aronoff

DoppelHouse Press • Los Angeles

TWO BOOKS BY
Maurice Rajsfus

Operation Yellow Star
Translated by Phyllis Aronoff and Mike Mitchell

Black Thursday, The Roundup of July 16, 1942
Translated by Phyllis Aronoff
Copyright DoppelHouse Press 2017

All translations of primary and secondary material, unless otherwise noted, are by the translators. Author's Preface and Note translated by Phyllis Aronoff.
Interview withMaurice Rajsfus translated by Isabelle Sellès.

Opération Étoile Jaune suivi de Jeudi Noir
Copyright LE CHERCHE MIDI EDITEUR

DESIGNED BY Curt Carpenter
PRINTED IN THE UNITED STATES

Publisher's Cataloging-in-Publication data
NAMES: Rajsfus, Maurice, 1928–, author. | Aronoff, Phyllis, 1945–, translator. | Mitchell, Mike, translator.
TITLE: Operation yellow star and black Thursday : the roundup of July 16, 1942 / by Maurice Rajsfus; translated by Phyllis Aronoff and Mike Mitchell.
DESCRIPTION: Includes bibliographical references | Los Angeles, CA: Dopplehouse Press, 2017.
IDENTIFIERS: ISBN 978-0- 9970034-9- 9 (pbk.) | 978-0- 9978184-0-6 (Hardcover) 978-0- 9978184-1- 3 (ebook) | LCCN 2016958418
SUBJECTS: LCSH Rajsfus, Maurice, 1928– | Jews-- Persecutions-- France. | Holocaust, Jewish (1939–1945)-- France-- Personal narratives. | Jewish children-- France-- Biography. | France-- Ethnic relations. | France-- History-- German occupation, 1940–1945.
BISAC BIOGRAPHY & AUTOBIOGRAPHY / Social Activists
HISTORY / Holocaust | HISTORY / Europe / France | HISTORY / Jewish
CLASSIFICATION: LCC DS135.F83 R36 2017 | DDC 940.53/1503924

 DoppelHouse Press
LOS ANGELES, CALIFORNIA

Contents

BLACK THURSDAY | THE ROUNDUP OF JULY 16, 1942

*The worst
is never sure,
but it is always
possible...*

Author's Preface to the English Edition

THE YELLOW STAR AND THE RED LANYARD

A S A SURVIVOR of the racial hatred unleashed upon occupied Europe by the troops of Nazi Germany in the late spring of 1940, I long hoped there would be a publisher in that country, now a democratic nation, that would inform young Germans of the results of the Nuremberg race laws decreed by Adolf Hitler in 1935. Of course, I was not expecting a German publisher of the twenty-first century to express regret for the genocide committed against the Jews during World War II, but publishing the book would have sent a message: "Never again such horrors in the name of the German people." That did not happen. What a shame!

I remember in the late 1990s accompanying various groups of German students visiting the camp at Drancy, where the Jews who had been rounded up in France were taken before being transported to the death camps. I always pointed out to them that a person didn't have to be German in those times to behave like a Nazi.

I can only rejoice that my historical research is being recognized by an American publisher. I see this as symbolic in that country where, in 1942, Black people were still victims of racial segregation, and thousands of Japanese families who had lived there for many years were interned in concentration camps following the outbreak of war between the U.S. and Japan. Quite clearly, there is no comparison with Nazi Germany, but the existence of such racist and xenophobic measures in that indisputable democracy during the presidency of Franklin Roosevelt casts doubt on the quality of American democracy.

***

Some seventy-five years ago, on May 29, 1942, a Nazi ordinance made it obligatory for Jews six years of age and older in the Occupied Zone of France to wear a yellow star prominently displayed on their chest. This racial violence was carried out by French police officers who were not inclined to question the orders of the occupation authorities. It should be noted that the tens of thousands of French policemen who sadly distinguished themselves by their zeal in acting as reinforcements for the Gestapo were never judged for their participation in that shameful policy of branding that harked back to the anti-Jewish hatred of the Middle Ages. How can one forget that, a few weeks later, these same policemen would be responsible for carrying out the roundups that would fill the extermination camps of eastern Europe?

After two years of German occupation punctuated with xenophobic and racial laws and numerous prohibitions, the yellow star made it possible, finally, to identify potential victims for a hate-filled police force that was always ready to hunt down pariahs. There would never be a trial of the French police institution, although it was faithful to the orders of the Nazi authorities. The Paris police, in particular, who were solely responsible for the roundups of May 14 and August 20, 1941, and July 16, 1942 (known as the Vél d'Hiv roundup), those carried out in September, October and November 1942 of Greek, Hungarian and Romanian nationals, who had until then been spared, and a massive roundup on February 10, 1943. There were also many smaller-scale police operations. These inhuman bullies would be decorated with the Fourragère Rouge, the Red Lanyard (a collective Legion of Honor), by General de Gaulle on October 14, 1944, after the liberation of France.

Now that this book is being published in the United States, it should serve as a challenge to those citizens whose prejudices against Blacks and Latinos are still cause for concern. History tells us that while genocides have not been rare, the "destruction of the European Jews," to use the American historian Raul Hilberg's words, represented an attempt to carry out the industrial elimination of an entire, purportedly ethnic, human group. This occurred in the face of a certain indifference on the part of the people of the countries concerned. To allow it to be forgotten would

xii

be an insult to the victims of this tragic past.

The French are committed to the Declaration of the Rights of Man of August 26, 1789: "Men are born and remain free and equal in rights. Social distinctions may be founded only upon the general good." This is different from the United States Declaration of Independence, July 4, 1776, which shows no interest in the situation of the American Indians or the Black slaves on the cotton plantations. The same omission is apparent in the Bill of Rights of December 1791. Furthermore, the second amendment recognizes the right of every citizen "to keep and bear arms," while expressing no concern for oppressed minorities.

The fact remains that the United States, along with the other countries of the Free World, voted in favor of the Universal Declaration of Human Rights in the United Nations General Assembly on December 10, 1948. Articles 3 and 4 of the Declaration state: "Everyone has the right to life, liberty and security of person" and "No one shall be held in slavery or servitude; slavery and the slave trade shall be prohibited in all their forms." This seems perfectly natural today, yet many countries fail to respect this fundamental text even though they are members of the United Nations.

While we must make sure that the abominations described in this book are never again perpetrated against the same victims, we must also remain vigilant with regard to the treatment of other groups of people while our democracies look on in embarrassed or shamed silence. As Berthold Brecht warned at the end of World War II, "Though the bastard is dead, the bitch that bore him is again in heat." These words are still true today, at a time when the enemies of human rights are once more gaining ground.

Note

Operation Yellow Star, conducted by the French police, did not begin on June 7, 1942, with the application of the recent 8th Nazi ordinance of May 29, 1942. The founding act unquestionably goes back two years to the conditions of the armistice signed on June 22, 1940, and in particular to Article 3, which states:

> In the occupied parts of France, the German Reich exercises all rights of an occupying power. The French Government obligates itself to support, with every means, the regulations resulting from the exercise of these rights and to carry them out with the aid of the French administration.
>
> All French authorities and officials of the occupied territory, therefore, are to be promptly informed by the French Government to comply with the regulations of the German military commanders and to cooperate with them in a correct manner. . . .[1]

This text is vague enough to support the strictest interpretation. However, there is no mention of making the French law enforcement authorities (police, gendarmerie, customs) part of the repressive apparatus for the ordinances of the German military authorities. Yet Article 3 would be applied indiscriminately by the Vichy administration, particularly by the police, against "Communist machinations" and then against

---

1. *Franco-German Armistice: June 25, 1940,* Yale Law School, the Avalon Project: Documents in Law, History and Diplomacy, http://avalon.law.yale.edu/wwii/frgearm.asp, consulted Nov. 14, 2015. All further quotations from the armistice agreement are based on this source. [PA]

Freemasons and Gaullists, all starting in the summer of 1940, before the Germans required it. The police in fact continued to enforce the anti-Communist laws and decrees that had been passed by the governments of Édouard Daladier and Paul Reynaud between September 1939 and May 1940. Then came the persecution of Jews, which was also not mentioned in Article 3 of the armistice agreement. However, the following words from Article 4 on the disarmament of the French armed forces should be noted: "Excepted are only those units which are necessary for maintenance of domestic order. Germany and Italy will fix their strength [numbers and weaponry]." While the police and gendarmerie are not explicitly named in this article, their participation is suggested, and General Huntziger [chief negotiator for the French], who signed the armistice agreement, saw nothing objectionable in it.

It is certain that the French law enforcement authorities immediately made efforts to apply Article 19 of the armistice agreement and did so extremely effectively: "The French Government is obliged to surrender upon demand all Germans named by the German Government in France as well as those in French possessions, colonies, protectorate territories, and mandates."

Operation Yellow Star

By Maurice Rajsfus

TRANSLATED BY

Phyllis Aronoff and Mike Mitchell

1

Honor and Discipline

O N JUNE 10, 1940, while the French government is preparing to evacuate Paris for Tours before going on to Bordeaux, Minister of the Interior Georges Mandel meets with the prefect of police, Roger Langeron, and gives him his final instructions, as it is only a matter of days until the Germans will enter Paris. The minister's words are clear: "You will fulfill the mission the government has given to you and that I communicated to you officially a few days ago at the Paris city council. Along with the prefect of the Seine, you will represent the government and France in dealing with the invader. There's no point saying more to you about it. I know you will carry out this difficult task."[1] On the same day, June 10, Roger Langeron notes in his logbook: "I visited the Republican Guard and the Mobile Reserve. I announced to the colonels that whatever happens, the Republican Guard will not leave the capital. It will work closely, as always, with the Paris police. The mood of these men is marvelous."[2]

On June 12, 1940, at the daily conference of General Hering, the military governor of Paris, important information arrives: by order of France's commander-in-chief, General Weygand, Paris has been declared an open city. Roger Langeron telephones Georges Mandel in Tours and gives him his guarantee that there will be no incidents in the capital.[3] He assures the fleeing government that he is in full control of the forces of

---

1. As reported by Roger Langeron in his memoir, *Paris, juin 40* (Paris: Flammarion, 1946), p. 11.
2. Ibid., p. 14.
3. Ibid., p. 25.

law and order. That evening, after visiting the police stations of Paris, he hosts a thousand inspectors, police officers and section heads at the prefecture of police to present the government's instructions, their spirit and their purpose. He explains: "The police have received orders to remain here so as to ensure the protection of the population and the tranquility of Paris, and, especially in the early days, to prevent individual incidents that would surely entail reprisals by the enemy, as well as to prevent looting of houses that have been abandoned and entrusted to our care."[4]

It is quite clear that this narrative, which was written after the war, was intended to show the integrity of the Paris police and its commitment to republican ideals. Prefect Langeron had a strong feeling that he was being listened to as attentively as in the past when he was setting up an effective service to maintain order during a high-risk demonstration. Having been prefect of police since March 1934, Langeron was well acquainted with the "Grande Maison" [Big House], as the police called the prefecture, and he stated, "The whole police force of Paris was there, with its strong conscience and sense of duty. We bid each other farewell with cries of 'Vive la France!'"[5]

The morning of June 13, 1940, Langeron posts two proclamations, the first one addressed to the population, stating: "In the grave situation that prevails in Paris, the prefecture of police continues to carry out its mission. It must ensure security and order in the capital. We will fulfill this duty to the utmost. Parisians, I am counting on you, as always, to support me in this task. Count on me."[6] The other proclamation, addressed to the entire hierarchy of law enforcement authorities, is written in similar terms.

On the eve of the arrival of German troops in Paris, Langeron notes that the administrators and officers in almost all the units of the prefecture have remained on duty, and he comments, "At this time when everything in the country seems to be collapsing, the Maison, as the Paris police call it, is more solid than ever. Its twenty-five thousand chiefs and officers are standing together around their leader . . . . How I admire them for the strength they give the country and the solid, unshakable backbone they provide in every neighborhood, serving a disoriented population that will certainly regain its confidence through their devotion to duty."[7]

Still on June 13, in the afternoon, a telephone conversation takes place between Langeron and Georges Mandel, the minister of the interior, in which Langeron reassures Mandel by confirming that there have not

4. Ibid., pp. 27–28.
5. Ibid.
6 Ibid., p. 29.
7. Ibid., p. 31.

been any incidents in Paris,[8] and concludes, "The police have never worked with such energy, cohesion and dynamism . . . . I am answering for my policing services as well as my intelligence services."[9]

On Friday, June 14, at dawn, the German troops enter Paris. At 11 a.m., Langeron is summoned to the Hôtel de Crillon by a German general. Their dialogue is brief. Langeron is asked to guarantee that order will be maintained in Paris. He agrees—he has no choice. In the afternoon, he confers with Charles Villey, prefect of the Seine: "We are taking certain measures. We are not hiding from each other our concern at seeing that the invaders are feigning respect for the conventions . . . . I would add that the Gestapo will soon come, and it will change the atmosphere."[10] In the evening, disregarding the police hierarchy, the German authorities summon the director of intelligence services.

On June 15, a police officer from the Gestapo goes to the prefecture of police to demand the police files, which Langeron had sent to Montauban when war was declared. On June 16, Langeron is very bold, devising a plan about which nothing more is ever heard. "I am developing a plan that is more ambitious than the preceding ones: the organization of an intelligence service that will work among the Germans and keep me informed about what happens there. There will be no lack of volunteers for this risky task in my departments. But it involves recruiting and holding on to well-placed informants. That is no small thing. We will start tomorrow. Those around me are very excited about this plan."[11]

On June 17, Pétain broadcasts his famous message on the radio: "I say to you today that the fighting must stop." Langeron immediately drafts an agenda for the various sections of the prefecture of police. The fact that the leader of the government of France has capitulated does not mean that public order will have to suffer. "In these grave circumstances, the Paris police have remained on duty in accordance with their orders. They have maintained, and are continuing to maintain, order and security in the capital. Order must be absolute, security must be total: this is your first mission. Administrators and officers, whatever your rank, you must, like myself, devote everything you have to it. You must be constantly vigilant. You must be tireless. Your firm attitude and strict discipline must reinforce your moral authority . . . . I know your motto: Honor and

8. On the same day, during a meeting of the council of ministers, General Weygand had stated that the Communists had taken power and Communist Party leader Maurice Thorez was in Paris at the Élysée Palace, the official residence of the president of France.
9. Langeron, p. 36.
10. Ibid., p. 48
11. Ibid., p. 66.

Discipline. I am counting on you!"[12] This is posted on the walls of the prefecture of police on June 18.

Also on June 18, 1940, Langeron states that he has heard General de Gaulle's appeal broadcast from London. He is careful not to speak of it to those around him, but many visitors come to his office and voice their "unanimous opinions as to the greatness of that action."[13] The armistice agreement is signed on June 22 at the crossroads at Rethondes, and its provisions are made known to the prefecture of police that evening.

On June 23, 1940, Langeron protests the arrest of several police chiefs by the German authorities. He tells the representative of the head of the Gestapo, a man named Turner: "I have promised full assistance and protection to the twenty-five thousand men who are here in Paris to protect the population and to maintain a calm that is also in your interest. . . . If my chiefs had done something wrong, we could discuss it. But they have done nothing. . . . If you do not turn these innocent men over to me, I will no longer have the moral authority required to command the others. I cannot see myself remaining their leader after allowing seven of them to be deported!" That very evening, Langeron is replaced for the interim by the director of the municipal police, a decision he says is "inconsistent with the principles of the armistice agreement."[14]

On July 9, the ambassador Léon Noël, Pétain's delegate-general to the officials of the Occupation, asks Langeron to return to his role as prefect of police, but Langeron refuses. Summoned by Turner of the Gestapo, he is ordered to resume his position. On July 13, again summoned to Gestapo headquarters, he is reinstated as prefect of police, but he interprets his return as tangible proof that it is possible to resist the Germans even though "they are quite prepared not to respect the clauses of the armistice agreement, never mind people's rights."[15]

On July 24, after a meeting with Boemelburg, who commands the Gestapo in Paris, Langeron notes: "The Gestapo is now solidly established in Paris. I must endeavor to watch them closely."[16] On August 8, he writes: "The prefecture of police has arrested four vendors of *Le Pilori* [a virulently anti-Semitic extreme-right weekly newspaper][17] who had gone into Jewish stores and overturned counters and displays."[18] He seems perturbed by

---

12. Ibid., p. 68.
13. Ibid., p. 72.
14. Ibid., pp. 96–97. This comment proves that this account was written after the war. In June 1940, there was not yet any question of deportation.
15. Ibid., p. 120.
16. Ibid., p. 131.
17. "The Pillory"; *Le Pilori* later changed its name to the rallying cry *Au Pilori* ("To the Pillory"). [PA]
18. Ibid., p. 144.

these anti-Semitic acts, and on August 18, he writes in his logbook, "The Gardes françaises [French Guards, an extreme-right-wing paramilitary group] continue to act as provocateurs. An attempt at an anti-Jewish demonstration in the street was aborted by the police."[19] On August 20, Langeron is summoned to the Palais Bourbon by a German military chief. He recounts:

> He told us that the German authorities denied responsibility for the recent anti-Jewish demonstrations and had no objection to our cracking down on them. I pointed out that we had done so but that other German authorities had demanded the release of the individuals arrested by us. This is not a very good way to suppress demonstrations or to prevent their recurrence. He assured me it was the last time this would happen and that we would have a free hand from now on . . . . Does he want to leave the responsibility for anti-Jewish repression to other Germans? Does he want to give the Jews a false sense of concern?[20]

Langeron seems quite decided not to allow these anti-Semitic actions to develop. At least, this is what comes out in his notes dated August 26, 1940. "Anti-Semitic flyers and pamphlets continue to be published and tracked by the police. The program of the new organization created by Pierre Clementi, the National-Collectivist Party: to remake France. The real program: to break windows of Jewish businesses, post flyers and create incidents. I have given orders to be firm and to prevent or suppress any form of demonstration."[21] He seems genuinely upset by all the agitation. On September 5, he notes: "Yesterday and today, violent anti-Jewish demonstrations by the PPF [Parti Populaire Français: French Popular Party]."[22] On September 23, he examines the anti-Semitic pamphlets and flyers found in Paris in the preceding few days.[23]

Things move quickly, and the active repression against the Jews becomes more clearly defined. On October 1, 1940, Langeron already knows what is to follow: "The German ordinance against the Jews will be made public. Despite the denial of responsibility for the demonstrations of recent days, they were the necessary precursor. The order came from

---

19. Ibid., p. 149. This involved the gangs of Robert Hersant, who during this period made a specialty of attacking women salesclerks in Jewish-owned stores on the Champs-Élysées.
20. Ibid., pp. 149–150.
21. Ibid., p. 155.
22. Ibid., p. 164.
23. More on these texts may be found in my book *Les Français de la débâcle* (Paris: Le Cherche midi, 1997), pp. 217–218.

high up. Doriot was not suggesting, he was carrying out. I am warning the Jews through various channels. I have already told them they were too trusting."[24] On October 2, he notes the logical outcome with calm lucidity: "The Council of Ministers too has announced a statute on the Jews. It is unlikely that it will be kinder than the German statute."[25] In his logbook, Langeron seems to have made himself the memorialist of the persecutions he foretells. October 4: "The German ordinance against the Jews has begun to be applied. Jews have been asked to declare themselves as such in the district town halls.[26] A black and yellow sign will be posted on every Jewish business." November 2: "Jewish storefronts are receiving small yellow signs from the Germans. They are being designated for attacks. We will have more difficulty protecting them."[27]

On January 2, 1941, shortly before leaving his position as prefect of police for good, Langeron no longer has any illusions about his troops' moral foundation of honor and discipline. He writes: "There are again rumors of the internment of Jews 16 to 45 years of age. Many young people are leaving Paris in the hope of getting to the unoccupied zone, regardless of the risks."[28]

On October 24, 1940, Pétain had met with Hitler in Montoire-sur-le-Loir. The old marshal declared with unfeigned gravitas: "I embark today on the road of collaboration!" Now there was no longer any ambiguity or pretense. It was no longer possible to say that Pétain in Vichy and de Gaulle in London were playing the same tune in different registers, the better to trick the enemy. Without any soul-searching, senior civil servants would fall into line. The same was true of police of every rank, who would swear an oath of allegiance to the marshal in January 1942. This was only an official confirmation, because the police as a whole had already taken the path of racial repression (the same was true for the gendarmerie), but the oath bound them institutionally to a state that had openly become a satellite of Nazi Germany.

---

24. Langeron, p. 173.
25. Ibid., p. 174.
26. When he was writing *Paris, juin 40*, Langeron seems to have forgotten that these declarations were made in the police departments that were still completely under his responsibility.
27. Langeron, p. 174.
28. Ibid., p. 202.

2

In the Service of Immoral Laws

AT EVERY STAGE OF RACIAL REPRESSION, the police of the country answer the call. Whether it is Vichy's legislation or the Nazi ordinances in the occupied zone, they show the same readiness to act. Following orders is perhaps an obligation for those who have not seen any need to resign from the police—and those who did resign were very rare. But nothing obliged these public servants to go beyond their orders to act as punctilious investigators and ruthless observers of physiognomy, constantly on the lookout for victims.

Starting in the summer of 1940, the French police show no compunction in enforcing the laws of Pétain's French State, which, at the beginning, are more repressive than the early Nazi ordinances. The best example is the nuances of the definition of a Jew. The 1st Nazi ordinance of September 27, 1940, recognized as Jews "those who belong or have belonged to the Jewish religion or who have more than two Jewish grandparents." Vichy's *Statute on the Jews*, dated October 3, 1940, and drafted mainly by the keeper of the seals, Raphaël Alibert, provided a somewhat different definition in its first article: "Is regarded as a Jew for the application of the present law, any person with three grandparents of the Jewish race or two grandparents of that race if the person's spouse is Jewish." Because the *Statute on the Jews* defines Jews by race and not religion, it is immediately obvious that the text is more racist than the one passed by the Nazis in the occupied zone.

The police, obliged to serve the French State of Vichy—which they wish to see as a continuation of the Third Republic—necessarily feel it appropriate to apply the repressive laws. Thus any citizen who is suspect is considered an "individual," while the new pariah is "the Jew," in contrast to other people, who are necessarily of the "Aryan race." In a few weeks, with complete equanimity, the French police master these nuances of language, which will soon appear on official documents such as memos, internal communications, circulars, reports and station logbooks.

Faithful to Vichy's orders, rigorously respectful of the laws decreed by the *de facto* state, police officers have the same attitude toward the Nazi ordinances. When the ordinance of September 27, 1940, requires that every Jew "must present himself by October 20, 1940, to the local sub-prefect of his district in order for his name to be entered in a special register," this does not pose any moral problem for the French police, who open the doors of their stations wide to carry out the census. The same is true for the gendarmeries in rural areas. Nor does the operation end with the formality of receiving the declarations, because the police also have to stamp the word *Jew* on every identity card.

The police are equally willing when it comes to "Aryanizing" businesses in accordance with Vichy's *Statute on the Jews*, whereas the Nazis require Jewish-owned establishments to post a sign intended as dishonorable: "Any business whose owner is Jewish must be designated a Jewish Business by a special sign in German and French." After receiving the various declarations, the French police officers go to work to complete the dossiers so that they are soon operational.[1]

Once the first steps are taken, the police of gentle France do not stop halfway. The laws are not mere declarations of principle; the next stage is necessarily repressive, and nobody shirks the task of making things worse for some three hundred and fifty thousand people who are already marginalized and will soon be defenseless.

The police's behavior is in line with some particularly trenchant comments by Christian Renaudin, the holder of an advanced degree in politics and economics: "This is not a legislative document designed to provide a basis in law for the legal relationship between different categories of Frenchmen, but a *law of exception* giving a special status to one category of citizens, who will then be marginalized in relation to the national community and expected to observe certain rules."[2] What he describes

---

1. The original French texts of these laws and ordinances—and those that followed—are reproduced in Philippe Héraclès, ed., *1940–1944, la loi nazie en France* (Paris: Guy Authier, 1974); Dominique Rémy, *Les Lois de Vichy* (Paris: Romillat, 1992); Serge Klarsfeld, *Le Statut des Juifs de Vichy* (Paris: FFDJF, 1990).
2. "Commentaire du statut des Juifs," *Recueil général des lois, décrets et arrêtés 11* (1941), p. 122.

8

with such cool composure is nothing less than the exclusion of an entire human group.

Renaudin's didactic approach was well suited to the servants of public order. Beyond his simple explanation, his comments on the law that would now control the Jews' everyday lives were an attempt to justify the exclusion of these men and women. Without compunction, he wrote: "The Jewish influence in the business of a country is harmful to its capacity for greatness and its ability to maintain its moral heritage. We will see that, in order to completely eliminate this influence in the French occupied territories, the German authorities, while leaving it to the government of our country to exclude Jews from public life, have from the outset issued ordinances so as to closely monitor the Jews living in these territories and exercise constant control over their activity."[3]

Why would the police, whose role was to see that people obeyed the law—even if it was that of the enemy of yesterday—be any less violent in their actions than the xenophobic, racist lawyers and politicians who drafted documents about applying the law? Especially since the Vichy authorities had paved the way for active repression: "It seems that after almost totally blocking Jews' access to the civil service through the law of October 1940, the government felt it appropriate in its turn to take the path traced and institute police surveillance."[4] For those who made the laws in Vichy, there could be no question of straying from the Nazi ordinances, and thus the best approach was to harden the application of the texts—whether they were French or German. Once these functionaries had accepted the principle of repression, they were determined to apply it as rigorously as possible: "We are justified in thinking that once the advisability of reducing the influence of the Jews in national life at this time is accepted in principle by the public powers of our country, the legislative measures adopted to do so can hardly ignore those prescribed for an essentially analogous purpose by the Authorities of the occupation."[5]

After the promulgation of Vichy's second *Statute on the Jews* on June 2, 1941, there can no longer be any doubt that the repression will only intensify. This is the Gestapo's intention in the occupied zone, and it does not displease the French police, who have already moved on to action, arresting several thousand foreign Jews in Paris on May 14, 1941. Renaudin expresses this bluntly: "It seems we may at this time consider, on the one hand, that two steps have been taken towards gradually making Jews second-class

---

3. Ibid.
4. Ibid.
5. Ibid., p. 123.

citizens, and, on the other hand, that the position adopted with regard to them has been reinforced from day to day, and in these conditions, the action against them has probably not yet reached its conclusion."[6]

One could hardly be more cynical, and legal experts like Renaudin, who explained almost didactically the laws they had no intention of challenging, paved the way for the repressive actions of the police who would be in charge of carrying out those laws. It is clear that the path taken by the Vichy government could only reassure those intransigent patriots that racial purification was possible in France. Of course, the police had no need of such lessons to carry out their orders. Personal feelings did not enter into it, because, as we know, "orders are orders." The police knew what they had to do, regardless of the fact that all of them, from the lowliest officer to the high command, were republicans—and had even, in many cases, been recruited during the time of the Popular Front [a coalition of left-wing groups that formed the government in 1936–1937]. Policemen are not ideologues; what counts is their capacity to exercise repression. Nor are they humanists; they have a strong propensity to despise foreigners, and if those foreigners are Jews, they don't hesitate to take action.

Since Daladier's decree-laws of May 2, 1938, the police have been accustomed to hunting down foreigners whose residence papers are not in order. What is being asked of the Vichy State, and in the occupied zone, the Gestapo, is the same repressive action. The target is simply more precise. Now, the priority is to hunt down Jewish foreigners, who have "a harmful influence on the national community." It is thus appropriate that the administrative authorities "protect the moral health of the populations placed under their control against these influences that are deemed pernicious."[7]

For the French police in the occupied zone, the Nazi ordinances have the force of law. Since ignorance of the law is no defense—especially for public servants in positions of authority—the law is rigorously applied. The Vichy legislators follow the Gestapo's edicts closely, and sometimes even anticipate them, so the police consider it their duty to support their position in favor of racial purification: "The Jews will increasingly have to be subjected to a reduction of their citizenship rights."[8]

Police officers are thus not torn between laws and ordinances from different sources. The conqueror and the conquered follow parallel paths.

6. Ibid.
7. Ibid., p. 130.
8. Ibid., p. 134.

While loyal to the Vichy State, the police are also respectful of the Germans, who are exercising a repression to which they are not opposed. They seek above all to convince themselves of this reassuring view. Since they often share the same hunting ground as the Germans, there is no place for thinking in the minds of the police on the path of racial war.

Faithful to their orders, the police are not particularly surprised when Vichy laws such as the second *Statute on the Jews* of June 2, 1941, reproduces the spirit of the Nazi ordinances limiting the right of Jews to exist in the country. It reassures them that Jews are under high surveillance in the unoccupied zone as well, and that this "fundamental" law provides for internment "in a special camp" for anyone who fails to respect the increasing numbers of prohibitions.

Ultimately, not only are violations of the law penalized; the mere fact of being a Jew becomes an offense. And then, to keep things orderly, the Vichy State decides—as the Nazis had done in the occupied zone—to take a census of Jews in the "free" zone. Renaudin dwells on Article 1 of that French racial law, extolling its boldness: "These provisions seem at first glance to go farther, in a certain sense, than those of the occupation authorities. The census they prescribe covers not only persons but also their assets; there was no mention of assets in the ordinances, at least not for individuals."[9] At this point, it becomes clear that the German occupiers could be less repressive than the Vichy government. Why, then, would the French police balk at obeying the Gestapo's orders? Police and gendarmes arrest and intern foreign Jews in the occupied zone, but their colleagues in the unoccupied zone operate exactly the same way, and the camps run by the Vichy regime are full in 1941.

Once again, Renaudin, this analyst who is so faithful to the spirit of Vichy's laws, calms any potential anxieties on the part of those who have to apply the laws in all their rigor. "The action undertaken by the government seems to have been guided above all by a concern to combat and eliminate racial influence on the country's business, which is considered harmful because of its *a-national*, if not *anti-national*, nature."[10]

Renaudin goes even further, encouraging unchecked repression: "The outstanding feature of the action carried out since last September, one might say, is its dynamism. It goes forward without ever stopping, getting stronger every day, and seems to arise out of a determination to reach and strike the Jews to the very limit of their freedom and their activity. What makes the situation they are in even more difficult is the impossibility,

9. Ibid., p. 146.
10. Ibid., p. 150.

11

due to the circumstances, of their leaving the country to seek somewhere else to put down roots."[11]

Here, expressed even more directly than in the ordinances, is the will to repress that is already being applied on the ground, although Renaudin considers the repression moderate. Even if the text is the same as that of the Nazi ordinance, it will be applied more stringently. The Jews' rights have been reduced to the right to breathe, but he still considers the sanctions insufficient. The total exclusion of the Jews would solve many problems:

> They are, in short, being doubly pursued. On this side of the line of demarcation, in the name of the military order required by the presence of an occupying army: a police pursuit. On the other side, in the name of the internal order imposed by the climate of the National Revolution: an administrative pursuit. The former seems to seek no justification than that of the old adage, "the end justifies the means"; the latter, begun at the same time and carried out, it seems, solely in the name of the immediate political necessities of the country, would lead, I believe, all things being equal, to a particularly severe judgment. Already, the indictment stage is over; sentencing has begun, and we are seeing it become even more serious with the appearance of a sentence that is not common in our criminal law: the *obligation of detention*.[12]

This, without the slightest ambiguity, means imprisonment. While the police officers aren't necessarily familiar with this explanation, it is gradually impressed upon them by a hierarchy unconcerned with legalistic niceties. From top to bottom of the chain of repression, there is a consensus, and the policeman, the last link in the chain, is ready to exert his repressive power.

11. Ibid.
12. Ibid.

3

The Stages of Humiliation

ROUNDUPS are the most visible police activity during the years of the occupation. With the publication of the first Nazi ordinances, it is already clear that the forces of law and order will devote a large part of their time to compiling files on the Jews and controlling them, even before the decision is made to force them to wear the yellow star. The Nazis feel they have to proceed in stages, and that logic suited our police.

When the decision is made to take a census of Jews in October 1940, the police are ready for that mission. When it is decided to add a humiliating stamp to their identification papers, the police are again ready. The Germans have been in Paris for only four months, and already the police are ready to carry out the first racially targeted missions. Even the Paris city hall is involved in this new legality the police are responsible for:

The German military administration of the city of Paris has ordered that, for the application of the ordinance on the census of Jews, identity cards or residence permits will have the word *Jew* or *Jewess* stamped on them. Therefore, all Jews who have made their declarations in the police stations will have to present themselves there again with their identity cards or, in the case of foreigners, their residence permits, on the dates indicated. Jews of French nationality who have not yet obtained the required card will have to present themselves with their identification papers and two witnesses who will vouch for the accuracy of their declaration.[1]

Once this measure is adopted, it is quickly followed by increasing numbers of identity checks based on appearance. Woe to anyone who "looks Jewish" who does not have an identification card adorned with the indispensable stamp. At the same time, the police are responsible for the "Aryanization" of businesses and have to see that the Nazis' orders on this are respected. On October 25, 1940, a notice from the prefecture of police extends the 2nd Nazi ordinance, issued a week before, on October 18. The prefect of police, Langeron, explains to the heads of Jewish businesses that they have to write their own declarations, under their own responsibility, and file them before October 31 at the police station in their neighborhood or, in the communes of the Seine, that of their district. Through this notice, the prefect of police delegates his powers to the chiefs of police in the neighborhoods or communes.[2]

The police also have to check whether Jewish businesses with storefronts and rural merchants' displays have posted prominently the small printed sign in black on a yellow background stating in French and German that this is a Jewish business. They closely monitor obedience to the Nazi ordinance, particularly in the markets, where they patrol constantly with a suspicious eye. This active surveillance is illustrated by a May 13, 1941 memo from the director of the Paris municipal police to the precinct captains of the city, the suburban districts and the special departments:

> I draw your attention to the need to advise the special department responsible for *Jewish affairs* (the Administrative Affairs Department of the general police) of all matters concerning Jews dealt with in your departments. With regard to foreign Jews, two information bulletins will be established, one for the foreigners' department and the other for the special department. As for Jews who are French nationals, it would be useful to indicate whether they are French or under French protection.[3]

---

1. BMO [*Bulletin municipal officiel de Paris*], October 20, 1940.
2. J. Lubetzki, *La Condition des Juifs en France sous l'occupation allemande* (Paris: CDJC, 1945), p. 143.
3. APP [Archives de la préfecture de police de Paris], series BA 1917 (dossier 68425). Document signed by Tanguy, assistant director of the municipal police. The distinction between being French and being "under French protection" is important, because the Jews of Algeria were stripped of French nationality and reduced to the status of an indigenous people, and were thus "under protection."

The files, which were set up in October and November 1940 by André Tulard and his collaborators, are quickly operational, and on May 14, 1941, some five thousand foreign Jews living within the boundaries of Paris are summoned to various centers for a "review" of their situation and then immediately arrested by the police and "entrusted" to the gendarmes, who escort them that same day to the internment camps in the Loiret (Pithiviers and Beaune-la-Rolande).

This first wave of mass arrests carried out on specific instructions does not preclude individual initiatives or stopping people at random or on the basis of their appearance. The following record, dated July 13, 1941, at 11:30 p.m., is from a voluminous file on police officers injured on the job—"victims of duty"—at the police station of the 20th district in Paris: "At 10:40 p.m., on the terrace of the Café La Vielleuse, 132 Boulevard de Belleville, some fifty young people were singing songs from the youth camps.[4] A crowd of about a hundred had formed and was immediately dispersed by the PJ [police judiciaire: judicial police, the criminal investigation division] and guards on duty nearby. Five arrests for refusal to circulate. Belleville police station made available." This is followed by the names of five young Jews, including Henri Chlewitzki, an electrician, born on September 22, 1915, in Paris.[5] In the course of these arrests, which must have been turbulent, a peace officer suffers a head injury.[6]

As the days and weeks pass, hunting down Jews becomes more targeted. When this does not threaten people's freedom, it ruins their everyday lives. On August 13, a Nazi ordinance orders that radios belonging to Jews must be confiscated. This new edict is issued by the head of the German military administration in France, but the French police are responsible for enforcing it. It states:

> By virtue of the powers vested in me:
> 1) It is forbidden for Jews to have radio receivers in their possession;
> 2) Jews having radio receivers in their possession must, by September 1, 1941, turn them over to the mayor (local police authority) of their place of domicile or permanent residence in return for a receipt; in the Seine department, to the prefecture of police or the district police station.

---

4. This is an error on the part of the police; they must have been songs from the youth hostel movement.
5. Henri Chlewitzki was one of my counselors at camp in 1937 on Île de Ré. He was the brother of the actor Maurice Chevit.
6. APP, series BA 873.

At the end of the designated period, Tanguy, who has become the director of the judicial police, communicates again with the precinct captains of Paris and the suburbs: "Following up on my telegram of August 30 regarding the turning over of radios by Jews, this must be carried out by them, and [the radios submitted] in your hands, by tomorrow, September 2, at 7 p.m. See that each radio has a descriptive label attached to allow the subsequent identification of the person."[7] This is another example of the constant harassment of a population that is already marginalized between the Nazi racial initiatives and the French police.

The episode of the "Jewish business" signs only lasts a little while; the next stage involves the "liquidation" of Jewish businesses and companies. On October 3, 1941, the precinct captain in the Père-Lachaise neighborhood writes to the director of intelligence services: "I respectfully report that I have not been informed of any incident provoked among the Jewish population by the liquidation of Jewish assets, and that no arrests have been made in my district in the past week."[8]

While it did its part in the mounting repression, the police find it necessary to bolster their position with reports intended to convey an image of public opinion, which during this period is actually very difficult to know with any certainty. One report by intelligence services, dated October 4, 1941, testifies to what may be described as sheer indifference with regard to the fate reserved for the Jews:

> The people of Paris in general did not like the Jews, but they tolerated them. Business people, especially, wished to be rid of the Jews because they were strong competition. In fact, the severe measures taken against the Jews by the German authorities and the French government did not give rise to any protests in the mass of the population, but the violent anti-Semitism of the Paris press goes beyond, indeed, far beyond, many people's antipathy toward the Jews and they find it excessive. The opinion of many people—particularly those in the Catholic milieu—is that the adversaries of the Jews generalize too much, and that by unleashing such anti-Semitism, they will soon provoke regrettable excesses. Thus, the news of the attacks committed yesterday against synagogues[9] caused no surprise or strong feeling

---

7. APP, series BA 1817 (dossier 51 B).
8. APP, series BA 1817 (dossier 68425).
9. On October 3, 1941, extreme right-wing groups attacked several synagogues in Paris, including the one on Rue de la Victoire, causing serious damage.

among the public. "It was bound to happen," people said with a certain indifference.[10]

On February 7, 1942, with the publication of the 6th Nazi ordinance, a new stage of exclusion begins for the Jews of the occupied zone. The French police will extend their repressive activity even more broadly. Article 1 of the ordinance imposes a curfew on Jews: "It is forbidden for Jews to be outside their apartments between 8 p.m. and 6 a.m." Article 2 states: "It is forbidden for Jews to change their usual place of residence." The Jews of Paris and the nearby suburbs had already lost the right to leave the Seine department. Article 3 states: "Anyone who contravenes the provisions of this ordinance will be punished with imprisonment or a fine or both. In addition, the guilty party may be interned in a camp for Jews."

The ordinance is German, but it is the French police who have to enforce it. They also try to show that the Jews are active in the black market, as is indicated in a memo dated March 20, 1942, and signed by Tanguy, director of the judicial police, sent to the precinct captains following the creation of a police unit specializing in repression and fraud in Paris and its suburbs: "In the procedures established against Jews for the illegal raising of prices, you must also record all violations of the *Statutes on the Jews* of which the offender might be guilty."[11]

They are determined to intensify the repression, and on March 27, 1942, Tanguy reiterates: "I remind you of the instructions in my report of November 13 concerning the Jews; these instructions have too often been overlooked. When there are Jews mixed up in judicial matters, you must closely examine their situation in light of the Jewish Statute. Record all violations observed, such as the exercise of a prohibited occupation, Jewish business, identification card, etc."[12]

A document dated April 22, 1942, clearly establishes part of the operation of the Department of Foreigners and Jewish Affairs at the prefecture of police. Under director André Tulard, who has moved up since the creation of the Jewish dossier in the fall of 1940, eight heads and assistant heads of departments implement a repression that cannot be left only to the Police for Jewish Affairs created by the Commissariat-General for Jewish Affairs. Tulard's department is involved in the reception and examination of declarations on persons and property, problems of public order concerning the Jews, the statistical file, periodic checks, intern-

---

10. APP, report of the police intelligence service, "La situation de Paris."
11. APP, series BA 1817 (dossier B 5 17).
12. Ibid.

ments of individuals, the camps, etc.[13] Of course, these are only the managers of the French anti-Jewish repression, and there are also a great many flunkies who busy themselves with all these tasks on the ground.

With the wearing of the yellow star, which is imposed as of June 7, 1942, there comes an additional form of humiliation: the obligation for Jews to ride only in the last car of the Paris metro. This segregation is the subject of several letters from the prefect of the Seine, Charles Magny. On June 10, 1942, he informs both the Vichy government's secretary of state for the interior and the Commissariat-General for Jewish Affairs of this measure:

SUBJECT: conditions of admission of Jews to the metropolitan railroad.

The German authorities have given specific instructions to the Metropolitan Railroad Company regarding the transport of Jews. From now on, Jews may only travel in the Paris metro in second class and in the last car of the train. The company has therefore distributed an order to the stations stipulating that conductors must not sell first class tickets to Jews, that supervisors must advise those wearing the badge that they may travel only in the last second class car, that guards or inspectors must politely ask those they may find to go to the last car at the next station. *No sign has been posted, and no message has been communicated to the public.*[14] These measures are merely the execution of an order of the German authorities on November 8, 1940, concerning Negroes and Jews, an order that as far as the latter are concerned, had not been implemented for lack of an identifying mark.[15]

On June 9, 1942, in *Le Cri du peuple* ["The Cry of the People"], the daily publication of Jacques Doriot's French Popular Party, the journalist Roger Nicolas expresses his satisfaction with this "healthy measure that will delight all Frenchmen who have good reasons not to rub shoulders with the racial brothers of Blum and his ilk."

Next comes a ban on Jews having telephones, or even using public telephones. At the beginning of July 1942, this decision by the officials of the occupation is explained by the Office of Telecommunications as follows: "On July 6, 1942, General Kersten gave the secretariat-general of the

---

13. APP, series BA 1817 (file 68425).
14. My italics.
15. CDJC [Centre de documentation juive contemporaine; Center for contemporary Jewish documentation], CXCIII 136.

PTT [Postes, télégraphes et téléphones: postal services and telecommunications] a note, dated July 3, 1942, demanding that all necessary measures be taken *immediately* to prohibit the use of telephones by Jews in the occupied zone. According to this note, telephone services subscribed to by Jews must be cut; access to the public telephone booths of the PTT must also be forbidden to Jews."[16] It would be an error to think the police are not involved in this discriminatory measure. A few days later, General Kersten gives a note to the secretariat-general of the PTT stating: "There are in Paris some 380,000 telephone subscribers, and some 150,000 Jews whose names are in a register held by the prefecture of police. In order to be mathematically certain that no Jewish subscriber escapes the review process, the prefecture of police (which alone can have access to the files) carefully compares the names of the 380,000 subscribers in Paris with its 150,000 files of Jews."[17] In addition, measures are taken to intercept mail.

One final touch remains to be added to this veritable mental—and now physical—imprisonment before the start of the roundups that will be carried out until the liberation of Paris. The police are also responsible for enforcing the 9th Nazi ordinance of July 8, 1942. The ordinance is short, but it allows for every possible interpretation—in the harshest sense, of course. This time, now that the Jews have been marked, they are to be totally excluded from the life of the city:

> It may be forbidden to Jews to enter certain entertainment establishments and, in general, establishments open to the public.
>
> Jews may enter department stores, retail stores or artisans' shops and make purchases in them or have them made by other persons only between 3 p.m. and 4 p.m.

The formulation "It may be forbidden," is interpreted as meaning "It is expressly forbidden," and the police lurk around theatres, cinemas, concert halls, museums, libraries, racetracks, stadiums, swimming pools, etc. These now-forbidden places see increased numbers of identity checks based on appearance. An unwary person who enters a café can end up in Drancy.

---

16. CDJC-XVIII 28–29 and XXXVIII 18–19.
17. Ibid.

THE SWEARING OF AN OATH TO PÉTAIN
BY THE PARIS POLICE

B Y 1942, the days when the priority of the police was to protect persons and property are over. It is no longer only a matter of maintaining order. The Nazi laws, which have been accepted by the Vichy authorities, must be enforced. The connection exists quite openly, because nobody has forgotten Pétain's meeting with Hitler at Montoire, and the police no longer need have any hesitations.

On August 14, 1941, a decree signed by Pétain has essentially made it an obligation for all public servants to swear an oath of loyalty to him. After members of the military, gendarmes and magistrates have done so, it is the police officers' turn to participate in an official ceremony, which takes place on January 20, 1942.[18] The administrator of the Palais de Chaillot, Pierre Aldebert, has graciously made its great hall available to the prefecture of police for the occasion, as is shown by the correspondence between Admiral Bard, the prefect of police, and Émile Hennequin, the director of the municipal police.[19]

This event cannot go unnoticed, and everyone of any importance among the collaborationists of Paris is there. The description of the occasion is eloquent:

> On Tuesday, January 20, at the Palais de Chaillot, 3000 delegates of the Paris Guard, the national police and the prefecture of police pledged a solemn oath of loyalty to the Head of State. At noon, saluted by the Paris Guards in full dress uniform, Monsieur Pucheu, minister, secretary of state for the interior, entered the room and took his place on the stage decorated with an enormous tricolor drapery with a portrait of Marshal Pétain in the center. At the minister's side were Messieurs Rivalland, secretary-general for the police; Admiral Bard, prefect of police; Chevallier, prefect of Seine-et-Oise; Chaugneau, prefect of Seine-et-Marne; and de La Rosière, director of the minister's office.
>
> . . .
>
> The call to attention having been sounded, the peace officers' band played "La Marseillaise." Then the minister made a speech in which he recalled the magnificent sacrifice of Marshal Pétain

---

18. Among the magistrates, only Judge Didier refused to take the oath. It appears that not one police officer avoided doing so.
19. APP, series BA 1784.

20

and explained the symbolic meaning of the ceremony that was taking place. The chief of the police division and head of the École pratique des gardiens de la paix [police officers' school], standing on a dais placed at the front of the stage, then pronounced the words of the oath: "I swear loyalty to the person of the Chief of State in all he commands, in the interest of service and public order, for the good of the country," and all those present extended one arm, saying, "I so swear." After a short silence, the national anthem rang out once again. The call to attention was sounded while the dignitaries made their departure, and the strains of "Le Régiment de Sambre-et-Meuse" marked the end of the solemn and moving ceremony.[20]

A representative of the rank-and-file policemen also swears the oath on behalf of his colleagues: "I swear loyalty to the person of the Chief of State and I promise to carry out my duties for the good of the country, in accordance with the laws of honor and integrity."[21]

20. BMO, Paris, January 22, 1942.
21. APP, series BA 1784.

4

Toward the Yellow Star

B RAND (VERB): "to put a mark on the skin of (an animal) to show who owns it . . . to describe or identify (someone or something) with a word that expresses strong criticism." This definition from the online *Merriam-Webster Dictionary* fits our subject perfectly. The branding of Jews for religious or political reasons occurred often in medieval Europe, where monarchs and popes alike would decide to brand a population that was distinguished by nothing other than the faith it professed. The "perfidious" Jews, "killers of Christ," must be driven out. This essentially began at the end of the eleventh century, with mass killings during the First Crusade, particularly in Germany and Bohemia, when armies were leaving to recapture the Holy Sepulchre.

After the bloodbaths and burnings at the stake, another means of repression was adopted. An order by King Philippe Auguste of France in 1206 stipulated that Jews had to wear a *rouelle*, a round cloth badge. The king appears to have been a trendsetter, because in 1215, at the fourth Lateran council, Pope Innocent III expressed concern about marriages between Christians and Jews and issued a decree forbidding Jews to dress like Christians. A round badge, sometimes red, sometimes yellow, was imposed. Later, it was replaced by a grotesquely shaped hood or hat in a bright color. In 1217, the papal legate in France spoke of a *rota* [Latin: "wheel"] worn by Jews.

The councils of Narbonne (1227), Arles (1234), Béziers (1246) and Albi (1254) all mentioned the *rouelle* of the Jews. In 1257, Pope Alexander IV made Jews wear a yellow one the width of the palm of a hand sewn onto their clothing.

In 1269, King Louis IX published an order requiring Jews to wear two distinctive yellow emblems in the shape of a wheel, equal to four fingers in width, one on the back and one on the chest. This measure included girls aged twelve and older and boys fourteen and older. In 1272, King Philippe III issued a reminder that the order of 1269 must be obeyed. In 1302, King Philippe IV ordered a return to the custom, which had fallen into disuse, and in 1315, King Louis X reiterated that order, but these orders were softened by King Philippe V in 1317. In the mid-fourteenth century, King Jean II confirmed the orders of his predecessors, but specified that the round badge, now red on a white background, would have to be worn only on the chest. In 1360, Pope Innocent IV required that Jews wear a red cape.

With the Renaissance, these obligations gradually died out in France; but in the [Papal State region] Comtat Venaissin, Jewish men had to wear a yellow hat, and women, a yellow headdress, until the end of the fifteenth century.

In many countries of Europe, the recommendations of the fourth Lateran council were generally applied. In England, throughout the thirteenth century, the kings required Jews to wear the *tabula*, a yellow badge that was supposed to represent the tablets of the law [eg. The Ten Commandments]. But in 1434, King Henry VI decided that they would have to wear a round piece of yellow fabric on their clothing. In Austria, from 1267 on, Jews had to wear a special hat, and from 1279 on, a round badge of red felt on the left side of their chest. In the other Germanic countries, Jews were forced to wear a special hat or a round red or yellow badge, depending on the emperor. In Venice, in 1394, they were forced to wear a round piece of yellow fabric on their chest. In 1496, the Venetian round badge was replaced by a yellow hat. In the sixteenth century, the doges decided that the hat would be red, and this remained the case until the end of the eighteenth century.[1]

During the second half of the nineteenth century, many Jews left the ghettos in which they had been confined and gradually integrated into various nations. It was then that an anti-Semitism[2] arose that was much more

---

1. Jean Forien de Rochesnard, *Les Signes distinctifs des Juifs* (Colombes, France: Jean Forien de Rochesnard, 1985); Léon Poliakov, *L'Étoile jaune* (Paris: Éditions du Centre, 1949); Serge Klarsfeld, *L'Étoile des Juifs* (Paris: L'Archipel, 1992).
2. This term was coined in 1866 in Germany.

political than religious. Its manifestations proliferated in Germany and Austria, and then in czarist Russia in the form of pogroms. In France, a climate of hatred became established with Édouard Drumont's ranting in *La France juive* and the Dreyfus affair. Anti-Semitic parties employing threatening language and violent practices sprang up and were supported by a vengeful Catholic press that refused to accept the Church's loss of influence. The content of the anti-Semitic articles in *La Croix* was every bit as foul as that of the later *Je suis partout, Au Pilori* and even *L'Action française.*[3]

In January 1933, Hitler took power in Germany with the explicit program to eliminate the Jews. The aim was, first, marginalization and branding, to be followed by exclusion and finally elimination. Following Kristallnacht[4] in November 1938, the Nazis envisaged "a scheme to label the person of each Jew in some way in order to facilitate the isolation of the Jews from the rest of the population."[5]

The start of World War II allowed the Nazis to move into action. On December 1, 1939, the General Government for the Occupied Polish Territories ordered Jews to wear a white armband at least four inches in width with a blue star on it. In the part of Poland annexed by Nazi Germany, Jews were forced to wear two stars, one sewn on the left side of their chest and the other on their back. On September 1, 1941, a similar requirement was imposed on German Jews, except that they only had to wear a single star, on their chest.[6]

THE PRELIMINARIES

I N FRANCE, in December 1941, the commander in chief of the army of occupation, General Otto von Stulpnagel, informs the Vichy government of his intention to make the Jews of the occupied zone wear a yellow star. This is not a new idea; in July 1940, the Germans had forced the Jews of Commercy to wear a yellow square on their backs, as is stated in a letter from the mayor of that town in the Meuse to the grand rabbi, Jacob Kaplan on June 7, 1945.[7] That was only a trial balloon.

Raymond-Raoul Lambert, one of the leaders of the Union générale

---

3. Names of publications: "The Cross," "I am everywhere," "To the Pillory" (previously known as *Le Pilori*), "French Action." [PA]

4. On the night of November 9–10, 1938, the SA and the SS broke the windows of Jewish stores in German cities and towns and arrested thousands of people. See Rita Thalmann and Emmanuel Feinermann, *Crystal Night, 9–10 November 1938*, trans. Gilles Cremonesi (London: Thames and Hudson, 1974).

5. Michael R. Marrus and Robert O. Paxton, *Vichy France and the Jews* (New York: Basic Books, 1981), p. 235.

6. Poliakov, pp. 18–19. As I mention in my *La Police de Vichy* (Paris: Le Cherche midi, 1995), it is unfortunate that the author did not cite his sources.

7. CDJC-XCII 22.

des israélites de France (UGIF)[8] in the unoccupied zone, reports in his logbook some information from Vichy regarding the racial measures decreed in the occupied zone, with a comment by Admiral Darlan, vice-president of the Council (and Pétain's heir apparent), expressing his concern about the measures. On January 21, 1942, Darlan had informed the Vichy government's delegate-general to the occupied zone as follows:

> Re: Measures against the Jews
>
> Ref.: Note No. G 78 of December 15, 1941, from the Commander-in-chief of the Armed Forces in France.
>
> 1. By the communication referred to above, the commander-in-chief of the Armed Forces in France asks that a certain number of measures be taken with regard to Jews in the Occupied Zone, such as: the obligation to wear a distinctive symbol, being banned from frequenting public places, excepting certain premises particularly reserved for them, and the institution of a special curfew.
>
> 2. I would like to inform you that I am not in agreement with these proposals.
>
> 3. I feel that the various strict measures already in force to date against the Jews are sufficient for the intended purpose, which is to remove them from public employment and from positions of authority in industry and commerce in this country.
>
> 4. There can be no question of going further without deeply offending French public opinion, which will see in these measures only humiliations without real efficacy, either for the future of the country or for the security of the occupying troops. The very excess of these decisions would certainly go against the intended purpose, and would run the risk of provoking a movement in support of the Jews, who would be considered martyrs.[9]

Admiral Darlan's anxieties are not taken into account by the Nazis, even though his reservations are quietly shared by those of Vichy's leaders who count "Israelites" among their personal friends.

On March 10, 1942, Colonel Knochen, head of the Gestapo in the occupied zone, writes to the German command in Brussels about a con-

---

8. On November 29, 1941, by decree, the Vichy government created the UGIF, the clear aim of which was to better control the Jews in both zones, on the pretext of community solidarity. See my *Des Juifs dans la collaboration* (Paris: EDI, 1980).

9. Quoted in Raymond-Raoul Lambert, *Diary of a Witness*, 1940–1943, trans. Isabel Best and edited and with an introduction by Richard I. Cohen (Chicago: Ivan R. Dee, 2007), p. 99.

ference of experts on the Jewish question that was held in Berlin on March 4: "As already agreed in Berlin, it seems opportune to mark Jews in the territories of the Netherlands, Belgium and France simultaneously. I have set the date of the conference, in which the expert on Jewish affairs of the Amsterdam *Aussenstelle* will also participate, for Saturday, March 14, 1942. Please send me your acceptance and the date of your arrival."[10]

On March 15, 1942, SS Captain Theo Dannecker, who attended the conference and headed the IV J department of the Gestapo [responsible for Jewish affairs], records the main decisions made there, which had only one subject: the identifying mark for Jews:

> At the conference of March 14 . . . the following points were adopted:
>
> a) In the ordinance that will be published in the Dutch, Belgian and French occupied territories, there will be no question of exemptions. The other ordinances will concern only "Jews."
>
> b) The yellow star (about 4 inches square) such as is employed in Germany will be used with writing in the language of the country; in Belgium, it will be bilingual.[11]
>
> c) The German embassy informs us that, for its part, it sees no problem in the exemptions granted to certain nationalities being stated in the ordinance. If it is not possible in these specific cases to avoid a special agreement with the country involved, that agreement will be defined in an internal administrative circular and applied without official publication.
>
> d) Mixed marriages will not be taken into account; the Jewish spouse will wear the star. . . .
>
> To summarize, the introduction of the identifying badge for Jews in the designated territories of the west will only be one stage of the Solution of the European Jewish question. Consequently, a presentation of the reasons, such as in the form of a preamble to the ordinance, is pointless. However, this does not exclude the use of propaganda. With regard to the penal provisions, in principle, for the sake of form, sentences of imprisonment and fines must be established. In any case, internment in a concentration camp must be possible.

---

10. CDJC-XLIX a 1.
11. Ultimately, the use of the letter J alone in the center of the star in the Belgian version would make it possible to avoid printing in two different languages.

Consequently, the following penal provisions must be drafted: "Violations of the ordinance are subject to a sentence of imprisonment and a fine, or one of the two. Internment in a camp for Jews may be envisaged." The German courts will not handle these cases; in order to produce the desired effect, offenders will be interned in a concentration camp. Plans must be made to set up women's concentration camps for Jewish women who violate the ordinance.[12]

What appears to have been most important to Dannecker was the introduction of an identifying mark for Jews as a stage in the solution to the Jewish question in Europe.[13] The description of the repressive actions envisaged for people who resist is interesting in that the almost identical wording is found in most of the arrest orders of the prefecture of police beginning in May 1942.

In Luxembourg, Jews are required to wear a yellow armband as of June 29, 1941, and the yellow star is only introduced on October 14. In the Netherlands, the yellow star is introduced on April 27, 1942,[14] and in Belgium, on May 21. If the measure only comes into effect in France some weeks later, the reason seems to be the reluctance of the Vichy government to promulgate the measure.[15]

On March 31, 1942, shortly before the appointment of Louis Darquier, known as Louis Darquier de Pellepoix, as head of the Commissariat-General for Jewish Affairs, the German ambassador to France writes to the commander in chief of the German army in occupied France, "We may hope that racial measures will soon be taken against the Jews, and that, thanks to more active propaganda, the French population will be better informed about the Jewish problem, so that, in a short time, it will be ripe to *swallow*[16] the introduction of the yellow star without any undesirable reactions."[17]

The new measure is already part of the Nazis' plans. With no apparent opposition from the Vichy government, the decision is made all the

---

12. CDJC-XLIX a 2.
13. Dannecker was alluding to the Wannsee conference, held on January 20, 1942, in the suburbs of Berlin, the subject of which was the "final solution to the Jewish problem." In the text quoted here, there is clearly a desire to code the message.
14. According to Jean Forien de Rochesnard, the Dutch resistance responded to the requirement for Jews in the Netherlands to wear a yellow star by distributing a printed badge with a yellow star and the words "Jews or non-Jews, wear the star!" The various groups in the French resistance never envisaged such an initiative.
15. Poliakov, p. 29.
16. In German, the word used was *schlucken*, which eliminates any ambiguity about his expectations with regard to the acceptance of this measure by the citizens of the country and the Vichy government. Incidentally, *schlucken* also means "to have the hiccups."
17. Quoted in Poliakov, p. 30.

more quickly because its instigators seem eager for it to be done. On March 20, 1942, a new note from Helmut Knochen shows how impatient the Gestapo is. "The treatment of the Jews in the occupied French and Dutch territories urgently requires the introduction of an identifying mark for Jews, given that the limited number of police officers for the Jews does not allow for real surveillance.[18] Furthermore, the introduction of an identifying mark for Jews, which is one more step toward the Final Solution[19] of the Jewish question, must take place simultaneously in all the occupied countries of the west. I am taking the initiative to propose that SS Brigadeführer Reder[20] be instructed accordingly, so that there are no new difficulties in establishing the proposed rules."[21]

On May 8, 1942, Dr. Zeitschel, an adviser at the German embassy in Paris, makes his thoughts known to a French department either at the ministry of the interior in Vichy or at the prefecture of police in Paris. Curiously, a false pretext is used to support Zeitschel's impatience to obtain the French authorities' agreement to administer the application of the measures regarding the yellow star. "As I have verbally informed Obersturmführer Dr. Knochen and Hauptsturmführer Dannecker, in view of the murder of a French police officer and the principal participation of the Jews in the Communist troubles in Argenteuil, the embassy has dropped its objections to the introduction of the star in the occupied zone. In addition, the embassy is asking you to carry out the introduction of the Jewish star as quickly as possible."[22]

The decision was made long before the final ordinance is decreed. On May 14, SS Captain Dannecker distributes a note to the Paris departments of the Gestapo, with a copy to Berlin. The note provides a preliminary draft that will serve as the basis of the 8th Nazi ordinance of May 29, 1942:

After a new discussion on the acceptance of exemptions, all departments concerned agreed that, in the interest of a single treatment in all the occupied territories, the rules that are valid in the Netherlands would be applied. Consequently, the 8th ordinance on anti-Jewish measures will read as follows:

---

18. Hence the implied need to have the French police do the work.
19. On the corrected copy of this note, the word for "final" is replaced with "definitive."
20. SS Reder had felt that there was no need to introduce the yellow star in the Netherlands and was waiting for orders from his superiors to give his assent. This detail is added at the end of the note.
21. CDJC-XLIX a 3.
22. CDJC-XLIX a 8.

PARAGRAPH 1

1. It will be prohibited for Jews over the age of six full years to appear in public without wearing the Jewish star.

2. The Jewish star is a six-pointed star with the dimensions of the palm of a hand and is outlined in black. It is in yellow fabric and has the word *Jew* on it in black letters. It must be worn visibly, on the left side of the chest, securely sewn on the clothing.

PARAGRAPH 2

Penal provisions:

Violations of this ordinance will be punished by imprisonment and a fine, or one of the two. Police measures such as internment in a camp for Jews may be added to or substituted for these punishments.

PARAGRAPH 3

This ordinance will come into force on June 7, 1942. At the same time, the press will publish the following notice: "Jews subject to the obligation to wear an identifying mark, by virtue of the 8th ordinance of May 29, 1942, on the measures taken against Jews, will have to present themselves to the police station or the sub-prefecture for their residence in order to receive badges in the form of a star, as provided in Paragraph 1 of said ordinance. Every Jew will receive three badges and will have to give in exchange a corner of his or her clothing ration card."

In the department,[23] it has been agreed that Jews who are nationals of the countries of North, Central or South America, as well as British nationals and nationals of neutral countries, will not be required to wear the identifying mark. This is in order to avoid reprisals against German nationals or those of neutral countries.[24]

Thus the practice of marking or branding men and women considered different, a legacy of the Middle Ages, is established without the slightest difficulty.

PREPARATIONS

FOR THE NAZIS, it goes without saying that the French law enforcement authorities will carry out the concrete tasks and then the repressive

---

23. The IV J department of the Gestapo in Paris, responsible for Jewish affairs.
24. CDJC-XLIX a 13.

actions. This is what the French ambassador Fernand de Brinon, the Vichy government's representative in the occupied territories, is told by General Oberg. On May 30, de Brinon passes along the orders and informs the prefects in the occupied zone and, in particular, the prefect of police, of these measures:

> Upon reception of these instructions, please, make all necessary arrangements to ensure, under conditions that will be defined by the German military authorities, the application of the orders they have decreed.
>
> In the first place, I particularly draw your attention to the importance of all Jews being in possession of their badges on June 6 at the latest. The German authorities have stated that the effective date of the ordinance below must be rigorously respected.
>
> Along with the official who will give you these instructions, I am sending to you: badges corresponding to the number of Jews you recently informed me were present in your department. This number being multiplied by three because of the prescribed number of three badges per person. . . . The issuance of the badges must be recorded. Each party concerned must sign a form in a register or on a statement. These documents must be kept in the files of the office that issued the badges. The form may be signed only in exchange for a piece of fabric that will be cut by the office distributing the badges . . . . [25]

The memo explains that this means the nearest police station.

The police stations in Paris and the suburbs prepare to issue ninety-five thousand yellow stars. For the whole of the occupied zone, four hundred thousand "special badges" are printed. There is a call for bids to provide some six thousand square yards of gold-colored cloth, which represent a weight of more than fifteen hundred pounds. The lucrative contract is won by Barbet-Massin-Popelin, a well-known wholesaler located in Paris.[26] The stars are printed and cut at the Charles Wauters et Fils print shop in Paris.[27] The zinc plates for printing the stars are provided by Deberny et Peignot, a well-known foundry in Paris.[28] High-quality work is delivered on a tight deadline; the prefecture of police only have to receive the merchandise. Everything is ready as scheduled, but in some cases, the process has to be rushed. While the order for the zinc printing plates is received by the foundry on May 4, 1942, and filled the

25. APP, series BA 1817 (dossier B 5 16).
26. CDJC-XLIX a 6. This bid is reproduced on pp. 114–155.
27. CDJC-XLIX a 12.
28. CDJC-XLIX a 9.

following day, and the order for the cloth is also filled quickly, the same is not true for the final production of the stars, and the printer calls on the services of the Gestapo through the chief of police for the Enfants-Rouges neighborhood, as shown by the following letter sent on May 13, 1942, by SS Captain Dannecker: "The Wauters printers, at 16 Rue de Montmorency, are now working on a very urgent order for the German authority. They must be authorized to work as late as necessary—even overnight—to allow them to finish this order for the deadline that has been set."[29]

Were the Nazis worried about how the operation of issuing the stars was going? The German military leaders were not all convinced of the support of the French police. This is what seems to emerge from a June 1, 1942 letter from the German military command, propaganda section, the addressee of which is not named in the archived document:

> Following four communications from French collaborators' circles, the Paris office of propaganda has given the impression that the anti-Jewish measures taken up to now have not developed as hoped because the ordinances were only carried out halfheartedly by the French police. On the one hand, it appears that a large number of Jews did not declare themselves as Jews but today, as previously, were placed on the lists of residents as Turks, Armenians, Romanians, etc. On the other hand, the appropriate departments of the French police have not done what was necessary to list all Jews living in Paris, without exception.[30]

This high-level military officer must have been brainwashed by the zealots of a collaborationist group who felt that the repression was not effective enough. However, the activities carried out by the French law enforcement authorities had convinced the Nazis of their good will for nearly two years, and examples of the police refusing to carry out orders were rare. His words are even less credible because, as we will see, the specialized departments of the prefecture of police have been preparing feverishly for the great day.

> The measures against the Jews were and are being carried out by the French police with an indescribable lack of enthusiasm. The prohibitions on going out and conducting business have essentially existed only on paper up to now. It should be noted that the

29. CDJC-XLIX a 12.
30. CDJC-XLIX a 19.

31

French police do not know that infringements of the decree by Jews constitute a first step. What has followed is not surprising; Parisians of the Jewish race more or less laugh off the ordinances. This has the effect of negative propaganda. The non-execution or poor execution of the measures taken by the military command does not improve the credibility of the German Authorities among the general population.[31]

It seems clear that the warped reactions of a group of active collaborators were used in order to make the point that the repression was not being sufficiently applied. The authors of the report knew perfectly well that the roundups of 1941 had been carried out wholly by the French police, whose willingness had been unfailing. But they wanted to speed things up and intensify the racial measures. That is what this message seems to suggest in its insistence that many French people were expecting much harsher actions against the Jews and that the police would therefore have to be more productive.

The adoption of the Jewish star, which, as we know, has long been demanded by all the collaborators' circles in the population, will only be seen as a propaganda action, and it will achieve the desired result only when its *brutal execution* reaches one hundred percent. But that means the police who have until now been in charge of these jobs should be replaced by new enforcement agencies we can rely on. We can observe that Jews who have not yet declared themselves continue to appear in public as non-Jews, and if, in addition, declared Jews do not wear the Jewish star, there will be very unfortunate consequences. We cannot yet judge the efficacy of the anti-Jewish police[32] the new commissariat will create, or know whether, with the help of the collaborationist parties, especially the PPF, it will be possible to create a new surveillance organization. In either case, it is still necessary that these measures be carried out with greater energy than the measures taken up to now.[33]

Yet, while he is speaking of a lack of zeal, the prefecture of police is already worrying about a shortage of stars for the designated victims pre-

---

31. Ibid.
32. This refers to the Police for Jewish Affairs, which was created by the Commissariat-General for Jewish Affairs and would soon become the Investigation and Control Section.
33. CDJC-XLIX a 19.

senting themselves at the police stations. This is stated in a June 4, 1942 memo from Tanguy, director of the judicial police, to the precinct captains of Paris and the suburbs as well as to the intelligence services and Jewish Affairs department of the police: "Starting tomorrow morning, for tomorrow, Friday, and Saturday, because of the lack of sufficient stock, you will distribute only two badges per person instead of three. This way, we will know in the future that those whose names begin with *M* have received only two. You will carefully keep the badges remaining after the distribution on Saturday and let me know by telegram on Monday the 8th, before noon, the number of badges that remain in your possession for subsequent distribution."[34]

Is the police leadership close enough to the concerns of the occupiers? There are indeed hate-driven collaborationist zealots who want to speed up the process, whatever the consequences for French society. Fortunately, these hysterical anti-Semites are often neurotics, and make difficult allies. This is the case for Captain Sézille, a First World War veteran named secretary-general of the Institute for the Study of Jewish Affairs, who shares his concerns with SS Dannecker on June 4, 1942:

> I had the pleasure of meeting Monsieur Heinrichson,[35] with whom I discussed the measures to be taken against the Jews. On this subject, I submit to you the following plan that the Friends of the Institute group intends to carry out. It is unacceptable to allow streets in Paris to bear the names of Jews, such as Boulevard Pereire, which I have myself asked, in four different letters to the prefect of the Seine, Monsieur Magny, to be changed to Boulevard Édouard-Drumont. This was naturally refused, on the pretext that the French government would not make any changes to street names until the end of the war. I feel it would be absurd that the French should be able to recognize Jews by the star they wear and not know the streets of Paris that bear the names of Jews (attached, a list of the streets bearing names of Jews).[36]

This was pure craziness. This madman who presided over the Institute for the Study of Jewish Affairs claimed to be fighting a police force and a government that were not fulfilling their obligations. Hatred

34. APP, series BA 1817 (dossier B 51).
35. A direct collaborator with SS Captain Dannecker and later his successor, Röthke.
36. CDJC-XI a 197.

often unleashes embarrassing passions that hinder the instigators of repression and their most faithful servants. Captain Sézille was a tenacious type, and even those who wanted to take him seriously must have been troubled by his logic:

> These streets should also be marked with a yellow star, and this work could be carried out by the Friends of the Institute. Naturally, we are going to encounter an impediment from the French police, but that will not stop us in our action to draw the attention of the authorities. We must, more and more, push the government to take measures, and it will only do so if it feels public opinion behind it. However, I ask you, Monsieur le Capitaine, to give me your opinion of this operation, and in case some of us should be arrested, to kindly grant us your intervention with the French police.[37]

On June 5, 1942, for the second time and in almost the same words, the propaganda section of the German military administration makes known its doubts regarding the commitment and the effectiveness of the French police in carrying out the tasks entrusted to it.[38] However, on the same day, a circular from the office of Émile Hennequin, director-general of the municipal police, warns the different departments about some Parisians who are determined to subvert the German ordinance on the yellow star: "If it is reported to you that young Aryans wearing the yellow star are demonstrating in the street, intervene immediately. You will proceed to arrest them, establish whether or not they are Jews and keep them at the disposal of the gendarmerie, whose headquarters you will notify at OPEra 21-29, extension 39. You will immediately report this to municipal police headquarters."[39]

This appeal for repression against non-Jews who dare make fun of the edicts is in line with a directive of the Gestapo. It shows the good will of the police authorities of Paris. They will not only exercise repression against Jews, but will also convince the French not to challenge the validity of the Nazis' crusade. The message is clear: whether they like it or not, the French must accept the exclusion of the Jews. If they oppose the measures implemented by the occupiers, they themselves will be treated like Jews.

Also on June 5, 1942, a report from the intelligence services seems

---

37. Ibid. Among the thirty-odd streets that Captain Sézille wished to have decorated with a yellow star were the following: Rosa-Bonheur, Halévy, Erlanger, Mendelssohn, Meyerbeer, Pierre-Louÿs, Chernowitz, Florence-Blumenthal, Georges-de-Porto-Riche and Rachel.
38. CDJC-XXVI 24.
39. APP, series BA 1818.

concerned about how the people of Paris will react when they see the first yellow stars in the streets of the city. It is clear that the inspectors are unnecessarily alarmist, so sure are they that the measure to take effect two days later will greatly displease people:

> The publication of the 8th German ordinance, on the obligation for Jews to wear a special badge, did not give rise to surprise in the Jewish community, where this measure had been expected for some time. However, various concerns were expressed about the methods of application of these new rules. Generally speaking, people were surprised by the discrimination between Jews of some nationalities, such as French and German Jews, who are forced to wear the badge, and others, such as Spanish or Italian Jews, who are exempted from doing so. Furthermore, people in general cannot understand why a French Jew who is a war veteran, and sometimes has even been wounded and decorated, should be treated worse than his Greek or Bulgarian coreligionist. Finally, the Jews are upset that the measure is applicable to children, who they fear will be exposed to bullying by their Aryan schoolmates.[40]

The report expresses pessimism based on the negative reactions of part of the population. One obsession is paramount: that the leaders of the underground Communist Party might seize the opportunity to stir up unrest "with the most turbulent elements of the Jewish community." The report also envisages the possibility that there will be a major fund-raising effort to promote a solidarity that perhaps would not arise of itself:

> The distribution of the Jewish badges should be finished on the 6th of the month, and it is foreseeable that the following day, Sunday the 7th, will be marked by some incidents. According to the intelligence gathered up to now in this regard, the Jews have been called on to gather en masse in the main streets of the capital and to circulate showing their badges in such a way as to create a real display. In the Latin Quarter, for example, it appears that the students have decided to show their disapproval of this measure against the Jews next Sunday by wearing mock badges at the center of which the word *Jew* is replaced by the word *swing* or by the name of the province where they were born: Normandie,

---

40. APP, report of the police intelligence service, "La situation de Paris."

Bretagne, etc. It is even possible that Aryan Communists may put on Jewish badges and display them in the Latin Quarter in order to provoke incidents if they have the opportunity to do so.[41]

Here again, the information gathered by the intelligence services is extremely uncertain. As we are relying on internal information, perhaps this was simply a case of self-brainwashing, the old police habit of exaggerating the danger or insecurity in order to justify the need for unchecked repression. The fact remains that the intelligence services overestimated the ability, or the desire, of the clandestine French Communist Party to get involved in this kind of agitation. Finally, they counted on the Jews themselves to accept wearing the yellow star without too much complaint: "The moderate elements of the Jewish community, eager to conform to the rule in order to avoid harsher measures, have already decided to stay home on the 7th and have canceled any meetings outside."[42] The authors of the report seem to consider this sensible, because the thugs of the French fascist parties could well be looking for trouble on June 7, 1942. Finally, the intelligence services still want to believe that things will go well, even if there might be a few incidents in certain places in Paris. "Ultimately, it is not likely that the Jews would respond to a general rallying cry and willingly expose themselves to sanctions whose harshness they can already envisage."[43]

As the fateful day approaches, the police services involved are on high alert. On June 6, 1942, a memo goes out to all offices—municipal police, police administration, intelligence services, special services, technical services, Jewish departments and neighborhood police stations—from the prefecture of police:

> *The occupying authorities have decided not to tolerate demonstrations or manifestations of any kind in favor of the Jews.*[44] Consequently, you will immediately recommend to your officers that they be especially vigilant and intervene immediately, quickly, decisively and firmly. You will proceed to arrest any Jewish or Aryan person who shows hostility to the wearing of the badge. You will do the same with regard to non-Jews who are wearing the star or a badge whose form and color imitate it, and also to Jews walking around in groups conspicuously displaying

41. Ibid.
42. Ibid.
43. Ibid.
44. Emphasis in original.

their badges. You will report any incident to PM[45] headquarters. You will receive subsequent instructions on the persons who are to be apprehended . . . .[46]

The words "Jews walking around in groups conspicuously displaying their badges" are particularly offensive, because the Jews had been notified that the "special badge" had to be worn very visibly. Unless "conspicuously" could have meant "with pride" or "without the slightest shame." This peremptory memo makes it clear that the aim was not just to obey the enemy's orders but to take special care to carry them out harshly. Obeying orders was no longer enough. The police had to be aggressive.

On June 7, 1942, Jews in the occupied zone will have to wear the yellow star. The prospect drives many of the designated victims to despair. Most will submit—how can they do otherwise when almost all of them are known to the police and have files? Some of them will decide to ignore the edict, which means that they will have to disappear, find a hiding place and live in fear more than hope. Others will decide to end it all and commit suicide. Police reports record the cases of these people, over whom they no longer have the power of coercion.

On June 6, 1942, a report to municipal police headquarters by the chief of police in the Goutte d'Or neighborhood states: "Today at 8:15 p.m., Jules Henri Weil, Esq., born 29-9-1896 in Paris, Jewish, living at 20 Rue Léon, in Paris, 18th, was discovered dead in his home. Suicide by lighting gas. I am investigating."[47] The cause of this suicide is perhaps not obvious, but a memo from the office of the prefect of police on the same day provides some details: "Weil, Jules, Jewish, was a lieutenant in the reserve, Legion of Honor, Croix de Guerre 1914–1918, liberated in August 1941. Refused to wear the *Jewish badge*,[48] committed suicide."[49]

Things are at a fever pitch at the municipal police headquarters, and alarming reports proliferate. Still on June 6, a "good citizen" anticipates that things will likely be hot the next day and says they should keep their eyes open: "An informant tells us that on Sunday, June 7, the Jews intend to hold a demonstration, backed up by the Communist Party. Their goal, if they are able to assemble, will be to go down the Champs-Élysées in small groups, conspicuously wearing the yellow star on black background with the word *Jew* on it, and the Communists will wear the same badge,

---

45. PM: police municipale; municipal police.
46. APP (dossier PJ 33).
47. APP, series 1816 (dossier B 51).
48. Underlined in blue pencil on this second note, which was handwritten in pen.
49. APP, series 1816 (dossier B 51).

but instead of the word *Jew*, theirs will show the region they come from or some other region."[50] Of course, no such demonstration ever takes place—it is a product of the fertile mind of the informant.

On Saturday, June 6, all police departments are on high alert. As if the application of the 8th ordinance the next day must take precedence over all other duties of the Paris police. At 5 p.m., Tanguy, director of the judicial police, addresses an urgent memo to the precinct captains of Paris and the suburbs as well as the technical services and the Jewish affairs section. Rioters, phony police officers and other troublemakers—there are a lot of them at this time—can operate freely; there are urgent matters elsewhere: "The application of the German ordinance concerning the wearing of the Jewish badge is entrusted to the municipal police, who will see to the direct internment of offenders. Only the contentious cases will be transmitted to us. According to our decision, the internment that will follow will also be the responsibility of the municipal police. Note that Aryans who demonstrate in favor of the Jews will be treated in the same way as Jews. On Monday and the following days, you will continue, until further notice, to issue badges to Jews who present themselves late. For this purpose, retain the extra staff placed at your disposal. Those people who are late will be subject to special treatment."[51] Sanctions, perhaps.

Still on June 6, 1942, one last circular, signed jointly by the director of the judicial police—Tanguy—and the director of the municipal police—Hennequin—reminds the precinct captains of Paris and the suburbs of their duty. Once more, the occupiers' intent to repress is mentioned and prioritized. This flurry of memos and circulars on the eve of the enforcement of the ordinance requiring Jews to wear the "special badge" shows the clear intention of the heads of the Paris police to implement this repressive measure.

The German authorities have stipulated that the ordinance concerning the wearing of the Jewish badge must be applied rigorously, with no exceptions. Any demonstration against the ordinance of the Militärbefehlshaber [military commander] must be severely repressed. Ridicule of the ordinance will not be tolerated. Various cases may arise:

1) Demonstration by the Jews themselves, wearing several badges.

2) Demonstration by groups of Jews, the gathering of whom constitutes a protest.

50. CDJC-XLIX a 65.
51. APP, series BA 1818.

3) Aryans unjustifiably wearing the Jewish badge.

4) Exaggerated greeting addressed to a wearer of the badge, constituting a criticism.

5) Wearing of an invented badge that, in its color and shape, mocks the regulation badge (the word *Jew* replaced by the word *swing* or by the name of a province: Normandie, Bretagne, etc.).

The German authority attaches extraordinary importance to the implementation of this order, and the German police in civilian dress will see that the *various police bodies fulfill their duty correctly.*[52]

For the Aryans and non-Jews arrested for various protests against the German ordinance, the following measures are to be applied:

The police chief for public order will place them at the disposal of the precinct captain.

The precinct captain will detain them and immediately notify the administration of the judicial police.

Any badges worn by Aryans (invented or not) will be confiscated and turned over to the administration of the judicial police with a detailed report.

The administration of the judicial police *will report the incident to the occupying authorities*[53] and will notify the precinct captain of their decision.[54]

Nevertheless, the priority remains hunting down any Jews who express resistance to wearing the "special badge"—who can only be identified by means of the racial profiling that has been favored by the police since the promulgation of the first racial laws in October 1940. In their final task of that preparatory day of June 6, 1942, Tanguy and Hennequin draft a last circular to the chiefs of police divisions, police chiefs for public order, and suburban precinct captains:

The application of the 8th ordinance regarding the wearing of the Jewish badge:

1) Men aged 18 and over.

Every Jew violating this ordinance will be sent to the cells by the police captain with responsibility for public order with a special,

---

52. My italics. These words clearly indicate the submission of the Paris police forces to the orders of the Nazi occupiers.
53. My italics. Again, these words clearly indicate the submission of the Paris police forces to the orders of the Nazi occupiers.
54. APP, series BA 1818.

individual arrest warrant, drawn up in duplicate. (The second copy being for M. Roux, police chief, custody section.) This document will set out the place, day, time and circumstances of the arrest, the first name, surname, place, date and place of birth, family details, profession, home address and nationality of the individual taken into custody. They will then be taken to Drancy Camp, along with the original arrest warrant, by the transfer section.

2) Minors of both sexes, aged between 16 and 18, and Jewish women.

They will also be sent to the cells by the captain with responsibility for public order, following the procedures set out above.

The staff on duty at the station will send the originals of the arrest warrants to the Department of Foreigners and Jewish Affairs which, after consultation with the German authorities, will decide on their case.

No release should be carried out without a written order from the Department.

3) Jewish minors under 16 years of age.

The captain with responsibility for public order will send Jews of both sexes under sixteen years of age to be dealt with by the precinct captain.

The precinct captains will proceed to conduct an investigation and will have the parent, or the person possessing parental authority, arrested once their responsibility has been established (cf para. 3, rider to art. 2 of the ordinance. PJ memorandum 475, p. 4).

The person whose responsibility has thus been established will be held in custody at the police station until a decision has been made by the Occupying Authority that will be sent to you by the Department of the Judicial Police. To this end precinct captains will submit a telegram to the Department of the Judicial Police with a summary of the incident and containing the same details as in the custody orders for men aged 18 and over as regards the person with responsibility who has been taken into custody.[55]

It is a huge administrative machine that is put in place for June 7 to crack down even harder than is demanded by the 8th ordinance promulgated by the Nazis. As soon as it is light, the sleuths of the French police will be on the racial warpath, while retaining full dignity and honor...

---

55. Cited by Serge Klarsfeld, in *Vichy Auschwitz*, Fayard, 1983, volume 1, p. 201.

5

Hunting Them Down

F ROM THE EARLY HOURS of this Sunday June 7, 1942, the first day when wearing the yellow star is obligatory, the Paris police are on the warpath. Their task is to see that the Nazi ordinance is observed. From now on men and women who do not have the right facial profile are questioned if they aren't wearing this "special badge" that has been allocated to them. The racist nature of this step is obvious and the physiognomists are at work. What other way is there of detecting those in the street who do not conform to the "Aryan" type, to use the terminology now adopted by the Paris police, than by an identity check, by the features?

Hour by hour the reports from agents of the police intelligence service and the details in the logbooks pile up in the district police stations and the city police headquarters. However, the fact remains that incidents, the possibility of which had been forecast several days ago, do not occur in the capital, which, according to the intelligence service, has retained "its habitual face." An early report suggests that the bloodhounds are indeed on the look-out and not losing any time: "Early this morning at the Gare d'Austerlitz, five Jews lacking the badge, who were getting ready to board the train, were put under arrest. They have been handed over to the police captain with responsibility for public order in the 13th district."[1]

At 10 a.m. a new report from the intelligence service. The police are

---

1. APP, series BA 1817 (dossier B 51 7).

keeping their eyes open. Incidents are rare, but the army of police sent out into the streets of Paris to try and hunt down the few foolhardy recalcitrants who venture to show themselves in public without the yellow star, have to remain on alert.

"The general state of affairs is normal in the principal thoroughfares of the capital. Jews wearing the badge proceed individually and do not engage in any demonstrations. Toward 9:30, on the corner of the Place de l'Opéra and the Boulevard des Capucines a Jewish street vendor wearing a badge that was not conspicuously displayed, a certain Prosper Ben-Ichou, was set upon by passers-by, notably by a certain Jacques Ernest Émile Berthet, bank clerk. The Jew Ben-Ichou and the above-mentioned Berthet have been taken to the Opéra police station for the purpose of an identity check."[2]

This incident tends to show that, for lack of possible victims, they need to make do with virtual offenders: Jews who attempt to conceal their star.

In the late morning a police captain called Delbrel from the 9th district, on special assignment like all his colleagues, sends a message to police headquarters, "I am taking Srul Bernard into custody; b. 10/16/1893 in Foltigonie (Romania), married, no children, shoe-vendor, he was proceeding along Rue Montmartre, outside no. 150, at 11 a.m., not wearing the Jewish badge."[3]

Another report from the Intelligence Service confirms the type of action taken by policemen on this morning of June 7, 1942: "At 11:30 a.m. on Place de la République the Jew Salon Lemmal, b. May 6, 1889, at Wertheim (Lower Rhine), French national, not wearing the badge, was arrested and handed over to the 2nd district police station. Meanwhile the following individuals: Szlim Migdal, b. 1912 in Zaroly (Poland), race Jewish; Elsa Pozyn, b. February 28, 1906, in Zaroly (Poland), race Jewish, were arrested by the local police for not wearing the badge and handed over to the 3rd district police station."[4] And then again: "a great many individual Jews are about in the streets of the more densely populated districts of the capital, notably in the Belleville district, Place de la République, Place de la Bastille and Rue Saint-Antoine. Others can be seen on Boulevard de la Madeleine and Rue Royale but they are not commented on. The Police Department for Jewish Affairs, in collaboration with the occupation police, is checking all the pedestrians on Place de la République."[5] This detail serves to prove that the police are not limiting

2. Ibid. Ben-Ichou's arrest record is reproduced on pp. 116–117.
3. APP, series PJ 33.
4. APP, series BA 1817 (dossier B 51 7).
5. Ibid.

themselves to checking the facial characteristics of the pedestrians. More than that, it seems that in certain districts it is the whole of the population that is being checked, far beyond a suspicion based on the "Jewish" looks sought by certain policemen.

This same report contains an item of information that will have satisfied both the French police authorities and the Gestapo officers: "Around 11 o'clock outside no. 1 Rue de Strasbourg, M. Charpentier called for a police officer to go and arrest his wife, from whom he was separated and who lacked any identity papers and the Jewish badge. The woman is Rebecca Charpentier, née Cogan, July 11, 1907, in Bolgrad (Romania), race Jewish, who has been handed over to the central police station of the 10th district."[6]

Throughout this first day there are repeated reports and press releases. The apparent calm in Paris appears to surprise the members of the intelligence service who, during the previous few days, had been influenced by alarmist reports. What is more, there are none of the protests that had been forecast: "At 1:30 p.m. conditions in the capital are still normal. Jews wearing the badge are going about their business without comment. No incidents have been reported from the densely populated districts, the Latin Quarter, the main boulevards, the Champs Élysées or the outer boulevards."[7]

In the central districts of Paris the same reports, in the same terms and the same pattern, keep coming in. At 12:40 Esther Solarz, born 1915 in Poland, "race Jewish," who is out in the streets without a badge, is stopped and taken to the police station of the 5th district.[8] At 4:30 p.m. a report with no precise details confirms that the municipal police are not the only ones hunting down Jews who are attempting to hide behind culpable anonymity: "During the afternoon two lieutenants from the section dealing with Jewish affairs proceeded to arrest Rebecca Safir, b. September 17, 1901, in Paris, race Jewish, and Schmul Kotler, cap-maker, b. May 15, 1883, in Vilno… Both of them were out walking in the streets of the 4th district. The first had two badges, the second none at all. These two have been sent to the precinct captain of the 4th district."[9]

There is constant emphasis on the state of calm in Paris. There is even a tendency to feel concerned at the sight of these Jews quietly going about their business in the capital. That is what is behind the note sent by the 3rd division to the headquarters of the Paris police: "Situation calm, a

6. Ibid.
7. Ibid.
8. Ibid.
9. APP, series PJ, 33.

fairly significant number of *Jews out for a stroll*,[10] notably at the Sébastopol-Saint-Denis crossing."

Around 4 p.m. the precinct captain of the 2nd district reports to his superiors that he has done his duty: "The French Jew Georges Svartz, b. 8/8/1925, single, living with his parents, had a piece of paper with *'on nez comme on est'* attached next to the yellow star [literally 'one nose what one is,' a pun on the nose, supposedly the most characteristic feature of the Jews; *'on nez'* and *'on est'* sound the same, so that read aloud it would sound like 'one is what one is']. He lent a Jewish star to the French Aryan Rebora. Svartz was handed over to me today."[11]

Even if routine seems to predominate, the scenarios vary, as can be seen from the case above, but in general it is always the racist sense of distinctions preceding the identity check which will be fatal for the foolhardy. At 6 p.m. a police captain from the 18th district informs police headquarters of his latest catch: "Plain-clothes officers Dolléans and Petit have arrested and handed over to me the Jew Aïm Fucks, b. 8/25/1922 in Odessa (Russia), living with his parents, who was out in the street without the regulation badge."[12]

In the course of the afternoon there is a report from the intelligence service about a demonstration organized by fascist groups. There is indeed an intention to create an incident, for lack of the disturbances predicted during the preceding days. This report is marked by its required matter-of-fact tone. As if the demonstration were a perfectly normal event—public opinion has to be allowed to express itself, even at the risk of some minor disorder:

"Since 4:20 p.m. a group of a dozen persons, wearing a badge with a horseshoe encircling a cornflower, have been walking along Boulevard de la Madeleine in the direction of Place de la Concorde booing at Jews. In a café on Boulevard des Capucines they urged the waiters not to serve Jewish customers. On the terrace of Brasserie Weber, Boulevard de la Madeleine, they slapped a Jew who was wearing the badge; they reproved a maître d' and one of the waiters. The group is continuing to walk in the direction of Place de la Concorde."[13]

The police take hardly any notice of this demonstration by French fascists; their sole concern is with people who were "visibly Jewish" who might venture out onto the main boulevards or those of them daring to "flaunt" the yellow star. It is certain that no arrest is made even if, hour

---

10. Ibid. Underlined in the text.
11. Ibid.
12. Ibid.
13. APP, series BA 1817 (dossier B 51 7).

after hour, the officers of the intelligence service take an interest in this demonstration that would delight the Nazi occupiers:

"Around 5:30 p.m. some thirty young people, led by two members of the Legion of French Volunteers[14] in uniform, marched along Avenue des Champs Élysées, on the right-hand side, as far as Rue de la Boétie. As they went along they booed at Jews and forced those who were on the café terraces to go inside. Then the group moved over to the left side of Avenue des Champs Élysées and continued as far as Avenue Georges-V. The Jews on the terrace of Café Tam-Tam were booed then the members of the group continued in the direction of Place de l'Étoile. The municipal police having been informed, a barrier was set up at the crossing with Rue de Tilsitt. The members of the group dispersed then formed up again on that road and continued in the direction of Avenue de Wagram, where they were once more dispersed."[15]

Another report, at 6:20 p.m., on this demonstration, now apparently flanked by police so that things don't get too out of control:

"[...] The group of about thirty, led by members of the Legion, that had been dispersed on Avenue de Wagram, managed to form again on Place des Ternes and continued their march along Rue du Faubourg-Saint-Honoré. The local police have been informed."[16]

That is no surprise. On this day the police do not suppress anti-Semitic demonstrations on public streets, except in cases where they refuse to keep moving. This resulted in a few hard-core members of fascist parties being detained for questioning:

"At 6:15 p.m. Joseph Mérienne, b. November 22, 1895, in Paris, 8th district, turner, French nationality, Aryan, who was distributing anti-Jewish tracts on the corner of Rue Astorg and Rue La Boétie remonstrated with two officers who had refused his tracts. He was handed over to the 8th district police station.

"At 7 p.m., a group of thirty anti-Jewish demonstrators was dispersed by the local police at the junction of Avenue des Champs Élysées and Avenue Marigny. Four of them, who refused to keep moving, were taken to the 8th district police station. They were:

"—Jean-François Bardot, b. November 16, 1918, in Versailles, student, member of the Anti-Bolshevist Legion, convalescing;

"—Gilbert Demars, b. November 16, 1923, in Vence (Alpes Maritimes), radio engineer, member of the MSR, 12th section;[17]

---

14. These are clearly members of the LVF, French mercenaries in the German army fighting on the Russian front.
15. APP, series BA 1817 (dossier B 51 7).
16. Ibid.
17. Mouvement social révolutionnaire [MSR—Social revolutionary movement] was set up at the end of 1940 by Eugène

"—Lucien Schlesser, b. October 19, 1922, in Versailles, clerk in the Commission for Jewish Affairs, member of the Ligue française.[18]

"Lucien Rosée, b. June 9, 1922, in Rouen, stage manager, member of the MSR, 10th section."[19]

What we have is doubtless only a small part of these reports. The fact remains, however, that throughout this first day when the yellow star had to be worn the repression is carried out by French policemen who could well have looked the other way. This desire to do well reflects the willingness of the police to carry out the 8th Nazi ordinance. Among the police stations producing the most results is that of the 5th district; moreover a report to the headquarters of the municipal police comes from the Panthéon precinct:

"At 6:30 p.m. a woman called Bacque, née Weintrand, b. 9/14/1887 in Serga (Poland), nationality French, housewife, has been arrested for not wearing the Jewish badge and kept in custody at the main station."[20]

At the end of the day the intelligence service concludes that in the end, everything has gone smoothly. The Jews as a whole have conformed with the edicts, without the authorities going so far as to suggest they have been reasonable. On the other hand the "Aryans" whom one might have thought would show their solidarity have not put in an appearance, despite the rumors that were spread. As for the provocative acts of the fascists, they were not considered a danger to public order. This is what comes out in the report:

"In the course of the day the Jews do not appear to have been obeying a general instruction aimed at making them appear en masse on public streets in order to form a demonstration. The breaches of the 8th German ordinance that have been noted appear to have been isolated actions. The incidents on the Champs Élysées that required the intervention of the police were provoked by young people belonging to anti-Jewish organizations. As for the general public, on the whole they appear not to have been particularly interested in the measures taken to enforce the German ordinance."[21]

This last report, dated June 7, 1942, is interesting in many respects. In the first place, it shows that the attempts during the previous days to work up public feeling were classic examples of attempts to provoke trouble.

Deloncle and financed by the Gestapo. The founders of the movement were mainly former members of the right-wing fascist terrorist organization la Cagoule, such as Jean Filliol, which had organized a series of attacks on synagogues in Paris in the night of October 2, 1941.
18. 'The French League'—a fascist-type party set up in the first months of 1941 by Pierre Constantini, former member of Action française, a far-right political movement founded in 1899. [MM]
19. APP, series BA 1817 (dossier B 5 17).
20. APP, series PJ 33.
21. Ibid.

Secondly, as we will see in the next chapter, very basic solidarity has only been expressed in the reactions of a few isolated individuals. Finally it should be noted that this report describes the demonstrators as members of "anti-Jewish organizations" and not of parties in favor of collaboration. This caution comes from the fact that at that time there were numerous fascist parties and they were literally at war with each other in order to establish a privileged relationship with the Gestapo. That explains the caution of the intelligence service.

In the late morning of June 8, the Municipal Police Department became aware that it hadn't really coped with the situation—at least on the administrative level, which explains this "general instruction" to the police stations of the city districts and the suburbs, to the police communication centers, and to the Jewish Affairs and Aliens section at police headquarters. It should be noted that the following document is marked *Confidential, not for general distribution:*

"Certain district police stations will not have had the time to distribute all the badges to the Jews who applied for them. When Jews who have been arrested claim that their police station was unable to issue the badges on the appointed day and told them to come at a later date, you must check their statements. If they are correct, those concerned must be taken to their district police station for the badges to be issued immediately."[22]

History does not tell us whether the Jews who were arrested for that reason the previous day will be released. The majority have already gone through police custody and been transferred either to Drancy internment camp for the men or, for the women, to Les Tourelles prison. With no hope of return.

A report from a "special department," doubtless the Gestapo, compiled on June 8, 1942, confirms that the French officers were not always alone in keeping an eye on pedestrians and looking for Jews who were shirking the requirement to wear the yellow star. These patrols, in direct collaboration with the German police, reveal the willingness of the French police to see that a Nazi edict is carried out:

"This morning some officers of the German military police were patrolling the 5th district and principally Boulevard Saint-Michel. With the assistance of French officers, they stopped all the Jews walking along the boulevard to demand to see their papers. Now many Jews are avoiding wearing the yellow star, so why not stop, instead of those who are

---

22. Ibid.

conforming, those who look as if they are not conforming to the ordinance. That is, we should be asking to see the papers of anonymous persons. A simple suggestion. On the other hand, public opinion is surprised at the considerable number of Jews there are in Paris, of which they had no idea. Many people, as a result of this measure, have begun to see the harm the Jews have caused us, they realize there are still too many of them despite the large number who fled during the recent events."[23]

On that day, two apparently anodyne reports from the intelligence service suggest that there is nothing about Operation Yellow Star that is not perfectly mundane. The police like to reinforce their certainties, as emerges from this internal reminder of the new obligations imposed on the Jews:

"The German ordinance no. 8, dated May 28, 1942, establishing for the Jews the requirement to wear a special badge reproducing the Star of David, came into force on June 7. Beforehand the Jews attended their local police station where their badges were handed out to them, three per person in exchange for one point of their clothing ration."[24]

The purpose of the second report seems to be to explain that life goes on, everyone having come to terms with the situation: the Jews and those who look at them since they have been wearing the badge.

"The public remains indifferent to the recent measures imposed on the Jews. Only those concerned have shown a response to them and expressed their fear that being marked out in this way might possibly expose them to harassment from certain elements in the population."[25]

On June 9, the office of the prefect of police, Amédée Bussières, keeps SS officer Dannecker informed of the retaliatory measures taken during the previous two days against those who disregarded the 8th ordinance. This letter amounts to clear proof of collaboration with the Nazis:

"I respectfully send you duplicate copies of the list of women and young people between 16 and 18 who were arrested on June 7 and 8 for not wearing the distinguishing badge of the Jews. *I beg you to be so good as to send me your instructions regarding them.*[26] Should we treat them in the same way as Jews found in the streets outside the prescribed times, as per the instructions I received from the commander of Greater Paris: V Pol 2/323-03, of February 16, 1942, that provide for police custody of at least 48 hours? As for men over 18 not wearing the badge, they are sent to Drancy Camp. The list will be sent to you every day following their arrival at the

23. CDJC-XLIX a 73. The poor translation of this report appears to confirm it was originally written in German.
24. APP, "The situation in Paris," June–July 1942 file.
25. Ibid.
26. My italics.

camp."[27] This letter is signed on behalf of the prefect of police by Tulard, the director of the Department of Aliens and Jewish Affairs.

In the archives of police headquarters is a station logbook with an entry dated June 10, 1942:

"Arrested this day at 10 a.m. on the premises of the prefecture of police, *for lack of the Jewish badge* by lieutenants Balcon, Turpinier and Kaiser of the intelligence service:

1) Gitla Sawicka, married name Mokrani, b. 1911 in Warsaw, French nationality, three children;

2) Chafo Alili, née Zyngier 1913 in Bialobrzegi (Poland), French nationality, one child.

Taken into custody. Signed Morisot, PI."[28]

As in other similar circumstances, the police are not the only ones out there, and there is no lack of good citizens who want to do their bit for the crackdown. Witness to this is a letter, dated June 13, 1942, and addressed to the head of police and the German SS, Avenue de l'Opéra:

"Take care, the Jews are not complying with your ordinance of 5/29/1942. There are a great many of them who are not wearing the Star of David. Round them up, demand their papers. *No more than 10% are wearing it*, and they are laughing at you. Be strict, send them to work camps in Germany and have a list of severe punishments published in the newspapers so that they will be a bit afraid. Why do you not also oblige those in the free zone to wear the badge? They've all taken refuge down there, and every day they are entering the zone without authorization."[29] This charming anonymous letter is signed: "A Frenchman who would like to see his country rid of this foul race once and for all."

On June 15 a report from the intelligence service notes, with a certain delay and imprecise dates, the new requirements affecting the Jews of Paris. It is as if they needed to be clear in their minds about a measure that had already been in force for a good week:

"Since June 6, the date of the implementation of the German ordinance obliging Jews to wear a special badge, Jews wearing this badge are forbidden to travel in the 1st-class carriages of the metro. They are only allowed to travel 2nd class in the last carriage of the trains."[30]

Keen to see the 8th ordinance properly enforced, the Gestapo officials in France keep the Berlin hierarchy informed, as is shown by this letter dated June 16, 1942, coming from SS officers Dannecker and Röthke,

27. CDJC-XLIX a 77.
28. APP, series BA 1817 (dossier B 51 7).
29. CJDC-XILX a 84 a.
30. APP, "The situation in Paris," June–July 1942 file.

but signed by their boss, Dr. Knochen:

"On the whole the introduction of the yellow star in the occupied zone of France on June 7, 1942, has passed without incident. Larger-scale demonstrations of sympathy, pro-Jewish marches or protests have not taken place. Preventive measures have been taken. The obligation for Jews to wear a distinctive badge has given rise to various reactions among the population. Wide areas of the population have shown little or no understanding for this distinctive badge. There are constant expressions of sympathy for the 'poor Jews,' especially Jewish children. People continue to see the Jewish question not as a racial problem but a religious question..."[31]

These somewhat dissatisfied reflections foreshadow even more drastic measures. In particular, the desire to impose the yellow star on people from certain countries that have avoided this rule (the British, North and South Americans, etc.), which, the authors of this letter say, would satisfy French anti-Semitic circles who cannot understand this leniency toward certain Jews living in France. However the SS report also contains certain signs of satisfaction:

"The yellow star has been favorably received in anti-Semitic circles, in particular, we have to say, by numerous small storekeepers and tradesmen who were most affected by the great economic influence exercised by the Jews. As a result of the distinctive badge, many people who had previously hidden their origin under cover of their foreign nationality turn out to be Jews. The population has not concealed its surprise at the high number of Jews there actually are."[32]

There is a tinge of regret in this report. The French population has remained more or less neutral with regard to the implementation of the 8th ordinance. For the SS, the lack of solidarity with those who have thus been made into outcasts is not enough. Fortunately, there are parties supporting collaboration:

"So far there have been no larger-scale anti-Jewish demonstrations, though anti-Semitic circles have suggested new restrictions to be imposed on the Jews. The measure finds approval in various political groups such as the PPF,[33] the RNP,[34] the MSR, but they are disappointed that it comes as the result of a German rather than a French initiative."[35]

On June 19, 1942, the SS officers Dannecker and Röthke count the

31. CDJC-XLIX a 90.
32. Ibid.
33. *Parti populaire français* (French People's Party), initially fascist then clearly pro-Nazi, created by Jacques Doriot, a defector from the Communist Party, in 1936.
34. *Rassemblement national populaire* (People's National Assembly), set up by Marcel Déat at the beginning of 1941. A defector from Léon Blum's SFIO in 1933, Marcel Déat was later to be labour minister in Pétain's government in exile in Sigmaringen.
35. CDJC-XLIX a 90.

number of yellow stars distributed by the French police. These results are in another note sent to the Nazi police authorities:

"According to information supplied by the Paris DNB on June 8, 1942, in total 78,699 yellow stars have been distributed to the Jews. According to information supplied by the prefecture of police (Tulard) on June 17, 1942, by that day around 83,000 yellow stars had been distributed. By November 1941, the number of Jews on record had grown to 95,000; at that date, there were said to be 15,000 Jewish children of between 7 and 15 years of age in the whole of the Paris district. According to the figures of November 1941 there should therefore be 95,000 plus 15,000, which is 110,000 Jews who ought to be wearing the yellow star. The difference between 83,000 and 110,000 would seem at first sight to be relatively significant, but it can be explained by the following facts:

1) Since November 1941, a certain number of Jews have managed to reach the unoccupied zone.

2) Furthermore, there are Jews who have been *evacuated*[36] to Germany.

3) It is also necessary to remember that the Jews of a whole series of foreign nationalities are not obliged to wear the yellow star.

4) Finally, there is in fact a certain percentage of Jews who have not yet collected their yellow star.

Furthermore, Tulard[37] indicated that he was personally surprised at the large number of stars handed out. He thought there would be a lot fewer Jews coming to collect their star. We have invited Tulard to send us in the next few days a precise and definitive official summary of the stars actually distributed."[38]

The Nazis attach great importance to the reactions of the French population to the anti-Jewish measures. Of course the extant sample is not the most convincing, but it does allow us to enhance what is contained in the files with material from Berlin. On June 24, 1942, the Gestapo department IV J issues to various German authorities some opinions gleaned in Paris after the introduction of the yellow star. This report comes from SS officer Theo Dannecker:

"*The Duke of M.* We can never be grateful enough to the Germans for having freed our country from these filthy Jews.

Marquis de la E. If we had to wear our cross, we would find that perfectly natural and wouldn't be unhappy with it.

---

36. My italics. "Evacuated" belongs to the Nazi coded language and means "deported."
37. The name of André Tulard, director of the Department of Jewish and Alien Affairs frequently appears in Nazi documents. In the present case it is perfectly clear that the creator of the Jewish file is constantly working.
38. CDJC-XLIX a 38.

A man of private means. The Jews ought to be proud at last to wear the yellow star, which they have for so long hoped for.

A collaborator. Well done, at last we can do business among ourselves without these filthy Jews.

A professional Swing dancer. It's a pity because of the Jewish girls, for there are some very pretty ones and now we can't be seen with them any more.

A housewife. It's sad for the children. Especially at school.

A Rue Lafayette jeweler. Why not the Turkish, Italian, Spanish, American Jews? Why this injustice?

An old worker. I didn't know my neighbors were Jews. Thanks to the star, I know now, and I understand why I felt an aversion toward the family, with whom we've never exchanged a word.

A Gaullist draughtsman. The yellow star? And why not a mark with a branding iron, as they gave convicts in the Middle Ages?

A small wine merchant. So much the better, now they won't be able to compete with us anymore."[39]

Always keen to do the right thing, the Paris police remain permanently on the alert. They wouldn't want their silent partners in the Gestapo to have the slightest reason to be unhappy with them. This concern can be clearly seen in a note dated July 10, 1942, signed by Émile Hennequin, head of the municipal police. This general instruction, sent out to the Paris precincts, the suburban police stations, the Jewish Department of the prefecture of police and the intelligence service, is particularly revealing:

"It has been reported to me that some Jews are secretly leaving their homes for the provinces. As of now, and until further notice, you will see to it that surveillance with particular regard to this is carried out by your plain-clothes officers:

A—at the Paris airports.

B—in the areas around railway stations and on the platforms for main-line services with no stops in the Seine and Seine-et-Oise departments.

All Jews not wearing the star or leaving the departments of Seine and Seine-et-Oise without authorization will be interned according to current regulations."[40]

The hunt for Jews proceeds in the most ordinary way, day-by-day, as a matter of routine, if one may put it like that. For the Paris police it's one task among others, like directing traffic or keeping an eye on the children when school lets out. A note dated July 21, 1942, from the police

---

39. CDJC-XLII a 96.
40. APP, series BA 1817 (dossier B 51 7).

station of the 13th district to the headquarters of the municipal police shows that, six weeks after the introduction of the yellow star, vigilance has not been relaxed:

"I am sending to the cells for a breach of the German ordinance of 5/28/1942, for not wearing the Jewish badge:

1) Warszawski, née Szarjarc, 3/14/1901 in Warsaw, Poland, no papers, residing at 12 Rue du Pôle Nord, Paris 18th.

2) Max Rosensztajn, b. 8/25/1924 in Paris 12th, French, son of Joseph and Adèle Kellner, bachelor, sheet metal worker, residing at 29 Boulevard Magenta, Paris 10th.

3) Chaïm Konstantyner, b. 3/5/1905 in Jokaroff, Poland, Polish, married, two children, dealer in secondhand goods, residing at 96 Rue de la Fraternité in Bagnolet.

4) Rouchla Konstantyner, née Rosentraub, 11/3/1899 in Lodz, Poland, Polish, two children, housewife, residing at 96 Rue de la Fraternité in Bagnolet, Seine.

Arrested this day at 11:30 a.m. within the precincts of Gare d'Austerlitz by officers of the 3rd section of the intelligence service."[41]

Each of these arrests on July 21, 1942, means the death of a man or woman, after a short delay and the classic tour: police cells, Drancy, Auschwitz. With the addition of a certain number of children. At 1 p.m. on that same day it appears that a young boy was arrested along with his parents. This is what comes out of a report sent by Lieutenant Hénin to the Department of Jewish Affairs at the police prefecture:

"I am handing over to Captain Dannecker, 31a Avenue Foch, the French boy Salomon Konstantyner, b. 4/24/1932 in Paris, 12th district, to Calen and Espera Rosentraub, living with his parents, Rue de la Fraternité, arrested today at 10:30 a.m. in Gare d'Austerlitz, for a breach of the ordinance of 5/25/1942. Not wearing the badge."[42]

The person in question is a boy of 10, easy prey for a policeman who has no scruples. Railroad stations are not the only places that attract policemen sent out to hunt down Jews who do not respect the ordinances. Still on July 21, the precinct captain of the 18th district informs Paris police headquarters that his men have done their duty: "1:15 p.m. at the main entrance to Bichat Hospital my men arrested a Jewish woman for selling goods in a public thoroughfare without authorization, Sarah Gutmann, b. 10/30/1915, living with her mother in Paris 14th, 25a Rue du

---

41. APP, series BA 1817 (dossier B 51 6).
42. Ibid.

Poteau; not wearing the star of David."[43]

On that same day the hunt has been fairly productive since further arrests for the same reason have contributed to the increase in the population of Drancy camp. It seems obvious that there will have have been many more station logbook entries of arrests and that we have not been able to access all the archives regarding people detained for this kind of questioning with its denouement. At 8:30 p.m., a policeman named Turpault in the station of the 4th district, calmly notes:

"Arrested today:

1) At 6 p.m. by officer Cambon of the 3rd section of the intelligence service on the premises of the PP [prefecture of police] for not wearing the Jewish badge: Lucie Dreyfus, b. 7/7/1900 in Strasbourg, French Jew, married, one child, housewife, residing at 20 Rue Danton in La Courneuve.

2) At 2:15 p.m. on the corner of Rue du Rocher and Rue de Laborde by cyclist officers Poulet and Bernard of the 8th district and taken to the 4th district by lieutenant Pierre Bedou of the 3rd section of the intelligence service for not wearing the Jewish badge: Robert Simon, b. 6/8/1894 in Vincennes, French nationality, of Jewish race, married, one child, track watchman residing at 144 Avenue de Paris, Vincennes.

They will be taken into custody."[44]

This document speaks for itself, especially the second arrest. It clearly shows that Robert Simon was checked by his physiognomy by two policemen on bicycles doing a routine patrol who 'collared' a Jew when that was certainly not the aim of their assignment.

As we have seen, a certain number of Jews coming from allied countries or those at war with Nazi Germany were exempted from wearing the yellow star when the 8th ordinance was announced. Collaborators regarded this as an 'injustice', and it has gradually been corrected. However, with the exception of Russian Jews, those coming from the allied countries were to remain exempted from wearing the yellow star until the end of the German occupation. Then there is a note from the national police department of the Interior Ministry in Vichy informing the prefects of the occupied zone that there was to be a development in Nazi legislation starting July 25, 1942:

"Item: the wearing of the yellow star by Jews of Hungarian nationality.

The head of the SS and the police, under the authority of the commander-in-chief of the military forces in France, has informed me of the

---

43. Ibid.
44. APP, series BA 1817 (dossier B 51 6).

following *advice*[45]: 'In completion of the arrangements in my note of June 1, 1942, I decree that, with immediate effect, Jews of Hungarian nationality are subject to the requirement to wear the distinctive badge of the Jewish star. I ask you to advise the French police and other authorities involved to issue instructions to that effect. I would be grateful if you would make immediate arrangements for those concerned to be provided with the badge that they are required to wear from now on.'[46]

There are no mundane arrests even if, quite often, they are carried out simply on the initiative of the police officers. Thus a strange note, dated September 27, 1942, with no indication of where it came from, shows that good citizens who like to see themselves as producing results, invent laws and decrees as their fancy takes them:

"At 3:30 this afternoon on Place de l'Opéra at the corner of Boulevard des Italiens two members of the Jeunesses du Maréchal[47] called for some police officers to arrest two Jews who were walking along Boulevard des Italiens. [...] These two Jews were taken to the central police station of the 9th district where they were discharged after the usual checks, the city police *not yet*[48] having received a directive forbidding Jews to use the boulevards. However, at 6 p.m. the central station of the 9th district was instructed by the municipal police that they are to proceed to arrest all Jews who were out on the grand boulevards."[49]

Ordinary arrests on no valid grounds are not rare. On November 19, 1942, Henri Bulawko, an official of a Jewish charitable organization, is detained for no apparent reason at the Père-Lachaise metro station:

"A police officer hails me. He sees my star and invites me to follow him. What crime have I committed? I learn that later. I am accused of hiding my star behind a book and a raincoat I am carrying over my arm. I try to demonstrate the absurdity of the accusation but the cop only recognizes one logic: his own. The roundup he has been charged with has to produce results. I am his only 'client' during the whole day, and he has no intention of letting me go."[50]

As 1942 comes to an end, an initial assessment of arrests due to Jews not wearing the yellow star can be drawn up. Since June 7, the Paris police have been paying particular attention to seeing that the 8th Nazi ordinance

---

45. A nice euphemism to avoid having to say "order."
46. APP, series BA 1817 (dossier 68 425).
47. The *Jeunesses du Maréchal* are the youth groups set up by Marshal Pétain on the model of the Hitler Youth. [MM].
48. This statement is not without interest. It indicates that the police are prepared, should the order be given, to take the repression as far as the occupying power may demand. That was seen on the occasion of the great roundup of July 16, 1942.
49. APP, series BA 1816 (dossier B 51). Such a directive is entirely a figment of the imagination for there are no reports of a ban on Jews using the grand boulevards.
50. In Henri Bulawko, *Le jeux de la mort et de l'espoir* (Encre, 1980), p. 44.

is observed. Although fragmentary, the bi-monthly reports of the intelligence service bring out this proactive vigilance. These reports appear with clockwork regularity and little real variation in the formulation.

—Report of June 12, 1942: "Sixty-six Jews who were not conforming to the provisions of the German ordinance requiring Jews to wear a *special badge* have been handed over to the Feldgendarmerie."

—Report of June 22, 1942: "Five Jews who were not wearing the special badge have been passed on to the Occupation Authorities."

—Report of July 13, 1942: 22 arrests.

—Report of July 27, 1942: 43 arrests.

—Report of August 10, 1942: 16 arrests.

—Report of August 24, 1942: 20 arrests.

—Report of September 7, 1942: 15 arrests.

—Report of September 20, 1942: 18 arrests.

—Report of October 5, 1942: 11 arrests.

—Report of October 19, 1942: 8 arrests.

—Report of November 2, 1942: 13 arrests.

—Report of November 13, 1942: 7 arrests.

—Report of November 30, 1942: 14 arrests.

—Report of December 14, 1942: 30 arrests.[51]

Thus these repetitive reports tell us that in a few months, apart from roundups, almost 300 people have been arrested, at random, according to chance identity checks based on their facial features. The officers carrying out these arrests had not necessarily been given this assignment. It is important to note that here there is no mention of the reasons for the arrests given in the station logbooks, for example the yellow star being badly sewn on or poorly cut out, as prescribed in the ordinance. Hunters like to assure us that during the battues the game has a chance. That wasn't the case for Parisian Jews from June 1942 to mid-August 1944 as they were hunted down by policemen motivated by the desire to see that the Nazi ordinances were respected. This hunt was to continue until shortly before the Liberation, and traces of these arrests can be found in the box files kept in the archives of the police prefecture. Proof, if need be, that during troubled times a police officer has no need of precise instructions to carry out this kind of action.

---

51. APP, report of the police intelligence service, "La situation de Paris."

A S A FOOTNOTE TO HISTORY we should point out that the small number of Jews identified on the Channel Islands (Jersey, Guernsey, Sark), with the help of the British police that remained there, were subject to the same German ordinances as the Jews of the occupied zone in France. Thus the 8th ordinance requiring the wearing of the yellow star with the word "Jew" at the center in black letters was registered with the Royal Court on Guernsey on June 30, 1942. It should also be pointed out that, despite everything, following the intervention of the governor and the crown prosecutor, this ordinance was not registered on Jersey. This is what emerges from a note dated June 15, 1942, by the governor of that island.

Finally, following an appeal by the administrator-in-chief of the government of occupation of the Channel Islands to the head of the German police in Paris, the English authorities in Jersey were ordered to impose the wearing of the star. This was done on Jersey on June 19 and, on Guernsey on June 30, 1942. However by August 23, 1942, the stars had still not arrived, as is emphasized by a document of the German authorities, nor by December 28. The stars were still not available, the German administrator wrote to his bosses in Paris on January 5, 1943, but that was not important anymore: "The deportation of the Jews being imminent."[52]

52. Summarized from research by Frédéric Cohen published in Le Monde juif, no. 168, April 2000, pp. 57–106, under the title "Les Juifs dans les îles de Jersey-Guernesey et Sercq sous l'occupation allemande, 1940–1945." It should be noted that one of the rare books devoted to that occupation, Vichy-sur-Manche by Jean-Yves Ruaux (Éditions Ouest-France, 1994), totally ignores this aspect of the history of the islands.

6

The Requests for Special Dispensation

T HIS IS A LITTLE-KNOWN ASPECT of the racial repression. While the Vichy government approved the measures taken by the Nazis in the occupied zone, they refused to pass them on to the so-called 'free' zone. Thus it is that wearing the yellow star was never the order of the day beyond the demarcation line, even when the Germans moved into that southern part of France after the Americans landed in North Africa on November 8, 1942.

Pétain, like Darlan, was loath to see French Jews of old-established families suffering the same repression as foreign Jews. This in no way called into question the intention to exclude them implemented by Vichy well before the Nazis promulgated their first ordinances in the occupied zone. For Darlan, the important thing was not to alienate certain senior officials who had given such proof of their loyalty to France as well as to the person of Pétain. This explains why, in the unoccupied zone, numerous exemptions to the Statute on Jews of June 2, 1941, were granted to academics, senior civil servants and renowned specialists.[1] This, however, only concerned the restrictions on numbers imposed by the statute.

Following the publication of the 8th Nazi ordinance, Pétain and his entourage are roused to action. The aim is not to protect certain celebrities in literature or philosophy any more than in the world of science, it is a matter of sparing the wives of persons close to power the humiliation of

---

1. See my *Sois juif et tais-toi!* (Paris: EDI, 1981), pp. 263–268.

the yellow star. This is the case with Mme. de Brinon, née Franck, who is living in Paris with ambassador de Brinon, but also with Countess d'Aramont, Marchioness de Chasseloup-Laubat, her sister, as well as Mme. Girot de Langlade, all of whom are intimate friends of the Pétains.[2] These, it seems, are the only special privileges granted by the Gestapo but that will not prevent shady characters such as Joanovici[3] being dispensed from the obligation to wear the yellow star.

There are amusing but sad episodes, such as the approach to a general in the German high command in Paris by Georges Scapini, a tool of Vichy and "minister for prisoners." While expressing his "approval in general of the measure imposed on the Jews" he asks for decorated veterans to be exempted. The better to convince the Nazis, Scapini pointed out that "wearing a French decoration next to a Jewish star was not fitting—*war nicht schöne*— and made the ordinance unpopular among the population." The Nazi general's reply was unambiguous: "You must forbid the Jews to wear medals, as is the case in our country, and that will solve the problem."[4]

From the end of May 1942 there are numerous requests to be exempted from wearing the yellow star with a variety of reasons given. Apart from Jewish figures close to the Vichy government—there are still some of those at the end of spring 1942—or those who are collaborating in the economic sector, there are some who think it natural to avoid this constraint that might ruin their economic activity or that of close members of their family. There are also those who, for a variety of reasons, try their luck—with little hope of success. This is not a question of casting slurs on those who attempted to avoid their fate, even if the way they went about it may seem distasteful. The exemptions granted are rare and in each case it is only for a limited, renewable period. Sometimes the requests come through Fernand de Brinon, but most often it is the Vichy minister of the interior who passes on the grievances directly to SS Captain Theo Dannecker, head of the Gestapo department IV J in Paris.

Some of these requests are poignant since there is no concern behind them that could be called dishonorable. On May 31, 1942, a young lady called Nelly Frankfurter writes to the general in charge of German military command in Paris. It is a very naive, moving letter written by a girl of less than seventeen years of age who imagines it is possible to touch the heart of a Nazi:

---

2. CJDC-XXV a 164–206.
3. A French Jewish iron merchant who supplied both the Resistance and Nazi Germany. [MM]
4. In *Vichy et les Juifs* by Michaël Marrus and Robert O. Paxton (Paris: Calmann-Lévy, 1981), p. 222. My italics; this letter was written in German. [MM note: The 'e' is a mistake in German. Presumably the extra 'e' is in the original document.]

"There is a request I would like to make of you. As you will know, starting June 7 it is forbidden to appear in public without wearing the yellow star. That grieves me very much because I am Jewish. I am a woman, and I find it hard to imagine that I will no longer be able to appear in public without arousing a feeling of animosity among certain people. I love all human beings without distinction, and to see myself rejected by those I love, above all by my classmates, causes me great distress.

My name is Nelly Frankfurter. I was born in Warsaw on September 19, 1925, and live in La Lande Camp (10 miles from Tours). I have permission to go to Tours every day to take classes. I therefore appeal to your kindness, to your sense of humanity, which, I am sure, is as strong in you as it is in me, and beg you to exempt me from this terrible measure. I would ask you to reply before June 7, the day on which the decree comes into force. In anticipation of a favorable reply I remain, Monsieur le Feldkommandant, yours sincerely, Nelly Frankfurter."[5]

The indirect reply will arrive over six weeks later. Nelly Frankfurter will be arrested on July 16, 1942, and deported from Angers to Auschwitz in the no. 8 convoy of July 20, 1942.

Some excellent French citizens, as they say, are annoyed at the 8th ordinance. It is generally a question of protecting good servants of the state, who are so much appreciated at Vichy, from being shamed. It must not be forgotten that, although the government has its offices in the town known for its spa, the ministerial departments are still in Paris, as if there were nothing separating the two zones. That means there are civil servants whose wives must be protected. This explains the petition, dated June 2, 1942, from the junior minister with responsibility for industrial production to the head of the economics section of the German military administration in France:

"...I believe the competent authorities have been happy to allow the principle of strictly exceptional exemptions to the above-mentioned ordinance for a certain number of Frenchmen whose position and family ties put them in a very special situation. My attention has been drawn to Mme. Henri Fayol, née Picard, the wife of M. Henri Fayol, senior distributor in the central office for the distribution of industrial products. There is no need for me to remind you of the magnitude of the task M. Henri Fayol has performed during the last eighteen months. During that time you yourself will have observed the competence, the high standards and constant devotion to the public interest with which M. Henri Fayol

---

5. CDJC-XLIX a 51 b.

has devoted himself to his mission at the head of one of the departments whose role is of vital importance in the circumstances the French economy must face."[6]

It seems perfectly clear that this Fayol is one of those zealous civil servants who, at the command of Vichy and the German authorities, are organizing the shortages in the occupied zone. To spare Mme. Fayol would therefore be of service to the collaborationist administration. In fact what is being requested here is an exchange of favors, as becomes apparent in the rest of this conniving letter:

"...M. Henri Fayol has come to inform me that, for sentiments of which I cannot but approve, he would find it impossible to continue to carry out his tasks if the requirements of the ordinance of May 29, 1942, were to be applied to Mme. Fayol. It was clear to me that such a consequence would be particularly prejudicial to the execution of the responsibilities of which I have taken charge. I would therefore be much obliged if you would lend me your distinguished support in approaching the competent authorities to see that the indispensable exceptional provisions should be granted to Mme. Fayol..."[7] The special dispensation was granted on September 8, 1942, subject to verification of Mme. Fayol's nationality. As we have noted, people at a much higher level have been disturbed by the measure. For Heaven's sake, these Germans Vichy is collaborating with could surely grant a few exemptions! Why this inflexibility that is of such an embarrassment to a number of those close to Pétain? It is with this in mind that the Marshal turned to Fernand de Brinon [the Vichy representative ("ambassador") to the German high command in occupied Paris] on June 12, 1942, begging him to persuade the Occupation Authorities to show a little humanity:

"My dear Ambassador,

Several times recently my attention has been drawn to the distressing situation that would be brought about in certain French families if the recent ordinance of the Occupation Authorities requiring Jews to wear a special badge were to be implemented without the possibility of natural and necessary exemptions being obtained.

I am convinced that the German authorities themselves understand perfectly well that certain exceptions are indispensable; moreover this is foreseen in the text of the 8th ordinance. And that seems necessary to me to ensure that the justified measures taken against the Jews should be understood and accepted by the French. I therefore ask you to press the

---

6. CDJC-XXV a 180.
7. Ibid.

matter with the general commanding the occupation troops that he should be so good as to allow the point of view that you will set out to him on my behalf, so that the head of the Department of Jewish Affairs can quickly be granted the ability to deal promptly, by individual and exceptional measures, with certain particularly distressing situations of which you could be advised..."[8]

A "distressing situation" for some, "justified measures" for others. There we have all the ambiguity of the powers of the Vichy government that would like to see the Nazi authorities show clemency toward old-established French Jewish families, all glorious veterans of the First World War. What Pétain and Laval do not seem to have understood is that the Nazis do not differentiate between the ones and the others. Even for the exemptions permitted, they demand proof of the French nationality of the ladies fortunate enough to be chosen, for this essentially concerns women. As far as men are concerned the Nazis are much more pernickety, whatever their status. The rule is clear: the Jews are of no use to society, even if their help is necessary to put out a fire, as we will later see. It is indispensable for the Jews to be marked out and the French authorities must understand that that is the price of their future in the new Europe. This is the sense of a letter of June 15, 1942, from General Oberg to Colonel Simonin, commander of the Paris fire service, who doubtless finds it shocking to send men wearing the yellow star to put out fires:

"In your above-mentioned letter you ask us, for reasons of discipline, to exempt the 28 Jewish reserve firefighters serving in the Paris fire service from the obligation to wear the Jewish star as foreseen by the 8th ordinance of the *Militärbefehlshaber*[9] in France. I cannot grant this request..."[10]

Even if, in a few rare cases, the Nazis do Vichy the favor, they have no intention of making these exceptions more widespread. There is a strange document in the CDJC archives reporting a conversation on June 17, 1942, between the German ambassador, Otto Abetz, and one of the advisers at the German embassy in Paris, a specialist in Jewish matters. Their intention to be firm as far as requests for dispensations are concerned is clear. In the course of the conversation it is possible to deduce that a dispensation might be granted to the widow of the philosopher Henri Bergson, who died the previous year. The subsequent discussion tends to show that the two Germans have only slight knowledge of the French cultural world. Thus they are talking about the wife of the writer de Jouvenel, "whether she

---

8. CDJC-XLIX a 90 a.
9. Military Commander. [MM]
10. CDJC-XLIX a 86.

really looks Jewish." The person in question is Colette, who is not Jewish at all, but a little later it is "the woman writer Gaulette" whose case is being examined, in the interest of the Reich. Then the two men wonder what reply to give the ambassador, Fernand de Brinon, as was finally suggested by General Oberg. For Otto Abetz, the solution could not be simpler: all Fernand de Brinon has to do is resign. For if they were going to get involved in the question of dispensations, he would start suggesting others.[11]

The Paris fire service is not the only official body affected by the 8th ordinance. On July 1, 1942, the prefect deputed to the occupied zone by the minister of the interior submits a request for dispensation through the channel of the Department of Jewish Affairs:

"I respectfully enclose a letter from the prefect of the Seine department concerning a request for dispensation from the obligation to wear the Jewish star made by three members of the security personnel at the law courts."[12]

The reply from the Department of Jewish Affairs, dated July 7, leaves no room for argument. Only the occupiers have the power to make decisions in that area:

"I respectfully inform you that dispensations regarding the wearing of the star of Zion rest on the German Authorities alone. The ordinance of May 29 was issued by the *Militärbefehlshaber* of France who alone has the authority to accede to the request of the three officers of the law courts."[13]

Equally interesting is the request submitted by the policeman Émile Seurat that is sent directly to the "Commander of the German Jewish Department," 32a Avenue Foch in Paris—his superiors know the right people to approach:

"I beg leave to request a dispensation from having to wear the badge for my wife, Ida Seurat, née Gutelmann September 7, 1915, in Paris, French of Jewish origin, married in Paris June 23, 1935.

I have one son, born in 1938, a baptized Catholic, enrolled in a Christian school. I have been a policeman in the Paris prefecture of police since January 4, 1932. I swear that my wife does not practice the Jewish religion.

In the hope of a favorable reply, I remain your obedient servant..."[14]

Seurat's approach is supported by a letter dated October 30, 1942, from the director of the city police, Émile Hennequin: M. Seurat is an

---

11. CDJC-a 91b; [MM note: The writer (Bertrand) de Jouvenel was the son of Henry de Jouvenel who first married a Jewish woman, then, in 1912, the writer Colette; they divorced in 1924, partly as a result of Colette's affair with her stepson, Bertrand de Jouvenel. Colette later married Goudeket, for whom she, subsequently in this chapter, is asking for a dispensation. "The woman writer Gaulette" is presumably just a German mishearing of "Colette."]
12. CDJC-CXCIII 72.
13. Ibid.
14. CDJC-XXV a 203.

excellent officer with a good attitude, dedicated and hard-working."[15] Dispensation granted November 4, 1942.

The Nazis are no less punctilious when it is a matter of granting dispensations, as is shown by the following certificate, dated May 1, 1943, and issued by Hagen, the head of the Paris SS:

"This present certificate exempts Madame de Brinon, née Jeanne-Louise Franck b. 6/23/1896 in Paris, at present domiciled in the Château de la Chassange, by Felletin (Creuse), from the measures governing the wearing of the Jewish star as laid down on 5/29/1942 in the 8th ordinance regulating the status of Jews. This letter is with immediate effect and remains valid until August 31, 1943, and will allow Madame de Brinon to establish, together with the attached certificate, her ancestry."[16]

Identical certificates are sent, through the channel of the ambassador, Fernand de Brinon, to Marchioness de Chasseloup-Laubat, née Marie-Louise Fanny Clémentine Marie-Thérèse Stern, residing in Chantilly, as well as to Countess d'Aramont, née Stern.[17]

Among the requests for dispensation some are in bad taste. That is the least one can say of the application coming from the famous novelist Colette. There is nothing more natural than that she should do everything possible to protect her husband, Maurice Goudeket, who is Jewish. Thus on December 12, 1941, after her husband has been arrested during the roundup of the 'notables' of the French Jewish community, she activates all her connections: Sacha Guitry, but also Brasillach and Drieu la Rochelle,[18] and obtains the release of Maurice Goudeket.[19]

Colette, who at that time was in need, she says, contributes to *Le Petit Parisien*, *Image de la France* and even *Gringoire*, an anti-Semitic weekly, and a little later will send her work to *Combats*, the newspaper of Darnand's *Milice*.[20] It is at this time that the successful author writes to the minister of the interior to request dispensation from wearing the yellow star for Maurice Goudeket. An edifying letter if ever there was one:

"I humbly beg to request that my husband, Maurice Goudeket, French Jew, born in Paris August 3, 1889, volunteer from 1914–1918, Médaille militaire, Croix de guerre, Croix du combattant, wounded, mentioned in dispatches, be dispensed from the requirement to wear the *Star of Zion*.[21]

---

15. Ibid.
16. CDJD-XXV a 206.
17. Ibid.
18. Sacha Guitry: a well-known actor and theater director, attacked after the war for being a collaborationist; Robert Brasillach: a writer executed after the war for his collaboration with the Nazis; Pierre Drieu la Rochelle: a novelist, proponent of fascism in France who collaborated during the Occupation. [MM]
19. Michelle and Paul Cointet, Eds., *Dictionnaire historique de la France sous l'Occupation*, (Paris: Tallandier, 2000).
20. The *Milice* (Militia) was a fascist paramilitary organization led by General Joseph Darnand and used by Vichy to combat the Resistance. [MM]
21. My italics. [MM note: This is the formulation used by the apologists of the extreme-right.]

"I am seventy years old, severe arthritis of the hip has progressively made walking very difficult for me. Which means I can hardly go out alone anymore, climb the stairs, attend professional engagements. It is thus for my own convenience, as well as for that of my husband, that I am asking for him to be authorized to accompany me, to give me his arm in all public places or, after eight o'clock in the evening, to support me in the metro, on the stairs."[22]

So far there's nothing much to take exception to in this petition that appeals to humane feelings, but the mask isn't long in slipping as the letter takes a perfectly obnoxious turn with winks and nods, meaningful reminders of the political choices of a celebrity from the world of literature, supposedly protecting her husband by begging for the support of those who are making every effort to get rid of the mass of Jews living in the occupied zone.

"I would like to add that my books and myself have always enjoyed a most favorable reception in Germany (lecture tour in Berlin, Vienna). Moreover, the occupying authorities have always, when the opportunity arose, shown me the greatest courtesy and kindness. Last year the *Pariser Zeitung* showered me with unreserved praise. For his part, my husband has the testimony of numerous people to prove that his life, both military and civilian, has always been devoted to honor, and I know that the occupying authorities attach importance to such details. I have no hesitation in vouching for my husband as far as the future is concerned.

"In the hope that if, during my long career, I have been able to render some service to literature, you will be so good as to attend to my request, and I remain your grateful servant..."[23] The letter is signed: Colette, woman of letters, commander of the Legion of Honor, member of the Royal Belgian Academy.

A waste of effort. A sorry argumentation. The letter quoted above has a curt "refused" scribbled across it in pencil. It is Joseph Antignac, secretary general in the Department of Jewish Affairs who takes up the pen to reply on June 19, 1943:

"In reply to your letter of May 31, 1943, asking me to intervene with the German Authorities to obtain dispensation from the obligation to wear the yellow star for Maurice Goudeket, I regret to inform you that my request has not been allowed, and I was told in reply that no dispensation was allowed..."[24]

---

22. CDJC-CXIII 9.
23. Ibid.
24. Ibid.

7

Non-Jews Wearing the Badge

FROM THE BEGINNING of June 1942 there has been no lack of reports from the intelligence service warning the Prefecture of Police. Above all, these reports raise the fear of possible reactions of the population following the implementation of the 8th Nazi ordinance. There is nothing that worries the French auxiliaries of the Gestapo more than to see a mockery made of the introduction of the yellow star.

As we have already noted, what concerned them was the possibility of large-scale demonstrations and important reactions in the student milieu. The finks and the snitches are on the lookout, and any little bit of tittle-tattle immediately becomes a serious piece of information. This self-induced neurosis also affects the Gestapo who then order the French police to keep their eyes open for French persons who wrongfully deck themselves out in a yellow star or any kind of mock badge.

On June 5, 1942, a note arrives at the Gestapo Office IV J. This warning has to be taken seriously since the note has been filed along with other subsequent ones: "According to a report from an informant, the teachers at the elementary school in the 5th district have urged their pupils to come next Monday, June 8, 1942, with some badge or other. It is assumed that this action is related to the introduction of the Jewish star and represents a demonstration of sympathy with the Jews."[1]

Another note, also sent to Gestapo Office IV J, sets the tone for that

---

1. CDJC-XLIX a 21.

June 5: "Today, around 7:30 a.m., the undersigned listened to a conversation between two young Frenchmen on the metro. They were talking about wearing the Jewish badge. One of them made the following comment:

'We'll have some good fun next Sunday, even the non-Jews among us will be wearing the star.'"[2]

Still on June 5, 1942, the propaganda office of the German military command eventually becomes concerned about these rumors and the possible effects of grotesque versions of the measure that has been announced. The language of the long note summarizing the situation indicates their concerns about an unacceptable campaign of resistance:

"According to the reports reaching us hour by hour, Gaullist and communist groups are making a massive propaganda effort to stir up trouble for next Sunday. The instructions they have issued are as follows: all Jews wearing the yellow star on the grand boulevards are to be greeted with *demonstrations of sympathy*. Following that, as indicated in an earlier report, the plan is for Gaullist and communist non-Jews to go around the streets wearing the Jewish star with, instead of the word 'Jew', the name of a French province. It seems that people in Gaullist families are busy making these yellow stars. Beyond that there seems to be a plan to ridicule the introduction of the Jewish star by having Jews wear not just the one star but, where possible, several stars."[3]

It is at this point in the note that the previously privileged information about the links between the Gestapo offices and those in charge of the Paris police, ever ready to carry out assignments with which they are charged, is brought out into the open:

"Given these reports, it appears to be necessary for the police to take all security measures necessary for next Sunday. Any demonstrations by Gaullist or communist elements must be put down; all those wearing false Jewish stars must be arrested and punished accordingly. It would have a very salutary effect for all individuals arrested in these circumstances to be deported to the east with the next convoy. It is also recommended to forbid Jews to be present on certain major thoroughfares such as the Champs Élysées, the grand boulevards, Rue de Rivoli and certain squares next Sunday. It is the sector between Place de la Madeleine and Place de la Nation that can be considered a center of possible disturbances."[4]

Of course these demonstrations did not take place, because the watchword had not been given. On June 6, 1942, the German military

2. CDJC-XLIX a 22.
3. Ibid.
4. Ibid.

commander of Greater Paris was so convinced that demonstrations of solidarity were being planned that it was considered useful to bring in the Gestapo, which explains this note addressed to Dr. Knochen, the head of the Gestapo:

"We have been informed that communist and Gaullist demonstrations will be held next Sunday to show their opposition to the introduction of the yellow star in the following way:

1) By wearing yellow flowers.

2) By wearing a yellow handkerchief in the jacket breast pocket.

3) By wearing paper Jewish stars. (In the optics factory on Rue Surcouf, fifty or so employees have been amusing themselves for several days now making a large quantity of Jewish stars.)

4) By wearing genuine Jewish stars that the Jews have been selling at 50F each.

In addition we have been informed that nationalists intend to beat up Jews and their friends next Sunday. If there is any truth in this rumor, the group concerned is probably the MSR, which has been banned and wants to show by this that it still exists..."[5]

Under the date of June 6, 1942, the Jewish journalist Jacques Bielinky notes in his diary: "As a demonstration of solidarity with a Jewish employee who has been sacked, all the staff—about seventy-five—at one of the offices of the Deposits and Consignment Fund went outside wearing badges made, following the 'official model', of yellow paper."[6]

The repression is unleashed starting on June 6 because a certain number of courageous Parisians have decided to anticipate the event.

Several police reports attest to this willingness of a minority to protest. The first arrest is of Alice Courouble[7] who, on the day before the 8th ordinance came into force, put on a genuine yellow star, to which she was not entitled:

"Plain-clothes officers Marquet of the 13th district, Nauzin of the 6th and Munier of the 5th handed over to the Sorbonne precinct captain Mlle. Alice Marthe Courouble, b. April 1, 1913, in Nyons (Drôme), typist... Arrested this day at 3:30 p.m. on Boulevard Saint-Michel for illegally wearing the Jewish star on her blouse. Mlle. Courouble being of Aryan race. When she was arrested she was accompanied by Mlle. Sophie Suzanne Moha, b. July 21, 1917, in Paris, 11th district; the latter, being

5. CDJC-XLIX a 25.

6. Jacques Bielinky, *Journal 1940–1942. Un journaliste juif in Paris sous l'Occupation* (Paris: Éditions du Cerf, 1992), p. 215. Information or a rumor that is difficult to verify.

7. After the Liberation Alice Courouble published her memoirs in a little book with the revealing title *Amie des Juifs*, [A friend of the Jews], Bloud et Gay, 1946.

Jewish, was wearing the Jewish star on her blouse. She has been released by precinct captain Zimmer. The badge worn by Mlle. Courouble as well as the blouse onto which it was sewn would appear to belong to Mlle. Moha..."[8]

To go by the note below addressed to the judicial police by the precinct captain of la Roquette district, cooperation between the German and French police is already very effective:

"I respectfully inform you that at 6:15 p.m. today officer Jurgens of the German Police for Jewish Affairs (Captain Dannecker's department) handed over to me Lazare André Villeneuve, b. May 26, 1919, in Monceaux-les-Mines, French nationality, denomination Catholic, semi-skilled worker, for wearing the yellow star, a badge reserved for Jews. When questioned, Villeneuve told us that 'just for fun' he had pinned one of the two stars that had just been given to his wife, née Chana Guini, b. 1/13/1920 in Smyrna, Turkey, French national by marriage, denomination Jewish, packer. Villeneuve is being kept in custody at la Roquette police station."[9]

On the morning of June 7, the police have a strong presence in the Latin Quarter. Target: the students. Despite everything the fact is that with some five million inhabitants in the Paris area (Paris and the Seine department) there are only about thirty-eight non-Jewish protesters. Thirty-eight free spirits or daredevils to defy the edict, to challenge the authors of this repressive measure and the police charged with enforcing it. Thirty-eight willing to resist openly.

No further comment is necessary.

It is a pity that no filmmaker has recorded the activities of the Paris police in the Latin Quarter where they were patrolling in great numbers on that June 7, 1942, in case it should be necessary to hunt down the students, as they were on all the major thoroughfares of Paris. I have found twenty or so daybook entries concerning the arrest of these "Aryans" who were presumptuous enough not to take one of the ordinances of the occupying power seriously. It is repetitive in style but I feel it is important to cite all of them.

Report of two officers to the central police station of the Odéon district: "We are sending to you young Paulette Voisin, b. September 6, 1923, in Tours (Indre-et-Loire), student, French nationality, of Aryan race, and Françoise Alexandrine Siefried, b. October 20, 1922, in Le Havre (Seine Inférieure), French nationality, of Aryan race. Both have

8. APP, series PJ 33.
9. Ibid.

been apprehended and taken to the Saint-Germain-des-Prés police station. These two women were proceeding along Boulevard Saint-Michel wearing paper badges representing a star of David on which the following had been written: 'Papou' and '130'."[10]

Another entry concerns Paulette Voisin alone who, when stopped, is said to have told Sergeant Pierre Giono and Officer André Perron, who had picked her up, "I just did it for a laugh because I think it's fun."[11]

Occasionally the police enjoy the cooperation of citizens outraged that people can mock the edicts, as witnessed by this report dated June 7, 1 p.m., from the police station of the 18th district:

"Around 11:35 a.m. outside 25 Rue de Clignancourt, Henri Muratet, b. October 24, 1903, in Sauveterre (Aveyron), married, three children, who was wearing a fake yellow badge with 'Auvergnat' written on it, was stopped and asked to remove the badge by a passer-by, M. Léonard Beynat, b. February 7, 1896, in Pavignac (Corrèze), storekeeper residing at 2 Place du Tertre (18th). M. Muratet having refused to comply with M. Beynat's demands, an acrimonious altercation ensued, and the two men exchanged blows. Taken to the station of the 18th district by the city police, M. Beynat lodged a complaint for blows and injuries, and M. Muratet has been detained."[12]

The reports multiply in the course of the day, particularly coming from the police intelligence service, which seems to be at work on June 7. Below is an inventory of arrests, all districts included, which can be found in the archives of the prefecture of police:

"For several hours after 1 p.m. the situation has been perfectly calm, and the capital has retained its usual Sunday appearance. Jews out in the streets, not in significant numbers anyway, have not caused any incidents."

That leaves the others, those who cause a problem by not realizing the necessity of observing the edicts:

"In the course of the afternoon the following occurrences were noted. At 4 p.m. at the Strasbourg-Saint-Denis crossing Mme. Jenny Micheline Wion, b. April 29, 1921, in Sérifontaine (Oise), shorthand typist, and Mlle. Denise Eugénie Recouvrot, b. November 3 in Antony (Seine) who were wearing white mock badges, one with 'Jenny' on it, the other 'Dany' have been handed over to the Porte Saint-Martin police station.

"At 4:30 p.m., at the junction of Boulevard Saint-Michel and Boulevard Saint-Germain, Madeleine Bonnaire, née Auerbach, August 29, 1919, in

10. APP, series BA 1817 (dossier B 51 7).
11. APP, series PJ 33.
12. APP, series BA 1817 (dossier B 51 7).

Paris, claiming to be a painter, French nationality, was arrested by the local police following an altercation she had with a black person, Simon Nazain. Bonnaire was wearing the badge even though her identity card does not have the word 'Jewish'. When she was taken to the police station and encountered a group of German officers, she thumbed her nose at them. She has been detained in the Saint-Germain-des-Prés station.

"At 6:30 p.m., Jeanne Le Pennec, b. June 13, 1918, in Paris 6th, who was wearing a badge with 'JP' on it and Marie Lemeunier, known as Anne, née Bordat, May 27, 1884, in Port-Saint-Vincent, who was wearing a badge with a cross were arrested and handed over to the 9th district police station."[13]

The police are on the watch in all districts, but it is in the Latin Quarter that their presence is most visible.

Sorbonne police station to PP, PM, PJ [prefecture of police, municipal police, judicial police]. A report signed Duhan at 4:10 p.m.:

"Mlle. Josephine Cardin, b. May 10, 1923, in Plaine-Haute (Côtes-du-Nord), student, of Aryan race, was arrested on Boulevard Saint-Michel for wearing the Jewish badge and eight little stars attached to her belt, each with a letter which taken together formed the word *victime*. She is being kept in custody."[14]

Sorbonne police station to the prefecture of police:

"Mlle. Paulette Pecol, 24, b. 11/18/1920 in Paris 18th to Louis and Antoinette Rochet, French nationality, Aryan, employee of the PTT [Postes, Télégraphes et Téléphones], has been arrested for wearing a Jewish badge in public."[15] Report signed Granvincent, 7:25 p.m.

Sorbonne police station to the prefecture of police, 5:10 p.m.:

"Henri Plard, b. August 6, 1920, in Dijon (Côte-d'Or), student at the École nationale supérieure and residing there, was arrested this day on Boulevard Saint-Michel for wearing a pocket handkerchief of yellow paper with no inscription. This handkerchief was sticking out of the breast pocket of his jacket.[16] This person was alone. Kept in custody at the central police station."[17]

Sorbonne police station to PP, PM, PJ, RG [prefecture of police, municipal police, judicial police, intelligence service]. Granvincent, 6 p.m.:

"Simone Liliane Decize, b. April 6, 1912, in Paris, employed in a paper

---

13. Ibid.
14. APP, series PJ 33. In another report the word is given as [an eight-letter word,] V.I.C.T.O.I.R.E. [VICTORY].
15. Ibid.
16. Clearly a sign of excess zeal on the part of officer Granvincent, who signed this report, and that we encounter during the whole of this day in the Latin Quarter.
17. APP, series BA 1817 (dossier 51 B).

mill, has just been arrested on Boulevard Saint-Michel for wearing a yellow rosette. She is being kept in custody."[18]

The hunt is also taking place on the grand boulevards on this Sunday, June 7, 1942. The police are on the alert from the Opéra to Porte Saint-Martin. Bonne-Nouvelle police station to PM:

"Lieutenant Charpin, seconded to the Jewish affairs police,[19] is hereby handing over to you Michel Begora, b. 3/7/1925 in Paris 18th, French nationality, Aryan, unmarried, residing with his parents, turner at the Compagnie électrique magnétique, in le Bourget, arrested on Boulevard des Italiens, outside the Marivaux Cinema, wearing the Jewish badge. He was accompanied by a Jew, Georges Svartz."[20]

Antonini, 1:25 p.m. Saint-Georges police station to PM. Maurice, 10 p.m.

"At 5:15 p.m., 16 Boulevard des Italians, at the request of M. Robert Amiraux, deputy head of the Department of Jewish Affairs, Mlle. Marie Lang, b. 11/24/1914 in Paris, newspaper vendor, non-Jewish, was questioned *as she was attaching a sheet of paper with the Jewish star to the collar of her dog.* She swallowed the piece of paper when questioned. It is a page from a brochure the distribution of which is permitted. Held awaiting instructions."[21]

Bonne-Nouvelle police station to PM: Kervich, 4:30 p.m.:

"Serge Robert Lapers, b. 11/15/1926 in Paris 10th, and Huguette Roberte Legallier, b. 11/11/1926, Aryans, were arrested on Boulevard Sebastopol wearing fake badges marked 'Swing'."[22]

18th district police station to PM Laine, 4:30 p.m.:

"At 3:50 p.m. on Boulevard Rochechouart Roland Bolivant, baker, French nationality, Aryan, wearing a Jewish badge has been sent to Grandes-Carrières police station for questioning."[23]

Finally there are brief station logbook entries like the one from the 3rd division of the municipal police: "Five Aryans arrested for mock badges," Silvestri, 5 p.m.[24]

At the end of the day, before all the arrests carried out on June 7 have been recorded, a list with numbers is compiled by the intelligence service:

—Jews without badge..17

—Jews with several badges or inscriptions...................2

---

18. APP, series PJ 33.
19. This detail confirms the fact that there were indeed links between the judicial police and the Jewish affairs police, which is generally denied.
20. APP, series PJ 33.
21. Ibid.
22. Ibid.
23. Ibid.
24. Ibid.

—Aryans with "Jew" badges..7
—Aryans with mock sign.....................................13 [25]

There is one question that has to be asked after this first day of the hunt targeting those crazy enough to want to demonstrate their hostility to the 8th ordinance. Had the officers who wrote the reports on the crimes under the rubric "Aryans with mock sign" been specially assigned to arrest this new kind of offender? Or was the fear of significant demonstrations so strong that the order to collar these Robin Hoods was given to all the police responsible for public order? It seems that the two approaches complemented each other. The fact remains that the police were highly motivated. With just the one exception, the reports on arrests that we have been able to see in the various archives are written using the phraseology used by the Nazis: the people stopped for questioning are all of "Aryan race." Which must be a matter of course for officers serving an ideological order in which "individuals" are classified by race. As the pariahs of the moment are "of Jewish race," it is appropriate to remind those who show surprising solidarity with them that they are "of Aryan race," and that as such their support constitutes an aggravating circumstance.

On June 8, 1942, there are still a number of those incorrigible dreamers who haven't understood the importance of eliminating the Jews. The intelligence service, which has informants in all areas of economic activity as well as in community organizations, drafts a revealing report:

"At the moment, the recent measure regarding the Jews is the principal subject of the conversations among militants in the proof-readers' and editors' union. Some, such as Louis Louvet, would like all Parisians to respond to the ordinance by walking around wearing a yellow star or one of another color. Jules Guérin, on the other hand, is against such a protest which, after all, he feels is unrealizable and, according to him, would only result in people being sent to concentration camps. Several others thought that the only result of making Jews wear the yellow star would be to arouse sympathy for the Jews, even among those who, until now, hadn't liked them. Some others remarked that for the Germans, having no worse enemies than the Jews, it was quite natural for them to take 'precautionary measures' against them. This point of view met with vehement protests, above all from Louis Louvet, who is known to have many Jewish friends."[26]

Is it to improve the performance of the French police that the German military police joins in on June 8, 1942? Here, one can see that the Nazis know how to go about these things, the result of long practice,

25. APP, series BA 1817 (dossier B 51 7).
26. APP, report of the police intelligence service, "La situation de Paris."

as is shown in this record of the arrest of a young woman by a German policeman who is sending his prey to the police in the 9th district:

"Mme. Don was arrested at the exit from the metro in company of a Jewish woman. She was talking to the Jew in a friendly manner and in such a provocative way that I have to admit that it was a challenge to my patrol. I told her that her behavior could be taken as a demonstration. The woman replied that there was no ban on talking to Jews. I left, and she responded to my departure by bursting into laughter. Fifteen minutes later she was still at the same place with the Jewish woman and, the intervention of French officers having produced no results, I handed her over to the French police to check her identity. The French police arrested her."[27]

Another report in the same tone again demonstrates the excellent coordination of the German and French police:

"Marie-Antoinette Planeix, b. April 17, 1920, arrested June 8, 1942, at 11:45 a.m. by a German military policeman. She was wearing a paper star with the initials JNRJ [Jésus de Nazareth, Roi des Juifs; English: INRI]. She has been locked up in Santé Prison. In her statement she says, "I made the star of David at home. I fixed it to my dress before going out. By that I wanted to show that Jesus Christ was the first royal Jew. I have nothing more to add.""[28]

And then:

"Renée Mignot, b. June 19, 1922, was arrested by German military police on June 8, 1942, for wearing the Star of David even though she is not Jewish. Apprehended during a check on Jews, she is locked up in Santé Prison."[29]

And yet again:

"Marcelle Galliot Camille, b. May 8, 1918, arrested at the same time, also wearing a yellow star. Brought immediately to trial, she declared in her evidence, 'I made the Star of David and attached it to my blouse. It was to be a protest against the anti-Jewish measures.'"[30]

However, the French police are not idle, and on the morning of June 8 the Père Lachaise police station informs the head of the judicial police:

"I respectfully inform you that today Jean-Pierre Simonet, b. December 13, 1910, in Valenton (Seine-et-Oise), electrician, was arrested at 8:10 a.m. on Place Auguste-Métinier, Paris 20th, under the following circumstances: as an officer was asking a Jewish woman, who had just had an altercation with a woman, to wear her 'Jew' badge in a more visible place, and

---

27. CDJC-XLIX a 30.
28. CDJC-XLIX a 71.
29. CDJC-XLIX a 29.
30. Ibid.

while she was doing that, the said Simonet came up and said, 'Madame, no law obliges you to wear that badge, the police are interfering in things that don't concern them. Moreover, this evening I will have one like you.' Simonet is being kept in custody awaiting further instructions."[31]

Always on the lookout for the slightest piece of information, journalist Jacques Bielinky notes in his diary after this wave of arrests, "It is said that one of the students arrested for wearing the Jewish star told the officer, 'That isn't a Jewish badge.' What do you mean? 'It's simple, these letters stand for Jeunesse universitaire internationaliste française.'"[32]

When the protest is made with humor the police fly off the handle. The law is no laughing matter even when the law in question is a Nazi ordinance.

In an intelligence service report of June 9, 1942, we read:

"Yesterday at 5 p.m. the German military police arrested the following in the Latin Quarter for illegally wearing the Jewish star:

1) Camille Marcelle Galliot, b. May 8, 1912, in Toulouse, painter.

2) Renée Mignaud, b. June 19, 1922, in Paris 5th district, student.

Taken to the central police station of the 5th district, these two young women were transferred to Santé Prison at 4:20 p.m. and handed over to the German prison service. Galliot and Mignaud have not previously come to our notice."[33]

The French police has not relaxed its surveillance at all.

On that same day, June 9, 1942, the precinct captain of the Saint-Martin district informs the head of the judicial police:

"I respectfully hand over to you Ginette Jeanne Orien, b. May 7, 1925, in Albi (Tarn) single, college student, 25 Rue de Passy, Paris, residing with her parents, of French nationality and of Aryan race. Stopped for questioning at 7:15 yesterday evening outside 63 Boulevard Magenta while wearing pinned to her blouse a yellow paper badge with the Jewish star with the word 'Swing 135%' on it. I attach hereto a report from the municipal police as well as the mock badge young Orien was wearing." In the other report, it says that the young girl has been sent back to her parents.[34]

Logbook entry of Grandes-Carrières police station, still June 9:

"Around 9 p.m. yesterday evening police officers arrested, outside no. 14, Place Clichy, Michel Ravet, b. October 9, 1921, in Paris, residing with

31. APP, series PJ 33.

32. Bielinky, p. 222. [MM note: The student claims the letters JUIF—the French for Jew— stand for "French Internationalist University Youth," presumably an invented organization].

33. APP, series BA 1817 (dossier B 51 7).

34. APP, series BA 1817 (dossier B 51 7) and APP, series PJ 33.

his parents, who was cycling wearing on his chest a badge of yellow cloth representing the Star of David with, written on it in black letters: 'Goy'. Taken to Grandes-Carrières police station; he is being held there awaiting further instructions. He has not previously come to our notice."[35]

On June 9, 1942, the police do not relax their surveillance and even take an interest in schoolboys. Boys of fifteen can be dangerously anti-authority, and nothing should be overlooked.

Report of the precinct captain of the Clignancourt district to the head of the judicial police:

"I respectfully advise you of the following facts. The municipal police have handed over to me:

1) Maurice Eugène Lombart, b. 10/8/1927 in Paris 2nd district, French nationality, schoolboy, residing with his parents.

2) Georges Louis Rabreaud, b. 8/31/1927 in Paris 2nd district, French nationality, schoolboy, residing with his parents.

These two children were arrested on Rue Ordener while walking wearing a yellow star imitating that of the Jews' badge with 'Swing 42' written on it. I immediately advised your department by telegram and, on orders received by telephone, I have sent the two juveniles to the station cells. Attached are the two confiscated badges."[36]

These two adolescents are joined by a third of the same age, picked up in the suburbs:

"Around 11:45 a.m. today police officers apprehended Serge Guider, b. January 9, 1927, in Boulogne, student, residing with his parents, who was proceeding along Avenue Édouard Vaillant in the same district wearing a yellow paper badge, imitating the Jewish badge, with the word 'Swing.' Taken to the Boulogne-Billancourt police station, he is being held awaiting further instructions. Guider, who is of Aryan race, has not previously come to our notice."[37]

The precinct captain to the head of the judicial police, June 9, 1942, 4 p.m. Report signed by Constant:

"Marcel Policar, b. 2/25/1925 in Paris 12th, student, of French nationality, Aryan, residing with his parents, was arrested today at 12:30 p.m. outside no. 77, Rue Saint-Louis-en-l'Île. He was riding a bicycle, wearing on his jacket a badge with the word 'Swing' on it. Young Policar is being held at the station."[38]

Among all these arrests there is one very special case. On June 10,

35. APP, series BA 1817 (dossier B 51 7).
36. APP, series PJ 33.
37. APP, series BA 1817 (dossier B 51 7).
38. APP, series PJ 33.

1942, the precinct captain of the Sorbonne district sends his report to the head of the judicial police:

"I respectfully inform you that at 6:25 p.m. today, on Place du Panthéon, police officers arrested Robert Pierre Brocheton, b. December 31, 1925, in Paris 5th, schoolboy residing with his parents. The above-named was walking on Place du Panthéon wearing on his jacket a Jewish star on paper with the inscription 'J3.' Stopped for questioning, he stated that, belonging to the Legion of Young Revolutionaries of the MSR, he had been encouraged by his leaders to ridicule the Jews, and it was with that in mind that he was wearing the confiscated Jewish star. He is being kept in custody for the head of the judicial police to decide what to do with him."[39]

It appears that the MSR, a fascist party officially banned, was hoping to gain some publicity on the occasion of the proclamation of the 8th ordinance, and young Brereton was not the only one to wear a mock badge for reasons that were far from friendly:

"Today, the police of Boulogne-sur-Seine proceeded to arrest the juvenile Jacques Henri Jean Fernand Devos, b. January 26, 1926, Paris 15th district, student residing with his parents. Together with the aforementioned Guider, who was arrested yesterday, Devos had made a yellow star with the inscription 'Swing'. As with Guider, Devos has been handed over to the German authorities. He has not previously come to our notice."[40]

In the archives of the prefecture of police I found the minutes of the hearing of Jacques Devos, who appeared in court immediately:

"Herewith the testimony given by the juvenile, Jacques Devos...never arrested nor sentenced, secondary education, residing with his parents, confession Catholic. At present a pupil at Ferdinand Buisson School, Avenue des Molineaux in Boulogne-Billancourt, pre-apprenticeship course. As to the facts, he declares:

'I admit to having made, for fun, a star on which I had written the word "Swing." I did this for perfectly childish reasons. I had absolutely no intention of using it to demonstrate against the measures taken against the Jews. Furthermore, I have no Jewish friends, my parents are of Aryan stock, and there are no Jews in our family. Moreover, after the arrest of my friend Guider, I tore up the star, realizing that I risked getting into serious trouble. I didn't think I would get into trouble with the police for this. Moreover, lots of students were wearing the star, just for fun. I wish to make it clear that my parents were in no way aware of this matter, for

39. APP, series BA 1817 (dossier B 51 7).
40. Ibid.

they would have been the first to scold me and forbid me to go out with an emblem like that. I would like to point out that we in our family are fairly anti-Semitic. Read, adopted, signed."[41]

Reading this evidence, one has the clear feeling that Jacques Devos signed a statement that was dictated to him by the police.

At the end of the day, they have to explain to the German authorities that the hostile reactions are not the rule. Proof was these mindless juveniles who made yellow stars to mock the Jews... Nevertheless, on June 10 the hunt continues, and if the police are teaching the little fascists of the MSR lessons, they do not scorn the kids' collaboration with their elders.

Faubourg-Montmartre police station to PJ:

"This is to inform you that at 4:05 p.m. today, at the instigation of Robert Coquier and Raymond Pescher, members of the Social Revolutionary Movement, 40, Rue du Paradis, Tony Basset, b. April 30, 1926, in Damas, Syria, schoolboy, of Aryan race, was arrested wearing a yellow star on his jacket with, written in the middle, 'Zazou'. Attached is the star worn by Basset."[42]

The captain of la Villette district to the head of the judicial police:

"In accordance with the instructions in circular no. 140–42 of June 6, 1942, and with the decision made by the Occupying Authority with regard to the minor, Raymond Robert, b. 10/22/1926 in Richelieu (Indre-et-Loire), we have driven the latter to 31a Avenue Foch in a vehicle of the municipal police, the reason being that he was arrested today at 11:15 a.m., by M. Grandjean, an officer of the 10th district, because he was wearing a mock badge made of yellow cardboard with 'Swing' written on it, a badge that he was displaying on his jacket. Stopped and questioned, he claimed he had done this in the belief that he was following a fashion adopted by some young people he doesn't know."[43] Attached to this report is an investigation into the moral standards of the boy's parents: "It has never been established that they could have communist tendencies."

Notre-Dame-des-Champs police station to the judicial police:

"Mlle. Solange Henriette de Lipowski, b. September 20, 1924, in Paris 15th, pupil at the Alsatian School was arrested while wearing in public two cardboard badges each with the words 'Buddhiste' and 'Budhist' on them. Awaiting instructions. Bucchini, 6 p.m."[44]

1st district police station to judicial police [PJ]:

"M. Lucien Augier, non-permanent employee in the Finance Ministry,

41. APP, series PJ 33.
42. Ibid. "Zazou" is a name given to the French fans of American swing music during the Second World War. [MM]
43. Ibid.
44. Ibid.

b. 11/25/1924 in Paris 1st, residing with his parents, was arrested by officers at 7:45 p.m. at 73 Rue Saint-Honoré wearing a badge similar to the Jewish star, with the inscription 'Swing'. Handed over to Les Halles police station."[45]

The precinct captain of the Sorbonne district to the head of the judicial police:

"I respectfully inform you that at 6 p.m. today on Place du Panthéon, the municipal police arrested the minor Charles Douard, b. August 24, 1925, in Paris 12th, of Aryan race. The above-named was wearing on his jacket a paper Jewish star with the inscription 'J3'. Douard stated that he belonged to the French Imperial Youth of the PPF and that he was wearing the confiscated star in order to mock the Jews."[46]

At the end of this day, June 10, Department IV J of the Gestapo can declare with a certain satisfaction:

"The introduction of the wearing of the Jewish star has proceeded relatively calmly. There have been no demonstrations, no expressions of sympathy. *The various divisions of the French police had received orders to be particularly vigilant and to intervene immediately and rigorously.*[47] [...] Checks on and surveillance of the measures by the French police were done at random on June 6 and 7, 1942. *There has been no cause for criticism.*[48] A certain number of non-Jews have been arrested and dealt with accordingly. Children and juveniles, kept in custody for 48 hours, after having been firmly reminded of the need to obey the ordinance, were released."[49]

On June 15, 1942, a report from the police intelligence service reflects the dominant mood in the capital after the introduction of the yellow star:

"Although it has left the general public apparently indifferent, the implementation of the ordinance obliging Jews to wear the yellow star has nonetheless gone against the feelings of a good number of Parisians who do not see this measure as necessary for the national interest. Recalling the common origin of their religion and that of the Jews, Catholic circles in the capital see this measure as rather uncharitable. It has, moreover, provoked several reactions in student circles, where some individuals have shown their opposition by wearing conspicuous mock badges."[50]

On June 16, 1942, the Paris office of the Gestapo sends a long progress

45. Ibid.
46. Ibid.
47. My italics.
48. My italics.
49. CDJC-XLIX a 33.
50. APP, report of the police intelligence service, "La situation de Paris."

report to the HQ of the Reich intelligence service in Berlin. The tone of this document is the same as that of the preceding report from the intelligence service and as that of the June 10 note of Department IV J of the Gestapo:

"...In about 40 cases so far non-Jews, minors for the most part, were wearing the Jewish star with inscriptions such as *Swing, Swing 135%, Zazou, Victoire, catholique*, etc. out of sympathy with the Jews and at the same time in order to express anglophile attitudes. Some French primary school teachers have ordered their non-Jewish pupils to show consideration for their Jewish fellow pupils. In some schools, *incidents* have occurred between French pupils and Jewish pupils. The attitude in the universities is partly a refusal to accept the measure, partly indifference toward it..."[51]

The few dozen protesters have been brought to heel; the time for penalties has come. On July 3, the central administration of the prefecture of police provides some initial information on the young women arrested between June 6 and 15 for wearing an illegal star:

"This morning Captain Dannecker has taken the Jewish journalist Jacqueline Mayer to Les Tourelles Center to be incarcerated there for an indefinite period. In the course of his visit he intimated that the words 'Friend of the Jews', imposed on women who have demonstrated their sympathy for the Jews, should be placed above and not below the yellow star. In addition, he required the inscription in use at Tourelles Camp to be replaced by a much more visible one like the one in use at Drancy Camp."[52]

Several men have already been interned in Drancy and treated like normal internees. Two months later, it seems that their release is not on the agenda. Indeed, in a letter dated August 13, 1942, the prefect of police asks Darquier de Pellepoix, the commissioner for Jewish Affairs, about the possibility of releasing men and women seen as having made a mistake and that they shouldn't be turned into martyrs:

"As agreed, I respectfully send you the list of *non-Jewish* persons who, in accordance with instructions from the occupation authority, have been interned in Drancy Camp (9 men) and Les Tourelles camp (11 women) for having worn a mock badge as a parody of the Jews' star. All those concerned, who are of French nationality, have been incarcerated for more than two months. Most of them are fairly young, students who did not realize the importance that would be attached to their act, that they would not be allowed to take their examinations because they were interned and thus find themselves having been severely punished. In

51. CDJC-XLIX a 90.
52. APP, series BA 1830.

these circumstances, I think a new request could be made of the relevant German departments in order, if possible, to obtain a gesture of goodwill toward them."[53]

His approach is fruitless. In reply, an underling at the Department of Jewish Affairs passes on a blank refusal to the prefect of police:

"...I respectfully inform you that the German Authorities have informed me that under the present circumstances this request could not be granted a favorable reply."[54]

It is not clear whether the Department of Jewish Affairs even passed on the request from the prefect of police. He must have had direct access to the Gestapo, since on August 24 he takes malicious pleasure in telling Darquier de Pellepoix that his appeal has been granted. Indubitable proof the office of the prefecture of police has better connections with and is taken more seriously by 31a Avenue Foch (headquarters of the Gestapo) than the unproductive fanatics of the Department of Jewish Affairs:

"I respectfully inform you that, by the letter IV J of August 15, the German Department IV J has just informed me that the non-Jews wearing mock Jewish badges will be released on September 1."[55]

The archives of the prefecture of police contain a number of reports following the cross-examinations of these "deviants," whom so few of the population of this country followed. The badge that Michel Reyssat made for himself out of very pale yellow paper was not in the right format and fairly discreet. But what was that to the sleuth who spotted him? He is the only survivor of this adventure whom I have been able to find. Sixty years later his memories are still intact.

On June 11, 1942, Michel Reyssat, aged 18, a student at the Violet School of Electrical Engineering is arrested in the Latin Quarter. Why? On the left side of his chest he is wearing a mock star with the word "Swing" on it. He has deliberately broken the law but has no idea of the seriousness of his offense. He has been disgusted by the promulgation of the 8th ordinance and doesn't accept that this humiliation can be added to the racial measures already taken "against the persons designated as Jews." Without consulting anyone else, Michel Reyssat decides to react in his own way and makes an entirely personal decision. He remembers:

"As soon as a reproduction of that star was published in the press, I cut one out of cardboard and colored it in, writing the word "Swing" on it, hoping to provoke derision. Usually I pinned this badge behind the lapel

---

53. CDJC-CIX 36.
54. Ibid.
55. Ibid.

of my jacket, but out in the streets I attached it where it could be clearly seen in order to encourage passers-by to reject this measure. Even hoping for a massive impact."[56]

Was the motivation of this student political, humanitarian or was it simply a matter of indignation? His response is immediate and direct. "It's a bit of all those at once. I had Jewish friends, of course, and my hatred of the Nazis contributed to my decision. You could learn a lot about them by reading Hitler's *Mein Kampf*. Everything you could read in that was unacceptable."

It is impossible not to ask Michel Reyssat whether he felt he was committing an act of resistance by wearing his star. His reaction is immediate: "I was in a permanent state of revolt. All my instincts were against that system. If I'd had a gun, I might have used it."

On June 11, 1942, Michel Reyssat is stopped for questioning by a policeman with a keen eye whereas until then, none bothered to ask him about the star he has been wearing for several days. He hasn't forgotten anything about that day or the days to follow, and he takes us back to that time of normalized barbarity:

"Five hundred, or perhaps a thousand people, including German soldiers and policemen, saw this mock star before I noticed, on the opposite sidewalk, the penetrating look of a man who hurried across the road and caught me after a brief pursuit. Did this very French plain-clothes policeman feel offended in his beliefs or did he have orders to hunt down people like me? Whatever the case, he took a firm hold of me to conduct me to the police station.

"I spent the night imprisoned in the basement of the prefecture of police on Quai de Gesvres, in a little cell with bars, like a criminal. The next day I ended up in Drancy Camp. Other protestors, around twenty, arrived there as well. All had been wearing a star with various inscriptions such as 'Auvergnat', 'Goy', etc.

"The SS officer and his assistant made us appear the next morning right in the middle of the camp square, in the wire-mesh gateway dividing it and allowing people to pass between the two parts of the building. Brandishing a revolver to intimidate us, bawling, shouting abuse, furious. This SS officer kept on asking us the same question: why were you wearing those mock stars? Not getting any reply, he got angrier and angrier, and I wondered if he was going to shoot and if so, who would be the first to be hit. Finally he calmed down and told us we would have to wear the Jewish star like the

56. Conversation with Michel Reyssat, March 30, 2000.

other internees with, in addition, 'Friend of Jews' written on a distinct white strip. It was the only time I met the man who was said to be SS Captain Dannecker. All the other persons in authority in the camp who were in contact with the detainees were French, including, I believe, the guards on the watch towers."[57]

Memories can fade with time, but how could he forget that internment that was to last for two and a half months, with the various repressive authorities determined to humiliate these rebels?

"In the camp, the people wearing mock stars were systematically isolated from each other. True, during the exercise hours we had the opportunity to chat in the yard, but it was difficult because the camp was crammed full. We mostly talked about problems of hygiene and food. When I arrived in Drancy there must have been between 1,500 and 1,800 men there, but with the July 16, 1942 roundup many more arrived. The camp was full. After the first deportation convoys we saw the internees from the camps in the occupied zone arriving, especially from Gurs."

Such an experience is bound to leave its impression on a young man of eighteen and make him aware of the way dehumanization works, as well as of his compatriots' lack of interest in this repression that they seem to feel has nothing to do with them.

"Our time in Drancy left its mark on us, of course. You can't forget the human misery under your very eyes, and all the rest. In such circumstances you learn everything about human beings. On the other hand there were some very moving acts of solidarity. In the rooms there were unchanging rites, as in the barracks: the roll call—morning and evening— by a room-leader, in the presence of a policeman. There was the sharing out of the bread: we used makeshift scales—I did it regularly. It was the daily task my room-mates had given me. It was the same with the soup with three peas each. And then the hygienic conditions were appalling: one trough with five faucets for fifty. Yes, I have experienced the life of a concentration-camp prisoner, but with one manifest difference: I was not at risk of being deported."

Apart from his memories, did his time in Drancy have an influence on Michel Reyssat's behavior after the war?

"Obviously. After that I found all persecution unbearable. It has made a lasting mark on me. You can't see things in the same way anymore, and men in particular..."

There can be no question of attempting a statistical analysis on the

---

57. Indeed they were French police, responsible for the external surveillance of the camp. The prefecture of police provided the internal administration. See my *Drancy, un camp de concentration très ordinaire 1941–1944* (Paris: Le Cherche midi, 1996).

basis of the thirty-eight names of these objectors who expressed their opposition to the Nazi ordinances in the most peaceful way imaginable, by thumbing their noses at the French police charged with their enforcement. One trend does, however, appear: the protesters are young, sometimes even very young, and there are as many women as men embarking on this adventure in which their moral courage is only outdone by their recklessness:

—Under 20 years old....................21 (of which 16 were under 18)

—Between 21 and 25......................10

—Between 26 and 40....................6

—Over 40...1

The distribution of those under 20 is as follows:

—10 at high school;

—8 students;

—3 manual or office workers.

The other daredevils include two painters (women), one architect, one female newspaper-seller, one housewife (at fifty-six the oldest in the group), ten women office workers and manual laborers of both sexes.

There were some demonstrations of dissent in a number of towns in the occupied zone, but it did not prove possible to compile a list of them. Despite that, we heard that in Besançon a young doctor spontaneously put on an authentic yellow star, thus risking deportation after his arrest by the French police.[58]

---

58. Conversation with Dominique Blum, January 24, 2001.

8

A Compliant Press

FROM THE MOMENT when the Jews of the occupied zone were forced to wear the yellow star the press had a field day, even more than for the roundups of 1941. Oddly enough, five weeks later that same press was to be very discreet after the so-called Vél d'Hiv roundup [named after the indoor cycling track and stadium where most of those taken were held].[1] In June 1942 it is advised by the *Propagandastaffel*[2] and the Gestapo to devote greater space to the enforcement of the 8th ordinance. Things are different after July 16, 1942, doubtless because public opinion is becoming more sensitive to the effects of racial oppression. A report to Berlin dated June 16, 1942, by Department IV J of the Gestapo shows that they are clearly satisfied to see the French press delighted at the recent measure:

"The Paris press has taken up the question of the obligation to wear the distinguishing badge in articles, some of which are fairly long. Several newspapers have pointed out that wearing a distinguishing badge was imposed in the Middle Ages by decrees of the kings of France and papal bulls. Further propaganda supporting the Jewish star by means of posters was refrained from for reasons put forward by the security police..."[3]

1. Maurice Rajsfus; Levy Laub (trans.) *The Vél d'Hiv Raid* (Los Angeles: DoppelHouse Press, 2017, originally published as *La Rafle du Vél d'Hiv* (Paris: Presses universitaires de France, 2002).
2. Propaganda unit. [MM]
3. CJDC-XLIX a 90.

Dailies and weeklies, whether they specialized in anti-Semitism or not, presented the news in a hateful manner with appeals for people to inform against Jews and for the oppression to be intensified. The tone is crude and bound to have an effect.

The passages quoted here are of course incomplete but expressive enough to show how pernicious this ideology, spread by a high-circulation press, could be.

From May 26, 1942, *Au Pilori*, which must have had the advantage of a number of leaks regarding the imminent publication of the 8th ordinance, attacks the Jews with tooth and nail, demanding even harsher measures in an article by Jean Méricourt entitled "A necessary and immediate measure":

"With Jewish, English or American propaganda (which all comes down to the same thing) becoming more extravagant with every passing day, with assassinations and sabotage on the rise and the situation in France therefore becoming more and more critical, we demand that the obligation to wear the yellow star be the first of the measures that must be taken against the 'cursed race'. We must first of all have a clear understanding of the situation. For several months now we have been receiving dozens of letters every day asking why this measure of the utmost importance has never been imposed. Clearly it was impossible during the Hebrew days of our member of parliament Xavier Vallat.[4] However, things have changed now.

"But beware, the mind of the Yid is fertile in trickery, subterfuge and camouflage. It is not only necessary that wearing the badge be obligatory but also that the color, size and shape, and the place where the ignominious badge must be attached (arm or chest) be clearly designated; that it be specified that the armband or badge must be worn at all times in such a way that it is visible on whatever article of clothing the Jew is wearing. And, of course, that the impact of the decree be made effective by serious penalties: fines and prison—imposed on the spot.

"At a later date we will suggest other prophylactic and sanitary measures of vital practical importance, of which some, which have already been introduced in several countries, have produced undeniable results, while other new ones turn out to be indispensable. So that there is no ambiguity, we demand that it be clearly specified that 100% or 50% Jewish men and women, adults and minors, be required to wear the armband or the badge. For we know our Jews and their devious and dishonest distinc-

---

4. An anti-Semitic right-wing politician, commissioner general for Jewish Affairs under Pétain until dismissed on German insistence in May 1942. [MM]

tions. We likewise express the desire to see the decree implemented in the non-occupied zone and in our colonies, which the government will certainly come to see as inevitable in the near future."

On June 4, 1942, three days before the yellow star has to be worn, *L'Appel*, a weekly whose sentiments were well in tune with the times, devoted a long article to this topic with the venomous title: "The Jews are beginning to pay!" The author, Jean Contoux, is a specialist in this kind of prose:

"It's done.

"Starting next Sunday, June 7, Jews over six years of age will have to wear the yellow star, the Star of David, clearly visible on the left side of their chest. Henceforth we will know whom we are dealing with. Henceforth Lévy, Blum or Cohen will no longer be able to worm their way into our confidence, abuse our good faith, even if they go by the name of Dubois, Dupont or Durand.

"The six-pointed star will identify them at first sight, and only those who want to be will be deceived, those who have been jewified, of course, and those incurable idiots who will feel sorry for the fate of these 'poor, eternally persecuted Jews'. [...] They have been warned: the Jews are merely TOLERATED—and that provisionally, for the moment. This is something every right-thinking Frenchman ought to be convinced of. 'We grant them the right of asylum, nothing more. Our affairs are none of their business anymore, not in any way at all. It is up to us to see that they do not interfere in them any longer. And when it comes to deciding their fate, they must not have a say in the matter.'

"But for us to be fully satisfied, it is essential that the same measure that is imposed on them here, in the occupied zone, be applied to those on the other side of the demarcation line. For—and this can never be repeated too often—though they no longer make the laws there, as in the days of Blum[5], their gold, which they carried off with them, and their wide-ranging influence, makes them all-powerful.

"The Côte d'Azur, which they have literally overrun, is systematically being bled dry by them. They are the only ones with enough to eat down there. The indigenous population is starving to death. From Marseilles to Lyons they have taken over the black market, turning it into a legitimate institution. With their thousand-franc notes they are snapping up all the properties, châteaux or farms, in certain departments of the southwest, notably the Lot, living happily there on the fruits of their plundering, an insult to the misery of the local population.

---

5. Léon Blum, Jew, French politician, prime minister of the left-wing popular front government (1936–1937) and after the Occupation; an opponent of Vichy. [MM]

"If those in Vichy really do not want—and on this point we have no doubts at all about the will and the good intentions of the head of government and of M. Darquier de Pellepoix—there to be two countries called France, divided by the Jewish question, it is essential that the Jews, all the Jews, those this side and the other side of the line, should henceforward wear the distinguishing badge. On the day that this is done, something will truly have changed, and we will be convinced that the national revolution is finally under way. And now, when will we have the armband of shame for the '*freemasonners*'?"

On that same day, *Au Pilori* loudly celebrates the imminent coming into force of the Nazi ordinance. The headline of the article is announced on the front page: "The Star for the Jews in the occupied zone. Will something have changed?" The author, again, is Jean Méricourt:

"For two years the Jewish question has been treated with moderation, balance and other democratic methods. Now is the time to take up the club and bring it down on the spines of the Jews, ever ready to stand up again when faced with weakness. The decrees have been circumvented by the Jews, aided by the complicity of the officials charged with enforcing them. It is time to employ other means to rid ourselves of these Jewish vermin: the star is the first of these means.

"People out in the streets are warned of all public dangers, why has it been that until now the Jews have not had to wear a sign? The vile Jewish beast must be struck down, and this victory must be the first revolutionary act of the new France. Our sole regret will be that we were not able or willing to do this ourselves.

"There is one question that arises at the moment: will it be enough for the Jews to cross the demarcation line for them to take off their star? Are the Jews any less dangerous in Vichy than in Paris? We do not believe that at all! We would, however, like some information on that subject."

With a slight delay the militant anti-Semitic weekly joins in the war dance on June 6, 1942. Lucien Rebatet is licking his lips at the thought of the measure that is about to come into force. The headline of his editorial is sober enough: "The yellow star" but the article is oozing hatred from the very first line:

"Today there is not a single Jew, whatever his origins, who is not acting as a sly or arrogant agent of bolshevism, who is not praying for its victory, who is not working for it by all means at his disposal. Thus the Jew reveals himself in all his viciousness. The decisive battle is being fought between him and the Aryan. The Aryans cannot leave such an enemy free to conceal himself.

"The yellow star that they are imposing on them is the natural consequence of Jewish duplicity. Faced with the Aryan, the Jew camouflages his race as far as possible, changes his name, but under the surface only thinks and acts for a single—Jewish— nationality, pursuing in his heart their permanent conspiracy against the Christian nations [...]

"In this magazine, last winter, I expressed my delight at seeing in Germany the first Jews distinguished by their yellow mark. It will be an even greater delight to see that star in the streets of our Paris where, not three years ago, this execrable race was trampling us underfoot.

"There is, however, one regret, a profound regret, and that is that the star is not being imposed by a French law. We are nationalists, convinced that Germany and France have a common enemy in the Jews and that France must carry on the struggle against them at Germany's side. If there is one area of complete understanding between the two nations, it is in this matter.

"There is no country that has suffered from the Jews as much as ours. They brought down upon us the worst of misfortunes: defeat. Since then they have aggravated our afflictions to an incredible degree, poisoning our minds, managing to exert the most baleful influence on our politics, spreading the scourge of the black market everywhere, profiting from our distress to build up new and vile fortunes.

"The steps we have so far taken against these wretches are as good as nothing. The few timid decrees published in the *Journal officiel* have hardly been enforced at all...There is one decision that is of urgent necessity: to extend the wearing of the yellow star to all the Jews in France. It is far more necessary on the other side of the Allier [River] than in this zone. THERE HAVE NEVER BEEN SO MANY JEWS IN FRANCE.

"This is a revolutionary measure? Possibly. But, after all, are we going through a revolution or are we not?

"The yellow star will make certain Catholics unhappy. It is easy to respond to them, to calm their troubled consciences. The yellow star goes back to the strictest of Christian traditions, that of the rondel which, during all the ages of pure and solid faith, the great centuries of pure Catholic civilization, marked out the Jews of the ghetto, and to that of the yellow hat of the Jews of Avignon, the pope's Jews. If the modern Church were to protest against the yellow star, it would have to disavow all the popes who devised, then imposed it."

And how can we leave out the choice morsel of this article, the vengeful tirade in which Rebatet rejoices in finally being able to differentiate between one person and another, with the conviction that all men are not equal:

"I cannot remember which politician it was who said, years ago: if the Jews were black or blue, there wouldn't be a Jewish question, everybody would be able to recognize them and exclude them. The yellow star will correct this strange situation in which a race of humans radically opposed to the others is not always discernible to the eye."

In capital form on the eve of the introduction of the yellow star, *Je suis partout* really lets loose in another article, unsigned in this case:

"The appearance of the yellow stars on the Jews' chests is going to create an opportunity, especially for nationalist revolutionaries, to show their colors in public. The measure is to come into force on June 7, but already the Gaullists are starting a compassion campaign. Instructions coming from Moscow and London are encouraging the French to show their sympathy for the 'Jewish victims'. We must remind, brutally if necessary, any of the French who might be tempted to follow these instructions that our thoughts must be above all for the prisoners, our sympathy above all for the prisoners, and that any demonstration in favor of those responsible for the war is an insult to our dead."

Le Franciste, the newspaper of the party of the same name led by Marcel Bucard, delights in the 8th ordinance coming into force. The gloating of this political nonentity, scorned by his fellow fascists, is very representative of this category of politician who have only one possibility in the occupied zone, and that is to conform unconditionally to the Nazi laws.

"Everything is changing. As I have already told you, they are going to be delighted to wear this six-pointed decoration. Perhaps they will find a new source of profit in it. It won't be long before you will see a black market in yellow cloth. The only amusing thing about this Jewish story is the one clothing coupon they have to use to get the star."

There are no newspapers on Sunday, June 7, the day when the wearing of the star is enforced. On Monday, June 8 the dailies fill column after column with this juicy tidbit. Buneau-Varilla's *Le Matin* stirs up its readers' hatred:

"The first day of the yellow star being worn. The thought it arouses: 'One would never have imagined that there were so many Jews in Paris.' Since yesterday the Jews have been wearing, sewn on their clothes, the Star of David, a distinguishing sign of their race, wrongly called the yellow star because it is in black on a buttercup yellow background. With the badge being carefully cut out according to the ordinances. [...] Yesterday morning this rash of yellow could mainly be seen in the outer districts, and in the ghetto, of course, in the Temple and Saint-Paul districts before spreading to the boulevards in the afternoon. Thus when they went to do their shopping, the non-Jews could identify the race of many people they knew, and had even met the previous day in the shops without paying special attention to them, and there were some surprises.

"There was another surprise in store for the Parisians, in the afternoon, when they noticed the significant number of Jews walking and talking, joining the queues outside the theaters and cinemas or just traveling on the metro. And only part of the Jewish population was out and about! We must not forget that in 1941 there were 1,200,000 Jews in France,[6] of which 350,000 were in Paris and its suburbs. Yesterday we could see once again what a short memory we have. Around 8 p.m. there were fewer and fewer yellow stars. By 8:30 the Jews had gone home."

A popular daily like *Le Petit Parisien* makes precisely the same points but in more measured tones:

"It was yesterday that wearing the yellow badge became obligatory for the Jews. Some were already to be seen towards the end of the previous week. But most Jews had waited for the exact date it came into force to conform to this requirement. For most French, this first day brought a surprise and, we hope, a cause for reflection: knowing the considerable number of Jews—which they had never previously suspected—that there were in some districts.

"Leaving aside the Saint-Paul, Saint-Antoine, Mouffetard, Lancry, Porte-Saint-Denis and Clignancourt districts, which are already known to have a high density of Jews, an unexpected blaze of Stars of David was to be seen in districts such as Les Ternes, Passy and Auteuil. And, also quite a few in Longchamp. Let us make it clear that this measure is of a general nature and applies to all Jews, no matter what nationality they might believe they can invoke to exempt them.[7] The Star of David is not at all a mark of derision but a racial symbol that has to be worn, having been cut out and firmly attached in a clearly visible way, on pain of serious penalties."

Paris-Midi, a midday newspaper, is as venomous as *Le Matin*. It is a paper that is sold above all by street-vendors on the grand boulevards, thus ensuring the official abuse is passed on so that no one can be unaware of it:

---

6. According to approximate estimates (on the high side) there would have been around 350,000 Jews in France in 1939, split equally between French nationals and foreigners.

7. A mistake. As we saw in the preceding chapter, those who came from the Allied countries (apart from the USSR) were not bound by it; the same, for the moment, applied to Hungarians.

"The abundance of Jews on Parisian sidewalks has opened the eyes of even the most blind. A Sunday stroll, but a surprising, astounding stroll. As your steps take you toward City Hall, along old streets with names still redolent of the Middle Ages, you see here and there a few of those much-vaunted yellow stars, recently imposed on the Jews. But as soon as you enter what one could call the Paris ghetto, the main thoroughfare of which is Rue des Rosiers, there are more and more of these distinguishing signs. Then, if you should happen to persist in walking to and fro, it will become an obsession, and it will not be long before you realize that it is you, you the Aryan not wearing a badge, who is the object of general curiosity.

"But leave this district and go to the grand boulevards. The stars appear there, beginning in the very early afternoon. Alone or in small groups, the Jews are out for a walk, all going in the same direction: west, along the Champs Élysées. From one moment to the next they become more and more frequent. The boulevard is abounding, teeming with them, something the true Parisian regards with amazement."

Les Nouveaux Temps, an evening paper directly financed by the Germans, edited by Jean Luchaire,[8] takes up the same refrain. In a long article entitled "Marking out the Jews across the centuries" a certain Maurice de Bannières, after having reminded the reader of the different stages of 'marking' the Jews across the centuries, proves to be even more violent than his colleagues in this anti-Semitic exercise:

"Let us be impervious to the hypocrisy of the moderates, the mediocre, the neutrals. According to the powerful statement of the Marshal, of which Robert Brasillach reminded us a few days ago, 'Life is not neutral'. For the Jews to remain mixed with the Aryans and to be mistaken for them represented a real danger. Drumont says at some point that the Jews, by their excesses, show a vague nostalgia for the *san-benito* (a term that in Spain designated the yellow garment the Inquisition imposed on them). This war, which they wanted, which is their war, which they support wherever they are and the insignia of which they are very careful not to wear, is going to grant their wishes to the full."

Jacques Doriat's *Le Cri du peuple* of June 11, 1942, doesn't restrict itself to expressing its rejection of the Jews. Behind the vengeful phrases you can sense the desire to impose even harsher repression:

"A scandal at the law courts. On her attorney's gown a young Jewish woman is wearing the yellow star. Quick to feel sympathy and to ascribe their own delicacy of feeling to the Jews, our liberal, right-thinking, naive

---

8. The great advocate of collaboration and openly pro-Nazi, Jean Luchaire was to be condemned to death and executed in 1946.

'goody-goodies' are generally doubly mistaken with regard to the Jews. In the first place they assume that the fifty-four Jewish attorneys permitted, despite their race, to enjoy the privileges of French nationality, must be justly proud of that. Secondly that the anonymous Jewish crowd must be appalled at having to go around in the open air wearing Solomon's seal. Well, that's all a load of nonsense. If the Jews are proud of anything, it's of being themselves. As to being embarrassed by the yellow star, all one had to do was to see the scorn with which the young Jewish advocate, sitting on the steps of the appeal court in her gown with the piece of yellow satin well placed over her heart, looked down on those beside her. Assisted by several Aryan ninnies, she seemed the very statue of pride filled with hatred..."

The weeklies take up the baton. On June 11, *L'Appel* lets off steam through an unnamed columnist: "When I heard that, at last, as we have been demanding in our columns since our first issue, the Jews were to wear a distinguishing mark, I was filled with a sweet sense of euphoria."

In the same issue Pierre Constantini, president of the Ligue française says he is satisfied, but demands more decisive steps be taken:

"I can see very well that the yellow star exposes some Jews. What remains is to make a census of all of them, then to expel them from Europe, for it is urgently necessary to make it impossible for them to do any harm. In the meantime they must all be sent to work camps, I say work camps, not concentration camps. The French want to see the Jews bending down over the soil of France, pickaxes in their hands.

"We have not forgotten the Jew-lovers. Nor the *freemasonners*, who must be the first to pay for their crime against their country. [...] It is our inflexible will to see all those who have dragged France down and betrayed her punished."

On June 11, 1942, *Au Pilori* has its banner headline: "They wear the star here. When will they wear it down there?" Like many of those institutions and individuals actively involved in collaboration, *Au Pilori* does not make a secret of its desire to see the obligation to wear the star extended to the unoccupied zone. This is expressed in a long article:

"Exposing the Jew will not be the only result of the obligation to wear the star; it will set off a winnowing process that should facilitate the revision of a census which was carried out under conditions (under the rule of X. Vallat) that made it a veritable act of betrayal. Thousands of 100% or 50% Jews did not declare their race and hope they will never have to.

"In the occupied zone, we are en route to complete purification. Very well. But what is going to happen in the so-called free zone. Invaded, contaminated, corrupted, ravaged, eaten away by the Jewish cancer, is it going to live on in its filth without reacting? Without hope of complete cleansing? We refuse to believe that.

"We demand, and firmly hope we shall obtain, a decree that makes wearing the yellow star obligatory for all Jews in the free zone. But the boundaries of this zone are not the Côte d'Azur or the Pyrenees. It goes beyond them, extending to Corsica, North Africa, to our colonies. These regions must be included in the decree. They are teeming with this base vermin. Have the inhabitants of these territories, including the natives, fallen out of favor? Have they been judged unworthy of being able to safeguard themselves from contact with Jews? For what reason? For no reason at all, as far as we can see?

"Not to impose the same measure as in France would do a serious disservice to our overseas compatriots. And all the more so because they are, every one of them, tremendously and justifiably anti-Jew, for one has to be born in Morocco or Tunisia or, above all, in Algeria (my splendid homeland) to know the Jew and what he is worth; to understand the devastation he can wreak and his power to corrupt."

Marcel Bucard's *Le Franciste* of June 13, 1942, returns to its ravings and its fears at not seeing the measure extended widely enough:

"The yellow star has started to show us all its colors! One newspaper has announced that the Jews from countries where wearing the star is not obligatory do not have to show the badge. This star, we are told, is a distinguishing mark. It is if all Jews wear it. It is not if it is reserved to French Jews alone. In no way am I standing up for them; but making an exception for all the dregs spewed out of the foreign ghettos during the time of the Popular Front is something I find disturbing."[9]

The same day *Je suis partout* puts on a show of surprise:

"All these Jews! All these Jews! The abundance of stars has truly amazed all those who were entirely unaware of the matter. You'd never have thought there were so many of them, the Parisians keep saying. The fact is that many Jews do not display their race in their features. They are the most dangerous ones."

An article entitled "The lesson of the yellow star" in *Les Nouveaux Temps* of June 16, 1942, by Guy Crouzat, rejects any humanitarian considerations:

"The wearing of the star of Zion makes any subterfuge impossible, tearing away the mask, patiently developed over the centuries, of Jewish

---

9. Obvious, deliberately misleading information. The great majority of foreign Jews have been wearing the star since June 7, 1942.

anonymity. This is what makes the day when it was decreed an historic day for us.

"Our anglophiles and our Gaullists keep repeating that it is an inhuman measure; we fail to see what is inhuman about imposing on a category of people, whose feelings, passions and interests are, to say the very least, not the same as those of French stock, the distinguishing mark with which the workings of nature and genetics do not always provide them. One cannot regard as abuse or a snub an arrangement which protects the French people against the pernicious influence of those who, for too long and without having been granted the hereditary right, have ruled the roost here and who today are the born enemies of this new European order in which it is up to France to ensure a place worthy of her. The common sense of the people has not been mistaken in this. Despite the provocative acts of traitors, fanatics and idiots, the yellow star has smoothly become part of our daily life, even if its profound significance mostly escapes those who come into contact with it..."

La Gerbe takes its turn in the discussion on June 18, 1942. Alphonse de Châteaubriant's weekly is lagging behind the rest so all it can do is to regurgitate the same arguments, though adding the stupidity of its own ignorance in ascribing the paternity of the so-called Star of David to Solomon:

"Last Sunday on the boulevards, on the Champs-Élysées, in the huge crowds at the cinema doors, at the racecourses, the people of Paris were made brutally aware of the immensity of the Jewish peril, as they counted with horror the number of yellow stars unmasking the racial origins of so many apparently harmless men and women. At first they counted them out of curiosity, then with amazement, finally with concern. And saying: What would happen in Marseilles or on the Côte d'Azur if they were forced to wear the star of Solomon..."

Under the headline "We must protect our race," Le National Populaire of June 20, 1942, again goes on about the "friends of the Jews," veritable traitors to their country:

"If there were any measures that enjoyed the almost unanimous approval of the French nation, it was those that were taken in the occupied zone to eliminate the Jews from the national community. However, despite the repugnance that the French as a whole feel for the Jews, there are still some young people, of what one might call the 'swing' generation, who, completely jewified because of the people with whom they associate, show sympathy for them and also wear the yellow star. It is the duty of the government to remove these undesirable elements

95

from the French community and satisfy their wish to join the Jewish community by providing them with genuine Jewish stars and registering them as such in the census. They will thus be in a position to enjoy all the measures we have the mind to implement."

Gringoire, a militant anti-Semitic weekly, felt obliged to add its contribution to this virulent press campaign. Associated with Action française during the thirties, this magazine had driven Roger Salengro, the minister of the interior, to suicide in 1936.[10] Under the Occupation it was the novelist Henri Béraud who was the great star of the paper. On July 3, 1942, *Gringoire* joined in with its own tirade:

"The requirement for the Jews to wear the yellow star has revived the face of Paris in one fell swoop. The badge is a fine golden patch casting its light all over the city. Every district has been able to spot its Jews. On the Opéra-Jean-Jaurès metro line the glitter of the stars is dazzling. Around 7:30 p.m. all the stars gather together in a quivering constellation. All the stars become shooting stars! They have to get back home before eight, if they don't want to end up on the damp straw of the cells."

Le Franciste of July 4, 1942, appeals to strange motivations in order to provoke hatred and rejection. Every Jew, even the most wretched, must be seen as a personal enemy:

"A gateway in a popular busy street. There would be nothing unusual about it, if there wasn't a beggar beside it. A beggar wearing the yellow star. It has a startling effect. It would not be surprising if some foreign propaganda organization were behind this beggar."

Le Petit Parisien of July 15, 1942, is delighted at the 9th Nazi ordinance, which has just been promulgated. Wearing the yellow star, the Jews are now excluded from public spaces:

"For a long time now too many Jews—young Jews especially—have been displaying their provocative insolence in public places, on café terraces, at the races. And when the ordinance requiring them to wear the star came out, too many Jews could be seen displaying, with ostentatious arrogance, the badge indicating their race on café terraces, in public places, sports grounds. It was the Jews who wanted the war, the maleficence of their race has plunged the whole world into a terrible conflict. Bearing this crime in mind, the latest measures seem mild. On the other hand, from the strict point of view of basic moral principles it seemed impossible that these people, of whom it is known from news items and court sentences that they

---

10. Roger Salengro, minister of the interior in the 1936 popular front, was attacked in a right-wing newspaper campaign based on the (erroneous) claim that he wasn't captured by the Germans in 1916 but deserted. No proof was ever shown. [MM]

account for 80% of the organizers of the black market that makes the plight of the poor even worse, should throw their ill-earned money around in places of amusement, while the great majority of the French people are suffering under the harsh conditions of life at the moment."

Economically the French are deep in destitution but the Jews, even though they can be spotted thanks to their "special badge," continue to live in luxury: that is the sense of an altogether edifying article in *L'Appel* of July 16, 1942, the same day as the Vélodrome d'Hiver roundup:

"Last Saturday on Place de l'Odéon two yid gang members, gleaming with unhealthy fat, the yellow star clearly displayed, were lounging on the rear seat of a bicycle-taxi, being pulled along by an unfortunate cyclist whose physique was a sorry sight. Humiliating as it is to see a human being reduced to this to earn a living, adding to that the extra humiliation of serving as a beast of burden for the Jews is too much. The offspring of the cursed race ought to be banned from using bicycle-taxis."

The aggressive comments in the press directed against a group of humans that was already decimated, terrorized, living in fear of the next day, are soon going to become scarce. On August 4, 1942, *Aujourd'hui*, which has gradually gotten rid of its brilliant intellectuals, publishes the declaration of one of the directors of the General Commission for Jewish Affairs:

"The wearing of the yellow star in the unoccupied zone is more than ever desirable. Then the French will realize how great the danger is. Even greater than one thinks if one takes into account the fact that certain marriages contracted since the armistice threaten to circumvent the law. No one is unaware any more that Jewish women today, panic-stricken at the thought of punishment, are arranging marriages with obliging Aryans. But for the measures recommended by the high commissioner for Jewish affairs to be effective we must have an anti-Jewish police force. The high commissioner for Jewish affairs is working on this as hard as he can..."

This long review of the press is by no means exhaustive. In fact, I have included only the most violently racist attitudes expressed in this collaborationist press where there is no place for shades of meaning. There was genuine rivalry between the journalists specializing in militant anti-Semitism with a very restricted vocabulary. As if they had to prove to the Nazis that collaborationist France could go farther than Germany in this rejection; this demonization of the Jews that would make it possible to solve many problems.

More generally, the whole of the press published this kind of news item in the same way as it did the reports of the German army's victories on the eastern front and in Libya. In the two zones, millions of ordinary readers were daily inundated with this racist propaganda, in both the general news sections and the most virulent editorials, and that could not but have a lasting effect.

For its part, the Resistance press did not dwell on this new approach to repression. This kind of news was not a priority for the little newspapers in which space was limited. How could they take an interest in this further attack on human rights when Europe and Asia were being laid to waste by war? Even the churches were careful not to react. In the final account, this lack of interest reflected the desire of the broad mass of the French people to concentrate its efforts solely on getting supplies and having their coupons for fresh meat and sausage or cheese stamped—are we going to get any potatoes or pâté this summer? Who had the time or will to get indignant about this very visible exclusion, the effects of which could only become more marked. Proof of this was provided by the venture of a mere forty—slightly mad—Parisians who had defied the 8th ordinance. At the end of spring 1942, when there was still no doubt about the victory of the Axis powers, the collaborationist press had circulation figures that would satisfy many of today's press barons. True, television had not yet taken its place in people's homes, while the radio—the much-vaunted wireless—was not yet truly widespread.

The circulation figures that are available, from one of the many investigations of the intelligence service, are for the end of December 1940 but seem still to be reliable for the period under consideration:[11]

DAILIES		WEEKLIES	
Paris-Soir	970,000	La Gerbe	135,000
Le Petit Parisien	635,000	Au Pilori	95,000
Le Mati	532,000	Signal[12]	420,000

---

11. These circulation figures, given by Roger Langeron in his book *Paris, juin 40*, pp. 198–9, only refer to the occupied zone. Moreover some of the papers noted here were to disappear or be changed as the months passed. *La France au travail* became *La France socialiste*, thus losing a significant portion of its readership, as did *Aujourd'hui* to *Le Petit Parisien* and to *Paris-Soir*, which later developed its noon edition, *Paris-Midi*. Among the weeklies that are not noted here there was, of course, the nauseous *Je suis partout*, but none of these newspapers ventured off the beaten track of run-of-the-mill infamy.

12. *Signal*, a weekly published by the German army, was a bit like *Match*, which explains its strange success. The *Propagandastaffel* (propaganda unit) tried, with greater difficulty, to establish another paper, *Der Adler*, the Luftwaffe weekly.

L'Oeuvre	196,000	*Le Réveil du peuple*	42,000
Aujourd'hui	110,000	*La Terre française*	50,000
La France au travail	92,000	*Tout et tout*	130,000
Le Cri du peuple	35,000	*L'Atelier*	47,000
Les Nouveaux Tems	30,000	*Le Fait*	30,000

9

Toward Liberation

L ET US PASS over two years. As liberation approaches it doesn't seem as if the nature of the assignments of the police force have changed. Similarly the behavior of individual officers is hardly any different. Any traces of resistance in the ranks of the police are so unobtrusive as to be barely visible. If that had not been the case, we would have had much more writing on the subject.[1]

The hunt for Jews goes on, as vicious as ever, and the wearers of the star continue to be stopped for questioning for any and every reason, as if wearing the "special badge" were a misdemeanor, whereas in fact it is an obligation. Nothing has changed in the way they stick to their orders, and the hunt for communists is still in progress. The victories of the Russian army on the eastern front and the Normandy landings have not produced any real turnaround in the state of mind of those responsible for maintaining public order. It is not until the end of July 1944 that those who, for more than four years have seen to it that the edicts of the Occupier and of Vichy are respected, gradually become less strict.

True, after the Allied landings on June 6, 1944, a certain casualness begins to appear among the rank-and-file officers. Not a revolt. Not yet. Simply the realization by certain policemen that the time has come to restore their precious republican virginity.

The great resistance fighters that are the policemen of Paris, at their

---

1. See my *La Police de Vichy* (Paris: Le Cherche midi, 1995), pp. 217–262.

head the prefect of police, Amédée Bussières, are concerned about the inadequacy of their weaponry. Evidence of that is a long letter of July 4, 1944, to the minister of the interior. That is six weeks before the first battles for the liberation of Paris and one month after the landings:

"I respectfully bring to your notice the extremely important question of the armament of the Paris police. The attached report will provide the necessary information on the present state of affairs and the seriousness of the situation, of which you are well aware. The Occupation Authorities will certainly look favorably on this. General Oberg has specified the weaponry he was authorizing, but we have to procure these armaments. [...] If we cannot have everything we need immediately, we hope our requirements will be at least partially satisfied, and we will make all practical arrangements compatible with the weaponry given to us. May I remind you that the situation I have been bringing to your notice for more than two years is getting worse by the day..."[2]

This letter also contains a warning with no ambiguity about it, which shows the determination of the police to support the repressive operations to the very end:

"In the event of general disorder the forces of the prefecture of police will quickly be faced with insurmountable difficulties, and should this come about we will be almost unarmed while facing opponents who, at this very moment, have at their disposal a considerable quantity of guns and grenades."[3]

There is as yet no evidence of a huge change in the police force. The simple fact is that some individuals are starting to disappear, since at the height of the battle for Normandy it is becoming clearer and clearer that, despite the saber rattling from German army headquarters, the Allies are not going to be thrown into the sea. This half-hearted development in the hearts and minds can be seen in an internal report, dated July 13, 1944, of the prefecture of police:

"A number of policemen have abandoned their post and disappeared. They will be dealt with according to the recent law of June 15, 1944, in which the police force is included in the same category as the military for a certain number of offenses for which provision is made in army regulations. They will be sought out and, if found, made to appear before a special tribunal. As for officers who allow themselves to be disarmed, they will be subject to disciplinary action in the form of a 'technical suspension from duty', entailing temporary confinement at the station, with

---

2. APP, series BA 1800.
3. Ibid.

food brought in at their own expense. They will continue to receive their pay, increased however by certain allowances."[4]

Should we deduce from this that the Paris police are already in a state of open rebellion? That is not the case, even if, little by little, the officers are learning to look the other way, becoming less arrogant, less strict in the enforcement of Nazi law. It is clear that, as the day of reckoning approaches, the head of the municipal police can no longer control his troops in the way he would wish. It is with this in mind that Émile Hennequin makes himself heard, on July 25, 1944, in a note sent to the precinct captains of Paris and the suburbs:

"Despite instructions, which have been renewed several times, there have been attacks on the distribution centers for ration cards without the intervention of the police. It is unacceptable that servants of the state should be taken by surprise without reacting and allow themselves to be disarmed. Once again I draw your attention to the necessity of adding personal comments to the instructions supplied and reminding the personnel under your command to show the greatest vigilance. To avoid being taken by surprise, the officers charged with surveillance must at all times have their pistol in their pocket, drawn and cocked, with their hand on the grip."[5]

This does not mean that the usual repression does not continue. A report of August 7, 1944, from the intelligence service is very clear about this:

"*The Jews.* 33 new registrations from individuals have been received. 12 of them that were considered late have resulted in legal action. In the course of the last fortnight 77 Jews have been arrested and all have been sent on to Drancy camp to be interned."[6]

The hunt continues in all places as can be seen in the fact that during the last week in July and the first week in August, 2994 fines have been imposed on cyclists compared with 3306 during the previous fortnight. There were 24 arrests for begging and then "In the course of *battues*[7] carried out during the last fortnight by day and by night, both on public streets as well as in the metro and establishments open to the public, the municipal police stopped 52,208 people for questioning, resulting in 107 arrests, of which there were 40 concerned young men who had not satisfied the requirement to register for military service, workers in disagreement with the German authorities and some who were avoiding the compulsory service."[8]

---

4. APP, series BA 1818, documents from the trial of Émile Hennequin.
5. Ibid.
6. APP, report of the police intelligence service, "La situation de Paris."
7. As in hunting; my italics. [MM note: A battue is a hunt in which the prey is driven towards the hunters.]
8. APP, report of the police intelligence service, "La situation de Paris."

This report from the police intelligence service confirms that the casual approach to police work only concerns an ineffective minority. Which is enough to alarm Émile Hennequin and his fellow senior officials. After August 7 there are hardly any more reports from the intelligence service (at least reports that can be consulted), but this very complete last report is teeming with contradictions. It seems that there is a great desire to give the impression that nothing has changed in the normal activities of the police:

"The people of Paris [...] are particularly concerned that, as events develop, and particularly if it should be the case that the Allied forces approach the capital, subversive elements might stir up serious trouble and that, in giving free range to their desire for revenge, they might commit all manner of excesses..."[9]

In this, one can sense the helplessness of the police hierarchy after four years of loyal service. It seems that the bosses in the prefecture of police have finally come to understand the risks run by the force:

"...In this respect the assassination of M. Frantz, the prefect of the Department of Isère only serves to intensify the fears of collaborationist circles and of all those who have fallen in with the policy of Marshal Pétain."[10]

On August 13, 1944, two police stations in the Paris suburbs, Asnières and Saint-Denis, are overpowered by German military police. One is blocked, the other disarmed. Immediately there is an outcry from the "resisters" among the police. Those who, since June 1940, have carried out their duties with good grace find it unacceptable to be deprived of the tools of their trade.

Following this "incident" the officers at several precincts refuse to wear their uniforms anymore, while still working at the station. When this is brought to his notice, Émile Hennequin is keen to reassure his men:

"The information I have just received from the German authorities allows me to give you a categorical assurance that no police officer will either be disarmed or suffer any coercive measure at all. The measures taken against the two police stations in question are to be lifted without delay. I therefore ask you to continue to carry out your duties normally, wearing your uniforms and carrying your arms, in order to maintain, as you have up to the present, the security of the people of Paris."[11]

On August 14, 1944, Émile Hennequin distributes to the precinct captains of Paris and the suburbs the order of the day from the prefect of

9. Ibid.
10. Ibid.
11. APP, series BA 1818. Documents from the trial of Émile Hennequin.

police, Amédée Bussières. This document is directed above all at the rank and file, since it seems clear that the officers in certain precincts have found the insult constituted by the disarmament of their colleagues intolerable. The tone is firm but moderate. Their task is, once more, simply to ensure the security of people and their property. As if nothing had happened since June 1940:

"Police officers of all ranks, my friends. Once more I ask you not to listen to appeals that may be directed at you, inciting you to fail to carry out your duties. I have to say, however, that I have no concerns about this. I know you. We must continue to ensure public order with firmness and absolute devotion to our country. There is no risk in doing your duty. I can confirm that you will be neither arrested nor disarmed by the Occupation Authorities. They have given me their formal assurance on that. Your attitude will determine not only the honor of the prefecture of police but the continued protection of the people of Paris, who have absolute confidence in you. No lapses will be tolerated!"[12]

The following day, August 15, things start to happen quickly. The Paris police go on strike—five days after the railway workers. It seems, however, that they were firmly pushed into this by the communist officials of the FTPs[13] of the Paris region and that they were offered a contract they couldn't refuse. "On the order of the police Committee of Liberation the police stations are deserted. There are no police officers in the streets of Paris anymore..."[14] The pyramid organization of the Paris insurrection works well: at the top Colonel Rol-Tanguy already has means of giving orders to police officers. On the intermediary level another communist, André Tollet, president of the Paris Committee of Liberation, sees to it that the instructions are carried out. From that point on Émile Hennequin makes greater concessions than he would have liked: "Given the circumstances, officers are authorized to return to work in plain clothes."[15] There are two factors behind this climb-down by the man who will only remain head of the municipal police for a few more days: in the first place, the rapid advance of the Americans on Paris and, above all, the increasing hostility of Parisians toward "their" police force.

On August 19, 1944, a small notice is posted on the walls of the prefecture of police. The text comes from Rol-Tanguy, a former political commissar in the International Brigades in Spain. Highly symbolic. Oddly enough, an appeal is made to the spirit of resistance not only of the

12. Ibid.
13. Franc-tireurs partisans, irregular partisan guerrillas. [MM]
14. In *L'Insurrection parisienne*, (Éditions du parti communiste, 1944), p. 11.
15. APP, series BA 1818, documents from the trial of Émile Hennequin.

police officers, who have much to make amends for, but also to the most vile henchmen of the Nazis during the previous years. This text reveals a will to create a united front that deliberately omits the recent past. Veritable absolution for the police:

"Appeal to the Paris police, to the Republican Guard and the gendarmerie, the riot police, the GMR (Groupe Mobile de Réserve—mobile reserve unit of the riot police) and prison wardens.

"The hour of liberation has come! Many of you have already participated widely in the struggle against the invader.

"Today it is the duty of the whole of the police force to line up beside the patriots gathered together in the French Forces of the Interior (FFI). You must *henceforth*[16] no longer take part in any operation tending to maintain the order of the enemy. You will refuse to take part in arrests of patriots, in searches, roadblocks, identity checks, guarding prisons, etc. You will assist the FFI in shooting down all those who, in that way, continue to serve the enemy."[17]

On August 24, 1944, what seems to be the last report by the intelligence service before the Liberation reveals the caution and unease of those who, continuing to check which way the wind is blowing, have realized that change is the order of the day, but you can't be certain.

"The people of Paris would like to be better informed about the events that are taking place in the capital and which they do not overall understand very well. They are disturbed by the losses in the ranks of the defenders, losses which, for the people in the various districts who do not get around very much, do not correspond to the losses of the *germans*[18] nor to the gains made against them. The Parisians are equally concerned about the fate of members of the FFI taken prisoner by the Germans and would like to know whether there are any negotiations with them, and if so, what is the result.[19] Moreover, they want young people from 16 to 18 to be disarmed. One reason is that, since they shoot with their pistols at the German patrols when they are very far away, the return fire from the Germans is

---

16. My italics. This appeal from Colonel Rol-Tanguy, who appears as commander of the French Forces of the Interior, is extremely ambiguous. On the one hand it brings up the resistance, supposedly long-standing, of the police to the invader, while on the other it asks these same police officers no longer to take part in operations to maintain order dictated by the enemy. In fact the Resistance has always been suspicious of these policemen, whom it has constantly denounced and who for four years have relentlessly pursued Jews, communists, Gaullists, Freemasons, etc. When the Liberation approaches there is suddenly a desire to regard these policemen as allies. Which results in this veritable juggling act transforming these policemen into members of the Resistance.
17. APP, series DB 542.
18. For the first time in four years, "Allemands" is written without a capital. In all official or internal documents it had become standard usage to write "Autorités Allemandes" or "A.A." [MM note: In normal French, unlike English and German, adjectives of nationality are written with the initial letter in lower case.]
19. This is related to the truce negotiated by the Norwegian consul Nordling with the heads of the German Army in Paris and the Gaullist elements of the Resistance.

haphazard and often wounds passers-by and housewives doing their shopping. Despite everything, the people are showing great calm, but it appears that this situation is unlikely to continue without arousing reactions due both to the privations they have to endure and to the lack of unity that can be discerned between the various resistance groups."[20]

Having been turned into a concentration camp for collaborators since the end of August 1944, Drancy has around fifty policemen among its new residents. Oddly, the particular list of these internees has under the heading "motive" the note "unknown," which is strange to say the least. Furthermore, a November 18, 1944 note states that the police interned in Drancy have not been selected by any general commission but come solely from the Commission de l'épuration de la police [Commission on the Purging of the Police]. (There is a strong desire not to wash their dirty linen in public.) It is difficult to know how many of those officers who were a little more "efficient" than their colleagues under the Occupation went through Drancy. A list of internees who had belonged to the prefecture of police and were transferred from their station to Drancy camp, was drawn up on April 13, 1945; on it, there are thirty-one names, different from the preceding list. A list dated April 10, 1945, and bringing together all collaborators, mentions four special lieutenants who had belonged to the judicial police.[21]

Once the Liberation has arrived, the rank and file of the Paris police are not particularly worried, and they found it difficult to change their way of thinking. The reports of the intelligence service are written in a style showing the difficulty of breaking bad habits acquired during the previous years. Thus the intelligence service officer present at a gathering organized by the Union des Juifs pour la résistance et l'entraide (UJRE; Jewish Union for Resistance and Mutual Aid, close to the French Communist Party) cannot resist noting at the bottom of his report: "It should be noted that the Jews who spoke in French had a fairly pronounced foreign accent..."[22]

Still in the same tone, with the ice-cold style denoting the police bias in favor of whatever order is in place, there is this note of October 26, 1944, from the intelligence service:

"In the well-informed Jewish areas in the capital we learn that Jews who have been dispossessed of their property in accordance with the law of July 22, 1941, intend to demand accounts from the managing commis-

20. APP, report of the police intelligence service, "La situation de Paris."
21. APP, series BA 1831.
22. APP, series BA 1816 (dossier B 51 5).

sioners and the administrators who were appointed at that time. The majority of those concerned *consider*[23] that they have been despoiled by the managing commissioners, regarding them as legally responsible in their function as salaried representatives."[24]

Along the same lines but less crude, we have found this note of April 27, 1945, from the police captain of Saint-Ouen to the director of the judicial police:

"Re: demonstration of Jewish traders.

"I have been advised, in confidence, that the Jewish traders of the Flea Market, who were evicted from their stalls under the Occupation, propose to retake possession of their market stalls by force. This operation might take place tomorrow—Sunday—afternoon or on Monday. I will provide surveillance."[25]

During the feverish days of the Liberation there is a great desire to inflate the list of police officers who died bravely facing the Germans after the "storming of the prefecture of police" on August 19, 1944. On September 9, 1944, the director of the municipal police asks Luizet, the prefect, to remove from the list of "heroes" a policeman who died in his home on August 27, 1944, in the course of an air raid. In this note it says, "There are grounds for deleting him from the summary of September 30 (police officers of all ranks killed on September 19 and the days following) where he appears under no. 129. This means that the number of dead is reduced to 135 with effect from today." In other documents the number of dead is given at 156, while in a list of policemen who died in the course of duty, these comments can be found: "Killed in error by a member of the FFI" for one and "killed by the owner of a café" for another.[26] This would seem to support the hypothesis that a certain number of these policemen who "died a hero's death" for the liberation of Paris were simply shot down by Parisians who were well aware of their part in the repression during the black years...

The important officials in the prefecture of police will come out of this reasonably well. Amédée Bussières, the prefect of police, was to save his own skin, and all Émile Hennequin, the director of the municipal police and the great organizer of the yellow star operation, later the architect of the roundup of the Vél d'Hiv on July 16, 1942, will get is a sentence of eight years hard labor.

---

23. My italics. Starting the summer of 1941, it was the prefecture of police that supervised these operations and even appointed these sinister "managing commissioners."
24. APP, series BA 1816 (dossier B 51 5).
25. Ibid.
26. APP, series DA 873.

10

The Red Line

P OLICE ADMINISTRATION has the habit of preserving in its
archives very visible traces of its actions. From simply trailing a
suspect to the most important repressive operations there is the
same determination, whether it is the police of a democratic country or
that of a totalitarian state, to fill files the only purpose of which will be to
fascinate later researchers. True, that is not the initial aim, but after a latent
period—longer in France than in other democratic countries—these documents become very important for history from the moment when it is
possible to gain access to them. In more general terms, the role of the intelligence service is valuable because, in the short or long term, it allows the
preparation of the "state of the nation" reports to which power is so partial.
As for preserving the vestiges of certain operations bordering more on
political criminality than on the protection of people and their possessions, this resolve is mainly the product of an old bureaucratic habit, combined with the feeling that these documents are inviolable or will only be
used with prudence.

The archives opened most recently to researchers by the archive center of the Paris prefecture of police prove that everything or almost everything has been preserved. The least memorandum, the shortest report,
written by an unworried hand, simple routine, can appear terrifying so
many years later.

We knew everything—or almost everything—about the abuse of power by the French police during the years of the Occupation. We knew the manner and the horrifying results of the harmful practices of the French policemen who were obeying the orders of the Gestapo. There were still certain documents missing—apparently the most anodyne—that will allow us to complete the picture. The practices of the ordinary officers were equally well known, but the reports of the intelligence service allow us to see the extent to which the rank and file made an effort to render the repression harsher, even more inhumane. At that level there is no thinking it over, no qualms, plain viciousness is enough. Simply the desire to do the right thing, a little more than that sometimes, in order to satisfy their superiors.

So it is no longer enough to content yourself with applying the unjust laws; improving on them becomes a temptation. You go out looking for misdeeds, sometimes even provoking them. It is the standard method of every good police force, even when this zeal is put in the service of a totalitarian power occupying a country whose police are supposed to be protecting its citizens.

The law is the law, and that's that!

Once the red line has been crossed there is no longer any limit to the depths they can sink to, since the policemen can no longer distinguish between the laws of the country and those of the Occupier. Why talk about laws when discussing that period? Once repression has reached previously unheard-of levels, there is no longer any need for legality, for the laws, the decrees and the ordinances exist solely to justify the horror. And since the law is not there to explain why action should be taken, there is nothing to do but invent it!

The exemplary nature of police actions is not simply for the purpose of creating fear. The ordinary officer now has at his disposal means of coercion that he can exercise without having to consult his superiors immediately. It is enough for him to report after having enforced his interpretation of the law. Once this stage has been reached it is no longer a question of public order. The Jewish widows and orphans no longer need protection, for these victims are of necessity guilty. This is the way the tainted mind of the policeman works when he is seeking, or happens to detect by chance, people who refuse to wear the yellow star. The policeman has already become a center of power. Repression can increase its efficacy through the simple desire of a man in uniform who, having changed masters, becomes an unquestioning assistant to the torturer who calls upon his aid.

What meaning, then, can concepts such as the rights of man, human dignity, respect for people who are old or ill and for children have? Humanism becomes a word that is empty of meaning. There is, on the one side, unthinking brute force and, on the other, a defenseless population group that is easy to repress.

There is always a strong temptation to resort to anathema when dealing with this period in which the policemen of France were nothing more than adjuncts to the Gestapo operating in French uniform. It is best to leave hatred to those who proclaim it by their very nature. That hatred which is part of the normal behavior of the average policeman, allowing him to take part in all repressive operations. Without ever faltering. That was the case from 1940 to 1944. That was the case when the police organization distributed yellow stars on orders from the Nazis and, with a vigilance that was worthy of all the praise, saw to it that the 8th ordinance was respected.

Once in uniform and on duty a policeman changes his nature. He is no longer an ordinary man, a father, a loving husband like all the rest. The symbols of force—revolver and truncheon, teargas as well—turn him into a robot to whom no task is repugnant. With no difficulty whatsoever the same individual can be the protector of democracy (well, he can force himself to be one) and, the next day, the strong arm of a dictatorship. Far from restricting himself to the object of his mission, he is an active party in the oppression and shows his aversion for those who are designated as opponents of the established power.

Without trying to think—that is not his job—a policeman abhors the designated victim and makes something that is merely official business into a personal affair. His hostility quickly goes beyond normal rejection that is justified by having to obey orders. This hatred is simply asserted and has no need to justify itself by thought. A policeman thus makes himself on all occasions into the implacable instrument of a repression, which, through his agency, has no limits. The established order will be respected, even if it is at the price of the loss of liberty—for everyone. A policeman is not the instrument of liberty!

A policeman can easily persuade himself that those whom he has been charged with repressing are his own enemies. Thinking doesn't matter; his own power comes from the obligatory hatred. As party to a political line or an oppressive regime, a man sent on an aggressive assignment must ignore any humanitarian temptations—except for changing his job.

Just like a man hired to protect a gangland boss, a policeman makes himself a shield for those who give the orders, ever ready to resort to tougher methods. He gradually comes to see himself as the exalted avenger of a society scorned by the Jews during the time of the Nazi occupation, then, as times change, by the students, the intellectuals, the young people of the outer suburbs—above all if they're of North African origin—the illegal immigrants, the homeless, the unemployed or various other demonstrators of the following decades.

Criticizing the state becomes suspect, and a policeman is immediately transformed into the guardian of laws of which he doesn't necessarily know the letter. As an avenger, he wants to wash out the affront, and anyone who mocks or insults him is attacking the state. His logic is simple: being an opponent designated by the institutions is a serious crime. Anyone who has been rejected, marginalized, has of necessity to be eliminated. A policeman goes about this task as if he were satisfying a personal desire for revenge. State business is turned into a settling of private scores.

Convinced of his own importance, a man who sees himself as the custodian of the law becomes merciless. Not content with being just the armed defender of power, he means to dispense justice as well, on his own level, in his own way. In fact it is no longer necessary to wait for judges to dispense the justice of which the police see themselves as the best custodians. Armed with the conviction that he must play both roles, a servant of the established order assumes little by little a power that no one thinks of questioning anymore, such is the confusion between the established order and respect for the law.

Let us, however, question it. Is there a necessity to maintain order when it is not under threat? A policeman assumes he is the only person who can determine that. That means his mission is a timeless one and fear of the uniform is salutary. How could one dare to ignore it?

IN 1942, the Jews did not, by their existence alone, constitute a threat to law and order. Except for the Nazis and those carrying out their ordinances. Faithful to the power of Vichy, the police got behind the racist ideology and imposed the laws that were those of a totalitarian state, while pretending to enforce those of the country. Since one does not oppose the law, unless it is to become part of the resistance to it, putting one's job, one's freedom and perhaps one's life at risk, a policeman is making a choice he feels is reasonable. Which explains the low numbers of officers who were genuine resisters. And not to forget that this—tiny—minority was also carrying out the general repressive duties so as not to risk being dismissed.

There is no threat to law and order when the Paris police are instructed to take over from the Gestapo. Who cares? Anyway, it is no longer a
democratic but rather a Nazi law and order. A policeman is certainly not
going to get bogged down in such considerations, since you can't pick and
choose with law and order. However, is it just a matter of respect for the
law in force at the time, even if it is extremely harsh? That would be too
simple, given how difficult it is to limit oneself to instructions. Improving
on a measure is in a policeman's nature. We must not think that his only
aim is to satisfy his superiors, simply to produce results. No. A policeman
who has become a persecutor has already left the classic pattern. He himself is the state and the established order. He is the law. Better than that,
he decrees the law. His own law.

This approach makes a policeman inventive, available for any new
development. Appointed to repress, after the summer of 1940 the victims are subject to his free will. It has been explained to him that the
current enemy is the Jew, especially if he comes from abroad. All his
fantasies can then be released to allow the hounding of this tribe of
undesirables who for too long have been polluting the soil of France.
This image is very attractive to a policeman who has set himself up as
the defender of patriotic values—but no longer of the Republic. He is
faced with nothing but suspects, soon to be outlaws. The servant of law
and order now sees the Jews as nothing but corrupt people who buy
everything with their money, figures behind the black market that is
contributing to the increased shortages. All the clichés trotted out by
the collaborationist press cannot but reinforce his conviction.

Finally, looked at in global terms, the Jews are the most visible part
of the underworld, so there is no shame in harassing them. That is the
way in which they can start purging the country of those profiteers who
have contributed to the decline of France. It is necessary to keep a close
eye on those predators with the sinister appearance who have brought
disorder on behalf of communism, or who are ruining us in order to
satisfy the ambitions of the American plutocrats. That may sound contradictory, true, but the roles are nicely shared out among these sons of
Israel who respect neither the law nor religion. This anti-Semitic dis-
course has left its traces in the ranks of the police: the Jews arrived in
France without a cent in their pockets, and we allowed these parasites
who are destroying us to prosper. We have had cause to regret it.

In ruminating on the rhetoric of hardened racists, the police officers
of 1942 feel they are entrusted with a great mission: to make a clean sweep

of things. A task that is made all the easier by the fact that the Jews are now very visible because of the yellow stars they wear. The lectures from their superiors are not even necessary anymore. The maintenance of order is merely a pretense, the law a vague pretext. Priority is henceforward given to this pseudo-law that allows the police to hunt down men and, very soon, women, children and even bed-ridden old people. There is no limit to their authority and the most villainous decrees are applied to the letter. Intended to reassure the people, the Paris police contains almost as many little tyrants as identity numbers, and the Jews, hounded, have no choice but to hug the walls.

To keep an oppressed group under the yoke, to make them feel the weight of the edicts, is an ambition that is well within the compass of an ordinary policeman. He has not been trained to comprehend but to constrain. He makes the law, which he is appointed to ensure is respected, even harsher. That is the price of authority. Citizens have to toe the line and look upon the policeman as the true holder of power. The man in the street has to be timid when faced with a policeman if he doesn't want to be seen as a troublemaker, a possible terrorist. But that is not enough: he has to let things go ahead without trying to understand, close his eyes, turn away, if he doesn't want to be suspected of complicity in acts contrary to the public good. As for the Jews, already very visible because of that yellow patch that can be seen from a distance...

A policeman in 1942 does not compromise. In those troubled times the law is replaced by force. Force is the law! As is well known: might is right. Anyone who is recalcitrant is a dangerous agitator when Pétain is governing in Vichy, and it is the Gestapo that decides the course to take in occupied Paris.

On October 12, 1944, General de Gaulle awarded the Paris police the Fourragère Rouge [red lanyard of the Legion of Honor][1]—forgetting that the members of that elite force paid particular attention to ensuring that the Jews respected the Nazi ordinance obliging them to wear the yellow star...

1. The Fourragère Rouge is still collectively worn by the Paris police.

To Captain Dennecker
Head of Department
GERMAN SECURITY

*[handwritten:
presumably Dannecker's
initials and 4.5.42—ie
May 4, 1942, presumably
date of receipt]*

Sir,

I respectfully inform you that we are in a position to supply you the 5000 square meters of CLOTH, samples attached;

Old gold at 120 cm width

PRICE...21.70 Fr. per meter

White at 120cm width

PRICE...13.05 Fr. per meter

Goods to be collected from our shops, net cash prices.

I remain, Sir,...

Handwritten:
5000 m cost
65,250 Fr
then presuably Dannecker's initials

Offer submitted for the sale of cloth used to make the yellow stars.

BARBET MASSIN, POPELIN & Cie Succ^{rs}

FONDÉE EN 1700

SOCIÉTÉ À RESPONSABILITÉ LIMITÉE AU CAPITAL DE 20.400.000 FRANCS

3, 5 & 7, Rue Saint-Fiacre _ PARIS (2e)

SUCCURSALES à LILLE . LYON . ROUEN _ TISSAGE de RENANCOURT à AMIENS

TELEG. ESBAR-PARIS-98

TÉLÉPH. { GUT 74-80 (7 lignes groupées)

Cte POSTAL PARIS : 1758

CODES { LIEBER 5 LETTRES CODEF LUGAGNE 1914

PRIÈRE DE RAPPELER
LA MARQUE CI-DESSUS

REG DU COM SEINE N° 13 780

REF PRODUCTEURS SEINE 3 AMIS 038

PARIS, Le **4 Mai 1942**

Monsieur le Capitaine DANNECKER
Chef de Service
à la SURETÉ ALLEMANDE
72, Avenue Foch.
à PARIS (16°)

Monsieur,

Nous avons l'honneur de vous faire connaître que nous sommes en mesure de vous fournir les 5.000 mètres carré de TISSU dml'échantillon ci-joints -
soit : Vieil or LSMA- en 120 cm de large
PRIX....Frs 21.70 le m.
Blanc - 13A - en larg. 120 cm de large
PRIX.. Frs 13.05 le m.

Marchandise à prendre dans nos magasins, prix nets et comptant.

Recevez, Monsieur, nos salutations distinguées.

F^{re} BARBET-MASSIN, POPELIN & Cie

Application of the ordinance of the COMMANDER of the
MILITARY FORCES in FRANCE concerning the
WEARING of a BADGE by the JEWS

MEMORANDUM no. Two

Arrests carried out on June 7, 1942
at the disposal of Captain DANNECKER

POLICE PRECINCT	DATE OF BIRTH – RACE PROFESSION–DOMICILE	OFFENSE	DECISION of GERMAN AUTHORITIES
Faubourg Montmartre 6/7/42, 10:20 a.m.	BEN ICHOU, Prosper b. 8/5/1926 in Paris 12, French Jew, street vendor, residing at 26 Quai des Célestins Paris (4)	French Jew wearing the Jewish star on his shirt and under his jacket so that it wasn't visible. Sent to the cells for breaking the French law of June 2, 1941	To Drancy
FAUBOURG MONTMARTRE	BEN ICHOU, née ZAKOURI Julie, 4/30/1898 in Marseilles (B. du Rh.) eight children, French Jew, housewife residing at 26 Quai des Célestins, Paris (4)	widow, mother legally responsible for the above	To Tourelles
St.. GERMAIN des PRES 6/7/1942 11:20 a.m.	VOISIN, Paulette, b. 9/6/1923 in Tours (I.&L.) Aryan student residing at 234 Rue du Tolbiac Paris (13)	Aryan wearing a mock badge in the form of a star with, in the middle, the number 130	To Tourelles
GRANDES CARRIERES 6/7/1942 11:35 a.m.	MURATET, Henri, b. 10/24/1903 in Sauveterre (Aveyron) married, 3 children, Aryan, architect, 14 Boulevard Barbès Paris (18)	Aryan wearing a badge in the form of a star with the inscription: "Auvergnat" [from the Auvergne]	To Drancy
St. GERMAIN des PRES 6/7/1942 11:20 a.m.	SIEFRIDT, Françoise, Alexandrine, b. 10/20/1922 in Le Havre (Seine Inférieure) student, 234 Rue de Tolbiac (13)	Aryan wearing a mock badge in the form of a star with the inscription "Papou" [Papuan]	To Tourelles
BONNE NOUVELLE 6/7/1942 1:50 p.m.	REGORA, Michel, b. 3/7/1925 in Paris (18) Aryan, turner, residing at 6 Rue des 2 Gares, PARIS 10	Aryan, wrongfully wearing a Jewish badge that had been lent to him by the French Jew SWARTZ, Georges, b. 8/8/1924 in Paris, who has been arrested	To Drancy
SORBONNE 6/7/1942 4 p.m.	PLARD, Henri, b. 8/16/1920 in Dijon (Côte d'Or), student at the École Normale Supérieure, Rue d'Ulm, and residing there.	Aryan wearing in the top pocket of his jacket a yellow piece of paper with no inscription, the upper part of which was cut out in the form of a star	To Drancy

The signature, although pretty illegible, will be Dannecker—at least it begins with a "D".

*

This archive document shows, if it should be necessary, the direct collusion between the French police and the Gestapo. The arrests are carried out by French officers and, as well as date of birth and profession, etc., the memorandum also includes the "race" of the offenders. Similarly their contravention of the 8th ordinance decreed by the Nazis. The last column is reserved for the decisions of Hauptsturmführer [Captain] Dannecker, head of section IV J of the Gestapo: Nach Drancy [to Drancy] for the men—both for the Jews arrested without the badge and for the non-Jews who adorned themselves with a mock badge—and Nach Tourelles [to Tourelles] for the women. For the last two it says "beid nach Drancy" [both to Drancy].

DIRECTION de la POLICE
JUDICIAIRE

36 Quai des Orfèvres

Télé. Turbigo 92-00
Poste 357.-

APPLICATION de l'ORDONNANCE du

COMMANDANT des FORCES MILITAIRES en FRANCE

concernant le PORT d'un INSIGNE par les JUIFS.-

EXEMPLAIRE à RETOURNER APRES DECISION à la DIRECTION de la POLICE JUDICIAIRE!

B O R D E R E A U   N° Deux

Arrestations opérées le 7 Juin 1942

à la disposition de M. le Capitaine DANNECKER .

COMMISSARIAT de POLICE	ETAT-CIVIL — RACE PROFESSION — DOMICILE	INFRACTION	DECISION des AUTORITES ALLEMANDES
Faubourg Montmartre 7.6.42, 10 h.20	BEN ICHOU, Prosper, né le 5/8.1926 à Paris (12°), français-juif, camelot, demeurant 26 Quai des Célestins à Paris (4°).	israélite français portant l'insigne Juif sur sa chemise et sous son veston, de façon non apparente. Envoyé au Dépôt pour infraction à la loi française du 2 juin 1941 .	Ned Drancy
FAUBOURG MONTMARTRE	BEN ICHOU, née ZAKOURI, Julie, le 30/4/1898 à Marseille (B. du Rh.), huit enfants, israélite française sans profession, demeurant 26 Quai des Célestins à Paris (4°) .	veuve -mère, responsable administrative- ment du précédent.	Ned Tavelle
St. GERMAIN des PRES 7.6.1942 II h 20.	VOISIN, Paulette, née le 6/9/1923 à Tours (I & L.), aryenne, étudiante, demeurant 234 rue de Tolbiac à Paris (13°).	aryenne portant un insigne fantaisiste en forme d'étoile, avec, au centre, le chiffre I30.	Ned Tavelles
GRANDES CARRIERES 7.6.1942 II h 35	MURATET, Henri, né le 24/IO/I903 à Sauveterre (Aveyron) marié, 3 enfants, aryen, architecte, 14 Boulevard Barbès à Paris (18°) .	aryen portant un insigne en forme d'étoile avec l'inscription "Auvergnat"	Ned Drancy
St. GERMAIN des PRES 7.6.1942 II h 20	SIEFRIDT, Françoise, Alexandrine, née le 20.IO.1922 au Havre (Seine Inférieure), aryenne, étudiante, dt. 234 rue de Tolbiac à Paris (13°)	aryenne, portant un insigne fantaisiste en forme d'étoile avec l'inscription	Ned Tourell
BONNE NOUVELLE 7.6.1942 13 h 50	REGORA, Michel, né le 7/3/1925 à Paris (18°), aryen, tourneur en métaux, demeurant 9 rue des 2 Gares, à Paris (IO°) .	aryen, porteur indûment d'un insigne juif qui lui avait été prêté par le juif français SWARTZ, Georges, né le 8/8/25 à Paris, et qui a été arrêté	Voir ned Drancy
SORBONNE 7.6.1942 16 h.	PLARD, Henri, né le I6/8/I920 à Dijon (Côte d'Or), étudiant à l'Ecole Normale Supérieure, rue d'Ulm, et y demeurant, aryen.	aryen portant dans la poche supérieure de son veston une pochette en papier, de couleur jaune, sans inscription, dont la partie supérieure était découpée en forme d'étoile	

SS-Hauptsturmführer

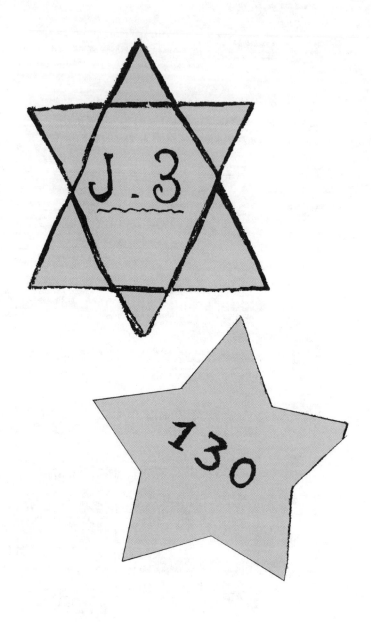

Some examples of false cardboard stars, made by a few Parisians on June 7, 1942.

French State
Prefecture of Police   Paris, June 10, 1942
Police precinct
Sorbonne district
No. 667

The police chief of the district
of the Sorbonne
to the Head of the Judicial Police

Re: illegal wearing
of the Jewish star

I respectfully inform you that at 6.15 p.m. today on

Place du Panthéon, officers of the Municipal Police

arrested Robert Pierre Brocheton,

of Aryan race   born December 31, 1925, in Paris 5

—schoolboy & living with his parents.

Arrest report from the Sorbonne police precinct.

ETAT FRANÇAIS

PRÉFECTURE DE POLICE

COMMISSARIAT DE POLICE
du Quartier

de la Sabonne

N° 667

SOMMAIRE :

Mod. 3).

Paris, le 19 Juin 19 42,

RAPPORT

Le Commissaire de Police du Quartier

de la Sabonne,

à Monsieur le Directeur de la Police
Judiciaire.

Port illégal de
l'étoile Juive

(en marge) race aryenne

J'ai l'honneur de faire
connaître que ce jour à 18 heures
15 sur la Place des Panthéon, les
Services de Police municipale ont
arrêté le n° Brocheton.
Robert, Pierre, né le 31 décembre
1925 à Paris 5°; — écolier, +
Demeurant chez ses parents

9 Rue de Beaujolais

May 31, 1943

Handwritten: [illegible] Refused

Monsieur le Ministre,

I humbly beg to request that my husband, Maurice Goudeket, French Jew, born in Paris August 3, 1889, volunteer from 1914–1918, Médaille militaire, Croix de guerre, Croix du combattant, wounded, mentioned in dispatches, be dispensed from the requirement to wear the Star of Zion.

I am seventy years old, severe arthritis of the hip has progressively made walking very difficult for me. Which means I can hardly go out alone anymore, climb the stairs, attend professional engagements. It is...

Excerpt from a letter of the novelist Colette to the Minister of the Interior in Vichy, May 31, 1943; the entire letter is reproduced in the book on pages 64–65.

9 rue de Beaujolais
31 mai 1943

Rejeté

Monsieur le ministre

J'ai l'honneur de solliciter,
de votre haute bienveillance, que
mon mari, Maurice Goudeket,
israélite français, né à Paris le
3 août 1889 — engagé volontaire
14-18, médaille militaire, croix
de guerre, croix du combattant,
blessé, cité, — soit dispensé du
port de l'étoile de Sion.

J'ai 70 ans ; une cruelle
arthrite de la hanche m'a progrès-
sivement rendu la marche très
difficile, de sorte que je ne puis
guère sortir seule, gravir des
escaliers, me rendre à des occupa-
tions professionnelles. C'est donc

123

David Brainin, who did this drawing toward the end of August 1942,

was deported on September 18, 1942.

See the extracts from the interview with Michel Reyssat, pages 81–83.

In pencil:

Reyssat very nice

Souvenir of "Drancy"

D Brainin

DRANCY VIII 42

Reyssat bien sympathique
souvenir de "Drancy"

J Brainin VII-42
DRANCY

125

Black Thursday

THE ROUNDUP OF JULY 16, 1942

By Maurice Rajsfus

TRANSLATED BY

Phyllis Aronoff

Preface

ON THURSDAY, JULY 16 AND FRIDAY, JULY 17, 1942, the French police arrested more than thirteen thousand foreign Jews in Paris and its inner suburbs. This was not the first round-up, nor would it be the last, but it was without doubt the most spectacular, the best organized, the one most faithfully carried out by France's servants of the Nazi regime. By the end of the German occupation, more than seventy-five thousand Jews residing in France had been deported. The vast majority of them would not return from the extermination camps. These tens of thousands of victims were part of the six million Jews exterminated by Nazism. Among them were my father and mother, two uncles, an aunt, a cousin and many friends and acquaintances living in Paris. All of my family that had stayed in Poland was also murdered.

This preamble is essential in order to make clear the scope of the disaster that devastated so many families. Our mourning during those tragic years should have been shared by all of humanity. Such was not the case. That is my feeling. But should the "coreligionists" of the victims therefore monopolize their memory, making hostages of the men, women and children who died and using them for propaganda? Although they died because they were defined as Jews, they did not give their lives for a Jewish cause or for the religion. It was barbarity that killed them without their being able to put up any defense, and their deaths must not be exploited.

There is no point trying to elicit pity from the generations that did not experience the pain inflicted on so many Jews living in France under the

Nazi occupation. Nor should future generations be expected to cry over the suffering of the Jews during the Second World War. No. To put it more simply—and more pointedly—it is important not to forget, to remember, every time it is necessary, where the racism of some and the indifference of others (the two are complementary) can lead.

The Jews were blamed for possessing an attribute that is hard to define because many of them do not declare their Jewish background, do not practice the religion of their ancestors and are not Zionists. Most of them simply consider themselves citizens of their respective countries. Be that as it may, skeptics will insist that they are still Jews, imagining some mysterious bond ready to be revived at the first opportunity. In this view, it is not individuals who decide on their Jewishness, but rather those who are determined to confine them in a ghetto that they will then criticize them for inhabiting.

Remembering does not mean cultivating hatred as if for a hereditary enemy. It means recognizing a catastrophic event in history and trying to understand why human beings are capable of persecution so brutal that the average person cannot imagine it. At the same time, there is a desire to conceal certain acts. This is true not only of those who deny the Holocaust, whom Pierre Vidal-Naquet[1] describes as perverts and flagellants. It goes well beyond the banality of evil. Indeed, it is not only fools—or connivers—who refuse to acknowledge an uncomfortable reality. The banalization of evil can arise out of habit, lack of interest or shortage of space in textbooks. I examine a chronological summary of contemporary history that is considered authoritative.[2] For the month of June 1915, I find the following information, which in its matter-of-fact tone may seem totally innocuous: "June 3, 1915. The Turkish government decides to deport Armenians." This sanitized historical fact is horrifying. As horrifying as the inaction of the democracies that, snugly enveloped in their intellectual complacency, have invariably observed genocide without reacting.

I will be told I am mixing things up, that I am naive, a whining humanist who understands nothing about anything, because the classic sufferings of humankind have nothing to do with the victims of the Nazi gas chambers and crematoriums. I couldn't agree more. The crimes of Auschwitz were carried out in the name of a perverse ideology that was opposed by democratic states whose mission was to bring about the reign

---

1 . French historian and activist who, in *The Assassins of Memory*, famously denounced Holocaust denial and historical revisionism. Vidal-Naquet belonged to a family of assimilated French Sephardic Jews. During the Second World War, his parents were deported to Auschwitz, where they died. [PA]

2 . Marcel Belloc and Jean-Pierre Bonnet, *Chronologie 1914–1945* (Paris: Hachette, 1973).

of happiness on earth. The slow deaths of millions of children in the third world show us that it is quite possible to behave as violently as the Nazi executioners without having to set up concentration camps or even make racist declarations. It is enough to ignore the suffering of others in favor of the columns of profits and losses on balance sheets—especially the *profits* column.

Those who insist on keeping sporadic persecution separate from grand economic operations will ask what racism has to do with these speculations. Traditional wars, neocolonialist conflicts and struggles for influence by lobby groups should be exempt from comparisons, and in any case, they cannot be accused of major perversion. War is clean, they will say, while racism is not. Which would mean, finally, that it is ignoble to murder Jews but it is perfectly acceptable to eliminate entire populations in a conventional war.

I have always had a horror of monuments to the dead, commemorations, flags raised or flown at half-mast, pompous words pronounced in honor of those who have been sacrificed or have died without really knowing why. I can't stand the deadly minute of silence (while people glance discreetly at their watches to see if the prescribed time is over yet). I have always considered those who brandish flags as gravediggers, and professional mourners (of both sexes) as superficial and intolerable. I abhor commemorative ceremonies; they are like an intrusion into my private life. I have sometimes expressed my view of such displays.[3] I am not a regular visitor to mausoleums. My remembrance cannot be collective, because I have no mourning to share. To mourn is already to prepare to forget: first, full mourning; then, half mourning; and finally, ordinary mourning. One wears black clothes, and then simply crepe, to let others know one has suffered a great deal and respect is due. One assumes a special manner. Finally, one begins to heal. I have nothing to do with those practices. My suffering is my own, and I do not have to share it. This being clear, I feel that forgetting is just as despicable as all that posturing.

More than six million Jews were murdered in Nazi-occupied Europe between 1939 and 1945. My parents were among them, and I came close

---

3 . In *Le Monde*, September 1, 1981, about a monument erected in Israel bearing the names of the Jews of France deported during the Nazi occupation: "I have always had a certain repugnance for monuments to the dead. The thought that the names of my parents figure on one of these major symbols of vengeance is especially intolerable to me . . . . My parents, who were Polish Jews living in France, did not die for France or for Poland, and still less for Israel. I therefore refuse anyone the right to use their names for any monument. I consider that it would be an insult to their memory to consign them once again, and forever, to that ghetto they had purposely abandoned in fleeing Pilsudski's Poland in the 1920s . . . . To me, the memory of my parents is a shelter with no address that is nothing like the Wailing Wall."

to going with them on their final journey and ending my days in one of the gas chambers that are so disputed by the followers of the infamous Holocaust denier Robert Faurisson. Since July 16, 1942, I can say I've been playing in overtime, after living on borrowed time until the summer of 1944. I have suffered, and I still suffer, the pain of a wound that will never completely heal. Around the age of fifty, however, I really became aware of the need for people to be reminded of history. I was unemployed, thus again excluded in a certain sense, but also, I had as much time to think as a prisoner does. At no time was I tormented by hatred for any human group as a whole, reserving my indignation for those individuals who had made themselves instruments of persecution and enabled its effects to be intensified.

I have tried here to reconstruct the day of July 16, 1942, in the unity of time and place, as it was experienced by a fourteen-year-old boy in a town in the suburbs of Paris. On that day, more than four thousand boys and girls, children of Jewish immigrants living in the Paris region, were arrested, interned and then deported, while I had the incredible luck of being released. Not one of those children would return to France, their country of birth, of which they were full and equal citizens. It is to their memory, and in particular that of my little cousin Denise Plocki, that this book is dedicated.

PART ONE

Twelve Hours of Dread

1

ALL THESE YEARS after the end of the war, it is still possible for me to contemplate on a white wall some fifty yards from my home, these words that make my blood run cold: "Jews to the ovens!" We have already celebrated the anniversary of the victory over Nazism several dozen times. A poor victory. The sad reality is that the racist beast is not dead; it has once again reared its head. It's true that imbeciles—those who are not in politics—often come to its aid. This graffiti will stay there for months—without bothering anybody, it seems. Has anyone even seen it? Neither the people living in the city nor the maintenance department is concerned about these words written in clear black letters. Apparently, nobody has thought of alerting the municipal authorities. There is a Celtic cross above the words of hate, no doubt to give that garbage an air of authenticity.

I know very well that there is no longer any truly anti-Semitic propaganda. There is no reason for paranoia about it. Rather, it is Arabs and African Blacks who are now the targets of racists in France. I realize this graffiti is the work of some poor jerk. I know very well that it will not necessarily have dire consequences. I know very well that things won't start up again as they did in Hitler's Germany and Pétain's France. I am totally convinced, but in spite of everything, I get shivers down my spine when I pass this white wall and this writing that is far from innocuous, even though it represents a minority opinion.

Beside those words that harken back to the past, there's another message: "Immigrants out!" The first message is an incitement to murder and purifying cremation, but it is a reminder of the past. In the second case, there is a pressing desire to expel the intruders who are eating the bread of the French; the message is brutal and uncompromising. Although I am deeply wounded by the words, which seem aimed directly at me, I am well aware that the second message represents a more immediate threat. It doesn't matter. When I come down from my apartment to go to the metro and when I come back in the evening, I am forced—unless I make a detour—to pass this vile thing. Of course, I could have gotten a can of paint and covered this wall that spews hate, but for a long time I was hoping that someone else, someone less directly concerned, would do it. I would have been touched by such an initiative, the reaction of a good white person, a true Frenchman, whether Protestant or Catholic. My hope was in vain. These messages are likely to remain on the wall of shame for some time. Perhaps, finally, they are representative of the population of my neighborhood, and while they do not win broad endorsement—which is reassuring—they don't receive condemnation either—which is distressing.

On April 15, 1945, so long ago, I already knew what "Jews to the ovens!" meant. The liberation of a number of extermination camps had already made information available about the horrors that occurred at Auschwitz and other places. In France, it had begun in the 1930s with "Jews out;" then, under Pétain, came the acceptance of the Nazi racial laws. Next, having gotten in the habit, the vast majority of people tolerated it when women, children and old people were arrested and sent far away to the east. Back to where they had come from? What harm could there be in putting things back in their places? When everyone knows their place, things are fine.

I haven't forgotten anything about that time. I will never forget it, even though I don't express my bitterness every day. I have learned to live with those who accepted the disgrace, because no one people, taken as a whole, is better than any other, or worse either.

Some may imagine that the memory of an old pain is leading me astray. They will say, with many arguments, that the demons of the past are dead and gone. Definitively. That they are part of a history that belongs in textbooks. Never again will such errors occur, we may be sure of it. Above all, we can envisage a happy future when man will no longer be a wolf to other men, whatever their color, their religion, their political views. Let's stop dreaming!

However, I do feel that racism can no longer take the forms we have known in the past. That seems quite clear to me. But the demons are waiting to be reborn. Of course, I will be told that Le Pen and his friends[1] are not anti-Semites, and that the lists supported by this representative of the Celtic race in the elections contain the names of some good Jews. It's an old song. If Le Pen does not openly express hatred for Jews, others do it for him, and their frequent malicious references to Badinter[2] in recent years, as well as to journalists of Jewish origin and to Simone Veil,[3] have been revealing. Before the Second World War, it was the fashion to say that Colonel de La Rocque[4] was not an anti-Semite because he regularly attended the commemorations of the great slaughter of 1914–1918 at the synagogue on Rue de la Victoire with his "Jewish friends." The fact remains that the Croix-de-Feu [Cross of Fire], the group he led, included maniacs such as Xavier Vallat[5] and Darquier de Pellepoix.[6]

---

1 . Jean-Marie Le Pen is a politician who led the extreme-right National Front party from 1972–2011. He is the father of Marine Le Pen, who is the current leader of the party and a top contender in the 2017 French presidential election.
2 . Robert Badinter is a French criminal lawyer, university professor, politician and activist against the death penalty. A member of the Socialist Party, he served as minister of justice and then president of the Constitutional Council under François Mitterrand. He comes from a Jewish family. During the Second World War, his father was deported and perished in the extermination camp Sobibor.
3 . Simone Veil is a French politician who served as minister of health under Valéry Giscard d'Estaing, president of the European Parliament and member of the Constitutional Council of France. As minister of health, she was instrumental in the legalization of abortion. She comes from a Jewish family. During the Second World War, her family was deported and many of them died in the extermination camps. She is a survivor of Auschwitz.
4 . Colonel François de La Rocque was the leader of the extreme-right-wing Croix-de-Feu, which was dissolved in 1936 by the Popular Front government.
5 . Xavier Vallat, a leader of the Catholic anti-Semitic extreme right in French politics, was the commissioner-general for Jewish affairs under the Vichy government. After the war, he was sentenced to ten years in prison for his role in the persecution of Jews.
6 . Louis Darquier de Pellepoix was a virulent anti-Semite; he was named commissioner-general for Jewish affairs by the Vichy government, succeeding Xavier Vallat, whom the Germans found too moderate. After the war, he was condemned to death for collaboration, but took refuge in Franco's Spain.
[All notes on this page are by the editors.]

2

HAVE YOU EVER WORN a yellow star on your chest? A large star, as broad as your hand, displayed prominently at heart level. Take a piece of fabric or paper, preferably yellow, and cut out a six-pointed star that fits into a circle four inches in diameter with a black border. Then pin this highly visible badge on your jacket. Make a few more for your coat or your shirt or even the sweater you wear between seasons. Look at yourself in the mirror to see the effect. Are you ready? Good. Now imagine that you're going to have to go out into the street identified in this way or else be forced to go underground, a dangerous clandestine existence in a country that is far from united, and whose inhabitants, if they are not outright collaborators, are at least playing a waiting game. What are you going to do? Today, all that would happen is that people would look at you strangely or take you for a provocateur or some kind of joker. So open your door and take your chances in the street.

When we heard, at the end of May 1942, that we were going to have to wear the yellow star, we were horrified; we had a couple of weeks to accept this almost immediate reality. We had to go to the city hall or the police station, which were hardly different from each other during this period. In exchange for one coupon from our clothing ration, we received three stars per person. A set of rules was put in place with the badges so that anybody could identify us from a distance. The edges of the star had to be carefully turned under, and the star had to be firmly secured to the garment. You couldn't just stick it on with a diaper pin or snap fasteners. Once indelibly branded, you couldn't alter your appearance, and using any artifice to do so was strictly prohibited. The slightest departure from these rules, which were laid down in the 8th Nazi ordinance in France, dated May 29, 1942,[1] was subject to the most severe reprisals: "Violations of this ordinance will be punished by imprisonment and a fine, or one of the two. These punishments may be supplemented or replaced with police measures such as internment in a camp for Jews."

In the supreme subtlety of Nazi language, the ordinance did not state that it was an obligation to wear the star, but rather that it was forbidden to appear in public—over the age of six—without wearing it. This meant that logistical problems were left to the discretion of the French authorities. The stars—which, it should be noted, bore the word *Juif*, Jew, in the center in black letters vaguely suggestive of Hebrew characters—were printed on square pieces of fabric, and those who made the mistake of sewing on the square piece of material rather than cutting out the star were subject to being picked up in the street. This often happened in the 4th, 11th and 20th districts, where the extremely zealous police would not tolerate such a breach of Nazi etiquette.

The signal to begin was given on June 7, 1942. The next day was a Monday, a school day. As in many other homes, our parents practically pushed us out of our little apartment wearing that decoration we had not asked for. Rare were those who disobeyed the Nazi ordinance. For that, they would have had to not declare themselves as Jews on October 3, 1940—but once they had been caught up in the machinery, there was no question of escaping it. Except by going away, for those who had a little money (the wealthiest were already far away, and they had good reason to flee to safety). In fact, the Nazi ordinance had become a French operation.

Once I reached the street, I hadn't gone ten yards when my schoolmates greeted me with the words "Here comes the sheriff!" It was neither an insult nor a joke, just a rather cruel observation from the mouth of a child. It was surely an expression of discomfort. I had the feeling everyone was turning against me. Especially because I was apparently the only person in Vincennes thus distinguished from everyone else that morning. Going to school, which was about three quarters of a mile away, would be a real ordeal. And above all, I couldn't cover my chest with my schoolbag. That definitely would have been a punishable offense, and I didn't want to hurt my parents. So I walked along in full view of the entire population, which actually showed little interest. I was very upset by the time I rushed through the door of the school. A quick glance showed that there were

---

1. See pp. 28–29, *Operation Yellow Star.*

three of us marked in this way, so not everyone was looking just at me.

With my jacket hung up, I wasn't out of jeopardy, because my shirt also bore the required mark. I walked into the classroom with an indescribable desire to disappear, or to see my classmates disappear. I think they were avoiding looking at me. I have never been as ignored as I was that day. The other boy in the class who was wearing a star had decided to present a jolly, rather provocative face to the teachers and the other students. It must have taken strength to clown around like that, and he wasn't really understood. So many years after, I still feel sick describing this memory. We were branded. A Nazi law applied in France had decided that I was different from the others and that this difference should be clearly known.

The few weeks until the end of the school year seemed like forever to me. Where I once wanted only to laugh and have fun, I had lost my high spirits. The worst of it was having to bear the silence and pitying looks of my schoolmates and the condescension of my teachers. I had the feeling that the whole world was against me. It was unbearable. Only the principal was on my side, saying to the children who were standing around me in a circle on the first day as if I was some curious phenomenon: "The first one who makes trouble will have to deal with me!" Which was paradoxical, because this decent man (that is how I see him) was wearing Pétain's medal, the *francisque*.

When I hear certain people today say they wore the yellow star with dignity and perhaps even pride, I find it so insulting that I prefer not to comment. Hitler and his henchmen in Vichy had revived the medieval baseness of the *rouelle* and the pointed hat,[2] but since everyone knew how to read in the twentieth century, the century of progress, they had added writing to the symbol—the word *Jew* in thick black letters. Everyone around me was fortified by the knowledge that they were not Jews because I was one, and they could see it without needing to take off my pants. Had I walked into the classroom with a rattle or bell attached to my knee like the lepers of old, it would have had the same effect. The silence was harder to bear, because the way they looked at me seemed stealthy, not out of treachery—surely not—but out of fear of looking directly at someone who is branded. I was humiliated but not dishonored, and my classmates were perhaps ashamed for me. Those who until then had seen me only as a foreigner's son whom they occasionally insulted (they were only a small minority) felt immediately confirmed because

---

2. See pp. 22–23, *Operation Yellow Star.*

they understood that, ultimately, I was doubly a foreigner.

These boys and I shared our everyday lives at school. What would they tell their parents that evening about the classmate who was wearing a yellow star on the left side of his chest? Once you passed through the doors of this temple of public education, there were two categories of students: the good French students and those who were not as good. I was regarded with a certain embarassment, but it had the advantage that I was not pestered anymore. It was as if a screen had been placed between us. Which didn't prevent two or three little brutes from making a nuisance of themselves. So it happened that on the infamous day of June 8, 1942, the most ignoble of the group said to one of our schoolmates, "So, Lévy, you've forgotten to put on your star!" and laughed spitefully. We never saw Lévy at school again.

There were other students who were occasional objects of curiosity in that class. One of the boys suffered from emphysema, and when he had difficulty breathing, he would take a little bulb out of his pocket and spray it into his throat. Kids would look at him, but he wouldn't pay any attention to them. There was also a stutterer, whom the teachers, out of pity, would rarely call on to answer questions, but who was greeted with gales of foolish laughter whenever he tried to speak at any length, that is, to get to the end of a sentence. I think the day I wore the yellow star was the day I stopped laughing at him. Another object of curiosity was a student who was a bit effeminate, who delighted us whenever he launched into his endless explanations. He later became an actor and was much admired in supporting roles, and he died in 1987. So I was now one of the oddities of the class, except that, unlike the other three, I seemed "normal." I was not relegated to the back of the classroom, my teachers all showed an appropriate attitude toward me and none of them asked any questions. I was the Rajsfus boy, nothing more. Or at least, that was what they tried to make me feel. But during the recreation period, I would find myself alone, because the others no longer invited me to take part in their games. The other boy in my class who wore a star remained alone at the edge of the school yard, because we felt no particular affinity with each other and there was no reason for us to go through this tragicomedy together.

With the passing days, those around us got used to our difference, because curiosity doesn't last. But I didn't get used to it. It was as if the yellow star was stuck to my skin. At night, in my nightmares, it became huge and shone like an autumn moon. During the day, I couldn't get rid of it or even hide it. It became impossible for me to act like other kids, even at the risk of drawing more attention. How could I play a prank like ringing the alarm bell when I was marked with this yellow brand? "You know, it's that little Jew, the one with the curly hair, who's enjoying himself at your expense!" Sharing my schoolmates' games was no longer possible for me, because my distinctive mark required that I exercise constant restraint. It's true that as soon as I left school, I wanted only one thing—to go home and be with my father and mother.

On Sundays when my sister and I went out with our parents, all four of us duly bedecked with stars, people moved away from us on the sidewalk, and my father, always the optimist, explained that, had we been identified like this in pre-1914 Poland or Russia, we would have had to fear for our safety, whereas here we could circulate without fear among the French. This relatively peaceful existence would last five long weeks before it was interrupted by more tragic events.

I didn't see that many yellow stars in our immediate environment, and the sight of them was perhaps just as unpleasant for me as it may have been for those who did not want to see it, perhaps sensing that they would one day be blamed for their indifference. Everyone lived in the present without imagining tomorrow, much less the outcome of this war that, at the time, did not seem to be going well for the Allies. When we went to Paris, which was less and less often, the landscape would change and there would be a lot more stars. On Rue des Rosiers, where my mother still sometimes went to buy poppy seeds, which she needed for making some traditional pastries, it was those who weren't wearing stars who stood out. It was a world peopled with uneasy shadows, and nobody even stopped to talk anymore in this street that had once been so animated.

Back in Vincennes, just a few metro stations from the Jewish quarter, we suddenly had the impression of having left one world for another. We were noticed again. How can you go unnoticed when you belong to a minority that represents barely two percent of the population of a city but that is indelibly marked? A bit like the one black duckling in a brood of yellow ones. We were already different. We were living in a state of inertia accentuated by the summer heat, until that day, the longest day of my life.

3

JULY 16, 1942. We had been wearing the yellow star for forty days, but the authorities did not need that mark to carry out the largest abduction in the history of Paris. The lists compiled by the French police were amply sufficient to guarantee the success of the operation. The day, which began at 4 a.m., would go down in history under the name Operation Spring Breeze for the police, and for the victims, Black Thursday, or in Yiddish, *Der Fintster Donershtik*.[1]

Like the people in other homes, we were asleep in spite of the heat of that summer night. It was a night like any other. Before 5 a.m., I was awakened by violent blows against the door. My mother was already up. The knocking continued, accompanied by shouts: "Open up, police!" Anyone who hasn't heard such an order at that time of day and with such brutal force cannot imagine our state of mind when we were awakened. Had they come for my father? Was it a repeat of the Billet Vert roundup of May 2 to May 14, 1941,[2] but this time in people's homes?

Upon opening the door, we were brusquely informed that this involved the whole family. A clean sweep. Still half asleep, I heard the order: "You have five minutes to pack your bags. Take only what is necessary!" We dressed quickly, and although it was the middle of summer, my mother insisted that we put on warm clothes. One thing I haven't

---

1. See Claude Lévy and Paul Tillard, *La Grande rafle du Vél d'Hiv 16 juillet 1942*, (Paris: Éditions J'ai lu, 1968), p. 68, which was the basis of a remarkable film. Also Maurice Rajsfus; Levy Laub (trans.) *The Vél d'Hiv Raid* (Los Angeles: DoppelHouse Press, 2017), originally published as *La Rafle du Vél d'Hiv* (Paris: Presses universitaires de France, 2002).
2. On May 14, 1941, nearly four thousand Jews from Eastern Europe who were living in Paris were summoned to the police stations regarding "a matter that concerned [them]." At the end of the day, they were all taken to the Pithiviers and Beaune-la-Rolande camps, in the Loiret province. Two of my uncles were arrested that day.

forgotten, although it may seem trivial or even ridiculous, is the new shoes I had to put on, which immediately hurt my feet. Wearing those shoes that whole day was a real ordeal.

As if he had been expecting this visit for a long time, my father did not react. He dressed mechanically, while my mother tried in vain to negotiate with the two policemen, who had orders not to listen to any complaints from their victims. To everything she said, they gave the same answer: "Be quick, Madame, we're in a hurry!" But my mother insisted, "Surely you're not going to arrest the children. There must be a mistake. You know, Sir, they are French." My mother kept speaking to the older of the two policemen who were standing on either side of the doorway; she knew him, because this man, whose name was Mulot, had been our neighbor on the same floor. I was already dressed, and I remember his irritated look; he must have had the same mission to carry out many more times and must have been eager to get it over with before full daylight. His mechanical repetition of "Dépêchez-vous!"—"Hurry up!"—sounded strangely similar to the Nazis' "Schnell!"

Our two peace officers were getting impatient while my mother, remaining strangely calm, started rummaging around. Obviously, she was trying to gain time. What was she hoping for? We never knew. Every minute might be valuable. How did she have the presence of mind to fold up the chair that was used as my bed? Was it just a desire not to leave things in a mess in the little bedroom my sister and I shared? She rushed back and forth from room to room in a strange ballet. While the two policemen stamped their feet and Mulot began to get angry, she had to go back to the kitchen for a package of biscuits and then to the bedroom again for a scarf. They stood in the doorway, following her every move with their eyes, because in our apartment of less than three hundred square feet, there was no way to hide anything.

The minutes passed until we were ready, my father first, I think. My shoes were already unbearable. Through the open windows—the heat was heavy—we could see the sun coming up. Although our windows looked out on the roof of a garage, we had a clear view of the sky, and our apartment was flooded with light very early in the morning. One last look at the familiar setting we might never see again. Though small, the apartment was cozy and filled with memories. How could we leave without regret, without a backward glance? We must have looked ridiculous in our new Sunday clothes, like peasants just arrived in the city. And the policemen, in a hurry, furious at still being there while other victims awaited. It had barely been five minutes since they had stormed in, but they found our movements too slow. "Turn off the gas, close the windows, turn off the electricity. Are there any animals in your home?" After these instructions, they pushed us onto the landing and closed the door themselves.

4

I LOOKED AROUND. I was dazed and still half asleep. It must have been a bad dream, one of those stories told to frighten children when they are misbehaving but that has a happy ending, because it's customary to have a happy ending. Alas, we were all awake, and my mother's expression and my father's sudden air of defeat left no doubt that we were the actors and spectators of a play of our own. It wasn't an illusion I could dispel just by rubbing my eyes. No. Nothing else would happen. I was torn from that room of some one hundred square feet, the universe where a good part of my early childhood had taken place.

Between my bed and that of my sister, the buffet, and the table and six chairs, there was hardly room to play. When friends or family came for lunch, everyone could only sit. When the beds were opened, you couldn't even circulate in the room. Yet it was in this little cubbyhole that I would do my homework when I didn't stay late at school, and where—a rare pleasure—I would curl up on my father's lap. We were happy there. Simply happy. It was where we talked, each one listening to the other. That was the sweetness of life.

When my parents weren't there, I would play in their bedroom—which was a bit smaller than ours—because my unrestrained activities bothered my elder sister. There was a narrow space between the bed and the mirrored wardrobe where I would sit by myself and play endless games of marbles under the bed. The glass marbles and the big steel ones would click against each other in the dim light, and I would plan surprise attacks against the clay marbles, foot soldiers in a battle they were doomed to lose. Marbles were a passion of mine when I was about ten, and because I was quite good, I rapidly accumulated a valuable collection that my friends sometimes envied. My other passion was bottle caps, which might seem ridiculous to little boys today. I played with them during recreation periods in the school yard on Thursdays but also under my parents' bed. The materials were simple; you just had to find caps from beer or mineral water bottles in good shape and fill the hollow part with putty, sealing wax or even compressed bread. They then became heavy enough to be catapulted by a flick of the middle finger against the thumb.

My other favorite place was the kitchen, a laboratory to be entered with fear and respect. It was a sad kitchen, a tunnel about eight feet long and not even five feet wide. A window that was sometimes opened a little, but rarely all the way, looked out on a dark little courtyard shared by several buildings, a sort of open sewer never reached by the sun's rays. We ate our meals in that kitchen and we washed in the sink, usually in cold water, because a water heater was a luxury we couldn't even imagine. On Sundays, my mother would heat big pots of water on the gas burner and bathe me in the galvanized tub usually used for laundry. Despite my complaining, that was a time of happiness, because my mother was there with me and spoke to me and teased me in Yiddish. The scrubbing was needed, because boys usually wore short pants in those days and my knees were more gray than pink. These ablutions, which supplemented the weekday mornings' quick dab with a washcloth, were a real ceremony, and my sister always teased her little brother who couldn't perform them by himself.

The spectacles that took place in that kitchen would have surprised our neighbors. The four of us ate supper there every evening; we were so crowded and the table was so small that it would have been hard to fit another person in. On Sundays and when friends came for dinner, the kitchen would be all lit up, and my mother, who was the best cook I could imagine, would prepare dishes that combined sweet and sour or sweet and salty flavors. When my homework was done, dashed off if not completely botched, I would hurry to the kitchen, forgetting my games and my friends waiting for me in the courtyard. I would stick my finger in the pots and taste the dishes, unconsciously consigning to memory the flavors I would later try to reproduce. It was hellishly hot in that temple of Jewish Polish cooking recreated near Paris, because the door was kept closed, and usually the window as well, to keep out the bad smells from the courtyard. I would watch the preparation of gefilte fish—including the painful moment when my mother would chop off the head of the live carp—and corned beef and cheesecake (which Russians call *vatrushka*, and which I knew only as *kaesekuchen*). And the simple appetizers, egg salad with onions, and chopped liver with or without onions.

The kitchen was also the starting point of another, less enjoyable activity. At least twice a month, it was laundry day. Early in the morning, the galvanized washtub would be placed on the gas burner and the little apartment would fill with the unpleasant smell. After the laundry had been scrubbed on the zinc washboard in the tub and then wrung out, came the next step in the marathon; lines were put up from the entrance across the two rooms to hang the sheets and larger pieces, with the rest being put in front of the windows. For two days, we would live in a kind of damp shed with a lot of passageways. When the mailman or the collector for the gas company knocked, we would have to pull the sheets aside to clear a path to the door.

There was another activity that couldn't be contained in the kitchen. When my mother had time, she liked to make fresh noodles, and every table available was commandeered for the sheets of dough dusted with flour to be spread out on to rest before they could be cut up. They would stay there at least half a day, taking up the table in the dining room, which also served as a bedroom for my sister and me. It didn't prevent me from doing any school work I had to do, because I had the peculiar habit, ever since I had started school, of doing my homework on the floor. Nobody stopped me, because that was the only place I could do it. There was always a risk of getting my notebooks dirty, but I learned very early to take special care with them, especially those for history and geography.

No space was wasted. Even the cabinets, which were tiny, had a second function; my parents would pile on them some of the merchandise they sold at the markets. You could get into them sideways, but just barely. Every inch of our space was put to use, including the little nook for the electric meter, which was filled with packages of stockings and socks. With the war, our space became even more cramped, because the collective heating system in the building no longer worked, and we had to find room in the kitchen for coal for the stove that had been set up in our bedroom (a tile was replaced with a pierced metal sheet so that the rusty pipe from the stove could be vented). When the wind blew the wrong way, the place was sure to be filled with smoke, especially if the coal was of poor quality.

This was our little universe, which is hard to fully recreate. We didn't complain about it, because we had never known any other. In spite of the disadvantages, we were happy in our small space. Now we suddenly had to leave this simple, uneventful life, this happiness that had already been shattered by the Nazi occupation with its succession of misfortunes, and face the unknown. We had to leave behind a whole part of our existence without really being aware that the break would be permanent. With that knock at our door, our lives were torn apart. But the fact that the four of us were arrested together was some consolation, and I clung to my mother while watching to make sure my father was not being taken away.

I remembered the arrests of my two uncles a year earlier. Their wives and children had not been worried, and they themselves, despite the uncertain conditions of their internment in the Loiret, had not been immediately deported. It was still persecution with a human face, supervised by Vichy and its police. Nobody could imagine that the Pithiviers and Beaune-la-Rolande camps in the Loiret, which had been opened in May 1941, and Drancy, opened in August 1941, were in fact the antechamber of horror. In the first two, the main problem was lack of food, but life there was not yet really that of a concentration camp, because for several months, many of the internees spent the days working outside the camp and could have run away. Few of them risked it, perhaps feeling that they were safer behind the barbed wire than outside. They also did not want their families, who were still free, to be subjected to reprisals. Escapes were therefore rare.

Most of those who worked outside the camps were employed on farms nearby, usually hoeing beets, taking part in the harvest or digging up potatoes. Their families could go see them while they waited for things to change. The situation was almost funny, as when a good part of our family, like many others, took a vacation in the Loiret in the summer of 1941, not far from the Pithiviers camp, so that my aunts could visit their husbands. The situation would worsen around the spring of 1942.[1] I still have a clear memory of that time, especially because one of my uncles had written to me in April 1942 for my fourteenth birthday and included a little leaflet with some drawings of the Pithiviers camp with its barracks and barbed wire. It was in the Beauce region, and behind the wooden buildings lined up in rows, there was a huge grain silo. From another angle, on a double page, there were other barracks in the camp, and the village very near, with its church steeple and water tower. (I do not think

---

1. David Diamant describes life in the camps of the Loiret in *Le Billet vert* (Paris: Le Renouveau, 1977).

the villagers of Pithiviers or Beaune-la-Rolande were unaware of these camps, because a lot of the internees worked for the farmers for a ridiculously low wage, which was pocketed by the gendarmerie. The same is true for some fifty internment centers that had been set up in the southern zone in 1941.)

While these were not yet extermination camps, the men suffered from hunger, their straw bedding was infested with vermin, there was a lot of sickness, the separation from families was hard and the winter was cold. It was France, the land of liberty, that set up these camps, without even any orders from the Nazis. In the southern zone in particular, the so-called free zone, the Vichy regime wanted to show it was capable in its own way of establishing the racial purity so dear to the Nazis.

5

THE SUDDEN INTRUSION of the police into our already troubled lives was not really a surprise. For months, there had been rumors of a coming wave of arrests in the Jewish immigrant community of Paris. This had created an unpleasant climate of uncertainty, especially because many families were already hard-hit, having lost their income when certain activities were barred to Jews. Not a day passed without our hearing—this time, for sure—that it would be next week . . . tomorrow . . . tonight. That it would only be able-bodied men . . . those under fifty . . . Russian Jews. In any case, one thing was certain: naturalized citizens need not worry. Most of the Polish Jews, who had been living in France for five, ten or twenty years, had tried repeatedly to obtain French citizenship, but few had succeeded in being accepted into the national community. The country had been quite happy to receive these foreigners (and to expel them on occasion), but as for making them French citizens, that was another story, and the war had put a stop to the flow that had continued in spite of everything. There were endless jokes between the newly naturalized and the others, which could sometimes become quite savage. They are part of my childhood memories, and there are some scenes that strike me as horrible despite the humor in them.

On September 2, 1939, our family was on vacation near Milly-la-Forêt. When the immigrant Jews went away in the summer, they never went very far; the Fontainebleau area or Sénart Forest was a respectable limit. Those who were better-off would venture to the beaches of the North Sea, but not many went that far. Very often, our wanderings took us no farther than Boissy-Saint-Léger or Noisy-le-Grand.

It must have been a little before noon when the rural policeman, between two drumrolls, fulfilled his duty of informing the population of the little village that war had broken out between France and Germany. After a stunned moment, humor came to the fore again and one of my uncles turned to a friend who had recently had the honor of being naturalized and said to him in Yiddish, with a broad smile, "You're French now, so get your gun!"

Naturally, we felt threatened, but all the unverifiable rumors seemed like nonsense to us. They could only sow panic in a community that was already sorely tested. Arrests had been increasing in Paris for more than a year, and on August 20, 1941, four thousand Jews had been arrested in the 11th district. Then, in December, some fifty Jews had been shot at Mont Valérien, where they were being held as hostages— but we didn't know that yet. There had been a break with the family living in Poland, and we had been without news of them for three years. All that took a toll on the morale of the adults. As for the children, the concern was to protect them from these threats, which were far from hypothetical.

What seemed certain was that the roundup would happen when it happened, with no warning. Those who hadn't yet fled Paris had finally resigned themselves to their fate, to an internment that, however painful, would last only until the end of the war. It would involve only the men. There had not yet been any women, children or old people rounded up. The only known cases of persecution of those groups were the pogroms in Russia for a period of some thirty years before the First World War. Even the children knew that. Jewish children, that is, because how could my schoolmates have been informed of these acts of violence experienced by millions of pariahs living more than twelve hundred miles from France, where life had a special sweetness? Like many children of immigrant Jews, I knew what a pogrom was. I had heard the terrible stories of murders committed in the streets for pleasure, of houses burned or pillaged, of women raped and old people abused. The memory of these horrors, some of which had taken place in our parents' lifetimes, was tenacious. Curiously, I do not recall hearing a lot of talk about racial persecution in Germany, but that was not yet part of my history, and the news sometimes lags quite far behind.

Since the Germans had occupied Paris two years before, we had all been aware, in a confused way, of the dangers. The repression had begun with administrative constraints and had taken increasingly brutal forms as the months went by. An analysis of the situation would have required that every family leave the Occupied Zone or, at any rate, disappear without a trace. That was not easy. People with money had been the first ones to leave. Others had followed as the danger intensified. But it's hard to imagine how the ninety thousand immigrant Jews in Paris could have taken to the road with no prospects, no money, in the case of many, and no real support, in the case of most. Political groups already had their hands full trying to protect their own members. It should be noted here that none of the immigrants' organizations, whether they were Communist, socialist, Zionist or religious, had given any instructions whatsoever when Jews were made to register in October 1940, and the same was true in May 1942, when we were informed of the coming distribution of yellow stars. As for any sign of solidarity from *la France profonde*, "deep France,"[1] we could have waited forever. Long enough, at any rate, for irreparable harm to be done. We were left to our own devices, and there was nothing to do but endure what came. My parents had already prepared themselves for this eventuality, but such was their optimism—natural or feigned so as not to appear worried in front of us—that no bags had been packed in case the fateful arrest occurred without warning.

We had been warned the night before the roundup. Friends, and then my father's sister, had come by the house to tell us of an imminent action against Polish Jews. Where could the rumor have come from? Was it through the grapevine, the "Rue des Rosiers radio"? Was it the Jewish Communists or the socialists of the Bund who warned their friends and relatives? Could the information have been leaked by employees of the UGIF?[2] Was it simply a leak from the prefecture of police, since they had known about the operation, which bore the lovely code name Spring Breeze, several days before? The latter hypothesis is probably incorrect, because only the senior officers had been prepared for the roundup, which should have brought in twenty-eight thousand foreign Jews. The rank-and-file policemen only learned the nature of the mission late the night before. The rumor could only have come from the

---

1. Small-town rural France. The term is used to designate an "authentic," often ethnically based national populace, much like the idea of "real Americans" as opposed to recent United States immigrants. [PA]
2. Union générale des israélites de France: On November 29, 1941, by decree, the Vichy government created the UGIF, the clear aim of which was to better control the Jews in both zones, on the pretext of community solidarity. See my *Des Juif dans la collaboration* (Paris: EDI, 1980).

Jewish community, then, but there had been so many false alarms that we didn't place any special importance on this latest one. Weariness was also a factor. Those who had not left for lack of the means or the will to fight back would not have left even if they were contacted. The police were able to round them up without too much trouble. They were sitting ducks, and they hardly resisted. While there were a few cases where desperate people jumped out of windows or shouted to alert their neighbors, they were exceptions.

The evening before, after a long walk in the Bois de Vincennes—we had to get home before the 8 p.m. curfew for Jews, which prevented us from enjoying the end of the overpoweringly hot day—we had talked as usual, but without mentioning the prospect of a roundup. We had this constant threat over our heads and we managed to live with it, just as people living beside a volcano stay there until it erupts, because there's no way they can go elsewhere. When the catastrophe came, we would see . . .

6

ONE OF THE POLICEMEN grabbed the keys: "We'll give them back to the concierge." We stood on the doorstep of our apartment, unable to move forward. "Go on," barked the one who was our former neighbor, and we had to go downstairs. The three flights of stairs seemed endless.

The building we lived in had been constructed on top of an old country house near the Bois de Vincennes, no doubt a bourgeois residence, dating from the previous century. On the ground floor, there was a broad stone staircase that was accessible from two sides, and at the other end of the floor, a smaller, more modest staircase to the upper stories. There were stained glass windows with frightening images of dragons on the first flight of stairs, and I would go up very fast, trying not to see them, but I couldn't help looking. The second floor was made up of apartments that must once have been luxurious but were now unoccupied. I had been in them with some of the neighborhood kids and seen their large rooms with ceiling moldings and walls hung with tapestries heavy with dust.

The upper levels of our building had been erected in 1930. It was a sad building, old even before it was lived in. The whole neighborhood had been built by the same entrepreneur on the same model. Most of the tenants were of modest means. The complex of six buildings around a courtyard where we lived was the least well-off in the neighborhood; the residents were mainly unskilled workers from the Kodak factory. Other buildings in the same group but of higher status housed low-ranking civil servants and various types of employees, as well as a few shopkeepers with businesses on the same street. In any case, all these houses were a blemish near the old residential area that had been built close to the Bois de Vincennes early in the century. We lived there because the rent—which in those days was always too high—was less than in other parts of the town. Whatever their economic level, people were happy to live near the wood, not far from the metro (since 1935) and in what was a major shopping area, because the entrepreneur had crowded the maximum number of tenants into two streets, making for a lot of potential customers.

Having moved into this building with my parents at the age of two, I didn't remember any world other than these already tired walls rising above a curious construction from the past. I felt at home here and would happily climb the three flights of stairs to our apartment. Obviously, we were aware, and the children perhaps felt it more, that there was a differ- ence in social status from the buildings on the street that had elevators, and we tried to redress this injustice by going and playing in the elevator that went up to the eighth floor of a building where we had no business. We had to watch out for the concierge there, who was on the lookout for us. It was worth it, though, because we found the stairs in our building very common.

It was those stairs that seemed to be resisting my every step as we descended them with our two escorts. They were in a hurry to get it over with, and we weren't moving fast enough for them. It seemed to me that every worn edge of a step, every nick in the paint exposing the plaster, every inch of the handrail, every broken piece of stained glass was a bit of my life that was disappearing. How many times this staircase had been the site of our endless games of tag. And now, suddenly, we were going down it toward the unknown. The policemen's steps seemed light. They were not at all troubled by remorse and were carrying out their work as if there were nothing out of the ordinary, as if we were criminals—except with no handcuffs. They were doing their job in that punctilious way typical of public servants who have no hesitations because the only thing that counts is following the rules. "You will be going to a labor camp in Silesia," Mulot repeated as if to prevent us from asking any further point- less question. "Faster," he added, in a hurry to be done with it, while his colleague, perhaps less proud of what he was doing—and surely less hard- ened—said nothing and simply walked behind us.

Despite the anxiety gripping us, none of us could yet imagine that we had begun a walk toward death. But fear of the unknown is just as oppres- sive. Our guardian angels knew that their victims were facing, if not immediate extermination, at least being put away, very far away. "Faster" was the leitmotif accompanying our descent. "Faster." There were others still asleep who had to be picked up before the sun had fully risen. "Faster." People mustn't see this legally organized kidnapping. "Faster." The National Revolution, the new France of Pétain and Laval, would not wait. "Faster." The road to deportation must not be obstructed, so we had to hurry. "Faster." We must have looked like a party of climbers descending a peak with one guide leading and the other bringing up the rear in order to prevent anyone from falling. But the two policemen didn't care for our well-being; their orders were to prevent us from escaping. They also had to make sure that neighbors or future victims were not alerted, so as to avoid scandal. People had to be kidnapped quickly and silently. "Faster." How many times did we hear that word in the ten minutes that had elapsed between our being torn from sleep and this descent that seemed endless? "Faster, faster." The one who kept saying this no longer had a face; he walked ahead of us without looking back, relying on his colleague behind us to keep us moving quickly. It was obvious that they were in a rush to go on to other victims. "Faster."

Just a few stairs left, a corridor and the steps outside into the court-yard. There was nobody there at this early hour to see us leave. The last few yards were the hardest. For my parents, it was a farewell to a whole life of work; for us children, the terror of being dragged into a perilous situation. To the left of the small stone staircase was the nook where my father stored his handcart when he came back from Aubervilliers on foot with his equipment and his stock. In front of us was the windowless wall of a garage. A few steps more and we would be out of this building where, though crowded, we had been so happy. Did these two policemen know what happiness meant? Nothing mattered to them but their orders, the mission they had to carry out. Without asking themselves any questions. "Faster." I can still feel myself being pushed as I went down the last stairs with my new shoes lacerating my heels. I mustn't be allowed to slow the progress of our little group. It was over, the building was behind us. Our destinies were already elsewhere. The essential thing was to walk quickly and not ask questions. "Faster."

7

THE LARGE COURTYARD we were now crossing under close supervision was where we had played every day. It had many features that made it ideal for our games. There was an iron door leading down to a former wine cellar, and the concierge, who would not tolerate our playing, would often chase us away from there. At the foot of the little stone staircase, there was a nook that was sometimes used to park a bicycle for a few hours or even overnight. This nook was the stuff of stories for us. Around June 10, 1940, when people were fleeing Paris, my mother had put her bicycle there and it had disappeared within an hour. Was it stolen? We were convinced that some desperate person had taken it to get out of Paris and put as much distance as possible between himself and the Germans. We had laughed about it, because the bicycle was an old piece of junk, but my parents sincerely pitied the poor devil who had been forced to rely on it. Two months later, when things seemed to have gone back to normal, the bicycle reappeared in its usual place. It had indeed been borrowed by someone who, once he no longer needed it, had wanted to make things right.

The courtyard had been the scene of my childhood games for more than ten years, and I had friends in every building around it. There were double doors at the end of it that were usually shut and which we watched closely, waiting for the day they would open, although we couldn't have said why. Behind these doors was a passage that led to the back of a cookie factory and, on the other side, to a garage belonging to the Kodak factory. The kids in the courtyard were always on the lookout, and every time the doors opened, they'd swoop down on the mysterious passage like a flock of swallows, with one of the concierges in hot pursuit. The courtyard was divided into two main parts, and at the center there was an old disused fountain we were forbidden to climb on. We would play cops and robbers there, and the girls would jump rope and get the younger boys to play hopscotch with them. The most daring boys would try out roller skates in spite of the curses of the concierge, whose constant refrain to those who lived in the nearby buildings was "Go play in your own yard." The modern signs forbidding playing had not yet made their appearance. Nevertheless, the kids were seen as a nuisance and sent to play in the street. The traffic wasn't very heavy, especially since the German occupation.

This play area represented my whole childhood. Street musicians would regularly come and sing us the latest hits or old standards. The tenants, who were far from rich, would always find a few coins to throw down for them wrapped in a piece of newspaper, and the children would rush to gather the little packages and give them to the singer, who was not considered a beggar. One day, a musician who only played the violin asked my mother if she would be interested in buying the instrument. We never knew why this man—who I believe was a gypsy—wanted to get rid of his violin. But my sister, who had until then sawed away on a crude three-quarter fiddle, now found herself with a very nice instrument. I then inherited hers, which I liked a lot less than my harmonica. This sad courtyard was in a sense the hidden face of Vincennes, which was largely middle-class. That hasn't changed, and today it is known as the "courtyard of miracles."

We had so many memories of this courtyard, with its buildings that were old before their time. Two of my father's brothers and their wives, one of whom was my mother's sister, lived there for several years before moving to Paris, and the third brother found a small apartment right nearby on Rue des Vignerons. We knew all these buildings. When we were very young and my parents were working at the markets on Thursdays, they would have us cared for by a woman who lived at the back of the courtyard. We called her simply "the lady who takes care of us." Her husband was Italian, and we would be especially delighted when she took care of us on Sunday as well, while my parents went to the big sales near the Porte de la Villette. That was like a party for us, because the husband of "the lady" was a great cook and he would make dishes that were new to us. He was a real joker, and he had a way of torturing the French language, making puns as my father did, playing with the meaning of a sentence when it was phonetically similar to something in his language. All I remember is his first name, Matteo. Was he a political refugee? Had he fled Mussolini's regime? I can't say. But he was generous with us, even though he had two children of his own, and we liked him a lot. Why do I remember this immigrant better than the French people from this court-yard? Maybe because I was never invited into the homes of the native French parents of my playmates.

Of the thirty-six families living in our building, we only knew two or three. On our floor, there was an employee of the prefecture of police who was later a prisoner of war, with whom my parents got along well (he may have given them a warning on the eve of the roundup). There was, of course, the policeman who was in charge of our arrest, but he had moved out a few months before. Later, in that apartment, there was a guy who dressed in a weird way and always wore boots, and who, in spite of seem-ing nice, belonged to the security squad of a fascist organization. I was later told he was a militiaman. Just before the war, there was a German couple living on our floor, and my mother would often have long conver-sations with them. The man was Jewish, or so his name suggested, but his companion was not. On the third floor, we knew a young couple who had been married not long before the mobilization; the husband was a cabi-netmaker and upholsterer by trade and became a prisoner of war; he had made the shelves around my sister's bed, which held the whole family's books. We didn't know anyone else in the building. People ignored us, which didn't bother us, because there didn't seem to be any hostility in our daily relations. Good morning, good evening. It was a bit short, but it was better than being insulted.

In the building on the courtyard that had its entrance on the street (hence the higher rents), there were a couple of elderly philosophers, German or Austrian Jews, that my father was very close with. But my parents only socialized regularly with a few people in their immediate environment. They didn't complain about this and found the relatively distant attitude of the neighbors rather reassuring.

8

W E CROSSED THE COURTYARD flanked by our two cops. The concierge, that witch who had interfered with my games, was at her window. She presided over the building on the street, but her windows overlooked the courtyard. Had the police awakened her early and told her what was going to happen? Because one of our two bodyguards gave her the keys to our apartment. My mother, always trusting, murmured to the concierge, "The keys to the cupboards are in the fruit bowl." The glass fruit bowl was prominently displayed on the obligatory Henri II buffet. The concierge had accepted the keys to the apartment with a certain coldness. She seemed to be saying good riddance to us. Maybe she was thinking that once these undeserving foreigners were gone, there would be more bread for the French, who were suffering so much under the occupation. Maybe she was thinking that in the current housing shortage, we could readily be replaced. Perhaps there were extenuating circumstances that would explain her unfriendly, even aggressive behavior toward us. Her twenty-year-old son, who had been conscripted in March 1940, had been killed at the front three months later. One day early that June, not long before, the Germans entered Paris, the afternoon calm had been shattered by the cry of a wounded animal; the concierge had just been informed of her son's death. Since then, this heavy, sullen woman had become even more surly, especially to the children who played in the courtyard, whose presence she would no longer tolerate. I don't think I'm exaggerating when I say she blamed her son's death on the foreigners who were living cozily in France without—to use a horrible expression that was popular during the war—lifting a finger to defend this country that had been so good as to accept them.

To the neighbors and even the concierge, we were Polacks, but not necessarily Jews. They saw us as different, but, aside from a slight accent, my parents were just like everybody else in behavior and dress. As for us kids, there was nothing that distinguished us from others. It was the yellow star that, in June 7, 1942, exposed to the light of day what most people who knew us had been unaware of. Sure, I had often been called a dirty foreigner, but that was about my parents, and these insults were part of childish cruelty. They hurt me, not just for my father and mother but because I considered myself a good Frenchman.

Now on July 16, 1942, the police were treating us like criminals, and the concierge, the only witness at this early morning hour, couldn't spare a kind word for us, not even a sad smile for our suffering. She merely took the keys the police handed her, the two perfunctory actions complementing each other. Her behavior expressed total indifference. Good riddance; now there would only be French people.

The cop and the concierge made a perfect pair. In fact, this was how the institution was imagined in the 1790s by the Committee of Public Safety during the Reign of Terror, or perhaps it was the humanists of the Committee of General Security. What could be better than a full-time volunteer stool pigeon to help preserve public order? The concierge, before the war, was usually a woman; she saw everything, heard everything, gossiped with everyone, and smiled sweetly at Christmas but didn't even look at the tenants after New Year's. She was also the ideal wife for the cop starting out: no rent to pay and odd jobs of painting or plumbing to be done under the table for the tenants, who were always looking for someone to do repairs. The concierge and her cop husband form a pair that is more common than it seems, and one that has always been a bargain for the police and intelligence services. Under the occupation, control of foreign nationals was a priority because any foreigner could turn out to be a terrorist or a black marketeer, as the collaborationist press never tired of pointing out. The power of Vichy depended on ensuring that the Nazi order was respected at any cost, and the concierge could be counted on to play a valuable role in that process. I am not saying that all concierges were supporters of collaboration. No. Simply that certain habits had been formed in the past, and concierges continued to be of service to the police without troubling themselves too much about trivial details. With both concierges and policemen remaining in the same positions, this fruitful cooperative arrangement continued.

My parents had twice been refused French citizenship despite their fifteen years of residence in the country and two children born in France. We had every reason to believe that one cause of these refusals might have been negative information our concierge gave to the inspectors during the customary inquiry by the police. My father had not been involved in political activity in France, he had not made himself conspicuous in any way, he had no suspicious acquaintances and we never made noise at night. Friends of my parents who had come to France later had no difficulty obtaining naturalization, and it was a mystery why we had been refused. But it's true we were blessed with a particularly xenophobic concierge. In her own way, using the means at her disposal, she must—even without necessarily being aware of the consequences at the time—have played a part in my parents' arrest and deportation; Jews with French citizenship had a better chance of avoiding capture than those who were foreign nationals.

My slamming of concierges is not without justification. I have already said on numerous occasions that during the Nazi occupation, the police were a reflection of deep France, and the same was true of concierges. Although there were a certain number of exceptions, they do not change my assessment of concierges—or of the police.

We have every reason to believe, although today there are no witnesses, that my cousin Denise and her mother, who had escaped the roundup of July 16, 1942, were informed on by the concierge of the building where they lived on Rue du Montparnasse.

When the raid took place, I had just turned fourteen. The awkward kid hadn't yet made way for the adolescent. There are certain factors that probably contributed to what was finally a genuine refusal to leave childhood behind. I felt so safe clinging to my mother's skirts and so protected in my father's lap. I was small for my age, and since the beginning of school, I had always been in the first row of the traditional class photograph. At the age when other boys were already little men with peach fuzz on their chins, my baby face had advantages and disadvantages. Nothing had prepared me to be thrown into life alone, far from my parents, defenseless.

I was easily recognizable, with my short pants, my beret always on my head, and in winter, my black cape. My curly hair and pink cheeks may have made my mother think her little boy would never grow up, and perhaps that pleased her. Nor had I matured much in terms of school; I took an interest only in subjects that were immediately accessible without much effort. Up to sixth year, that hadn't been a problem, because I had the gift of an infallible memory and I retained everything, even what I didn't study, merely by keeping my ears open when a classmate was sweating bullets during the dreaded question session at the blackboard. That worked for history, my favorite subject, and also for geography and biology. I did all right in literature if it was presented in the form of stories, and I did well in my first lessons in English. However, when it came to math and physics, the classes often went on in my absence, because my dreams took me far away from the teacher filling the blackboard with incomprehensible formulas. After completely failing the entrance exam for fifth year at Lycée Marcellin-Berthelot in Saint-Maur, I had still managed to get into the school in Vincennes. In fifth year, everything suddenly changed; you had to work hard, learn to be independent and divide your time well over a heavy workload. There was competition for the top places, even after the selection of students for entrance. Indeed, even in this school, the students represented a minority of the children our age, most of whom had already begun apprenticeships.

Aside from the subjects that aroused my curiosity, I had my head in the clouds, and I can't claim, these many years later, that I was distracted from my studies because of the war and the tension that for months existed in the house in spite of everything. I think I simply wasn't ready for the major changes involved in growing up. Events would take care of that. As an old Yiddish song says: "Oh, how quickly I grew old. I didn't have time to be a child. My youth is gone. Oh, how quickly I grew old." Another verse speaks of the sense of loss that accompanies growing up: "We hardly had time to live and now already we are old. Oh, how quickly life passes."

9

RELIEVED OF OUR KEYS, we were no longer part of the world we had lived in for more than twelve years. Years during which my parents' situation had gradually improved. We had gone from a minuscule apartment, one room with a kitchen, to this one, two rooms with a kitchen, which was not much bigger but seemed huge to us. Now we were torn from this cubbyhole where we had lived so happily. Little by little, honest poverty, the poverty that is unseen and bothers no one, had replaced the real misery of the early years. It was the beginning, not of a life of ease, but of freedom from the most immediate financial worries. We got enough to eat—in spite of the restrictions—and our clothes were decent though not luxurious. We were no different from the people around us. An ordinary family that did not stand out from the rest of the people in the neighborhood.

We were only a few yards from the street. To get there, we had to go through a basement corridor. There were no witnesses, nobody to turn to, no one who would give us a sympathetic smile or even a look of commiseration. Nothing. Four or five yards more and we would be outside. This corridor brought back memories of a lot of adventures. It had been the headquarters of our gang of kids. There, at least, we could escape the vigilant eye of the concierge.

It must have been just five in the morning when we reached the street. The sun was coming up, but nobody was out, except for a cyclist hurrying to work. None of the shops, not even the bakery, had opened their doors.

We were alone on the sidewalk with our two policemen bringing up the rear. My whole childhood had taken place in the little world between the courtyard we had just left and these few yards of asphalt. On the left was the shop of the pharmacist, whose son, a little younger than I, would become a journalist for the Europe 1 radio network some fifteen years later. On the right was a shabby hairdresser's shop where, a few years before, I had been brought by my mother and sat on two telephone books for a haircut. Beside it was a bookstore, and then a charcuterie shop whose owner's smile was so outrageously phony that it was a constant joke between my parents. Next were the wine merchant, the bakery, the grocery store and the local bistro. On the opposite side of the street were a photographer, a fishmonger, a Maggi dairy store, an herbalist and a dry goods store. Aside from a butcher shop, there was everything you needed to do your shopping on Rue de la Villa, and you just had to turn the corner at the bistro to find a horsemeat butcher shop and a poultry and offal shop on Rue des Vignerons.

Across from our group of buildings was Rue du Bois, at the end of which was the Bois de Vincennes, where every path, every brook, practically every tree, was familiar to me. This little street lined with detached single-family homes and other low-rise housing was filled with the pleasure of life; on summer evenings, people would bring their chairs out onto the sidewalk and talk until nightfall. It was renamed Avenue Anatole-France in the 1970s and given its share of concrete. It was one of the few streets in the city that was already completely paved, and we could exercise our roller-skating talents there without being afraid of getting run over by a car. As for horse-drawn carts, we could hear them coming from far off.

We crossed the street. No more words were exchanged. We looked around for a police car, because we weren't being taken along the road to the police station, which was then on Rue du Château. We must be heading someplace in the neighborhood, because we were going on foot. A few dozen yards on the lovely Rue du Bois, and our guards had us turn off into Rue du Donjon, where we could see the huge mass of the central smoke-stack of the Kodak factory to our right, with its big clock. In the morning, we would be awakened before 7 a.m. by the factory's siren warning its workers living in the area to hurry to work; a second warning would sound at 7:15, and ten minutes later, a third one, a nerve-shattering sound, would announce the imminent closing of the doors and punishments for latecomers. For years, these sirens had punctuated our awakening and breakfast and served as the signal to leave for school.

Our cops were not taking us in that direction; they were herding us along the other section of Rue du Donjon, from which we could see the drawbridge of the wall surrounding the Château de Vincennes. At the end of the street was Place Carnot. There had been air raid shelters there since September 1939, where people were urged to go when alerts went off during the night. But these damp, mildew-smelling tunnels were not very inviting, and the prospect of taking shelter in them beneath a foot of concrete didn't attract a lot of people. In the vicinity, there were several luxurious buildings with basement shelters deep enough that people could be safe from the bombs. There too, there was much to fear: the possibility of water pipes breaking and the anguish of dying by drowning, or gas pipes bursting and the certainty of dying by asphyxiation. The result was that, after the first false alarms of September 1939, hardly any people went to the shelters when there were air raid alerts. Especially since, often, by the time people got to the shelters, the anti-aircraft defense was already in action and shrapnel was fallling onto roofs, sidewalks and pavement. That is why the first American air raids on the rail junctions in the eastern suburbs of Paris found us at home calmly contemplating the flares that illuminated the targets.

Beyond Place Carnot was the Fort of Vincennes, with the sloping glacis around it that provided one of our favorite places to play. While walking, we could see all that at the end of the street, and maybe even the Nazi flag with the swastika that was flown from the inner tower, but our escorts made us turn into Rue Louis-Besquel, which seemed very far from our street, the sad Rue de la Villa. Today, Rue Louis-Besquel is still an oasis of calm, home to people of modest means, although its appearance may suggest that the bourgeoisie has moved in. On the sidewalk on the left side, there were detached one- or two-story houses, and on the right, apartment buildings more affluent than ours, where we sometimes tried to get into the elevators in spite of the threats of the concierges, who were terribly vigilant there as well.

Where would our escorts take us next on this morning walk? We soon found out. After only a few steps on Rue Louis-Besquel, we observed a certain animation, which contrasted with the calm of the neighboring streets. Small groups of people were arriving on foot with police escorts, like us, carrying suitcases as we were. Others were getting out of police cars; they had probably come from farther away. All these people passed through an iron gate to a house near one end of the street. What could be the meaning of this dense concentration of people in this place at such an early hour? At this time, we knew nothing of the huge roundup that had been going on in Paris and the suburbs since four in the morning, and we believed we were the only people this was happening to. Why had we been taken to this anonymous house? What were we going to do here? What could we expect to happen? For how long? All these questions were running through our minds, but the police weren't there to answer them. Actually, we didn't even ask them. The two cops who had snatched us up and brought us here in such a hurry seemed to be motivated only by the desire to get rid of us, to hand their prey over to their colleagues who were ready to receive us. There were other victims waiting. We were pushed forward past the sidewalk and through the gate, and we found ourselves at the foot of the steps to a house where we would never have gone, not even to ask for information.

On the other side of the street, in the oh-so-respectable apartment buildings that were so strange to us, windows were opening. The residents wanted to see the show and try to understand why all these people were there at an hour when even the dairy man had not yet come with his delivery for the shop at the end of the street. They were asking each other questions from one window to another. Why were these people being brought to this street whose peace was never troubled? Who were these suspicious people who were being imprisoned at the risk of ruining the street's reputation for decent folks? The sight of the children who were there with the adults raised other questions. It's true we didn't look like the gypsies who were chased from town after town. Very quickly, it became obvious: we were all wearing yellow stars. That one characteristic we had in common finally made them realize what was going on. Maybe these decent people leaning from their balconies were thinking that it was only Jews, nothing serious after all, not as if a fire had broken out in one of the apartment buildings that were so respectable.

Such a concentration of people on one of the quietest streets in Vincennes, and at such an early hour, was an unusual sight. We were causing a commotion that was disturbing people's sleep. The war and the occupation had already brought a lot of difficulties without this brutal awakening by the sounds of the police barking orders, the motors of the cars leaving to pick up more victims, the crying of little children clinging to their mothers. As much as we rubbed our eyes, we would not wake up from this nightmare. Clutching my mother's hand, I looked at my father, waiting for him to do something. There were a few families ahead of us, and there was something sadly comical about our being lined up waiting to go in, because the house seemed full of people already.

There were two uniformed policemen on guard in front of the gate, two at the foot of the stairs and two more on a sort of landing at the top. We entered the building as if we were walking into a train station. There was still some room; it was a bit like the Marx Brothers' cabin on the ship. When our turn came, we had to go up a few steps and into the unfamiliar building. Once over the threshhold, we found two large rooms on either side of a central corridor, one of which must have been the dining room and the other the living room, but both rooms had been emptied of any furniture so that they could be filled with people. The police pushed us toward the room on the left.

A Jewish family had lived in this house a few years before, and it had been requisitioned when they left for a happier place. In June 1940, the small brick building had served as quarters for German officers, and now, two years later, it was a temporary prison for Jews.

10

A T THE AGE OF FOURTEEN, I was a laughing kid, always ready to joke and have fun. I looked on the bright side of life, because I hadn't known the dark side. I was simply happy. Serious people bored me, and I didn't think much about the future. To me, the future was everyday life with my parents, and nothing else was really important. I was considered weird and scatterbrained, interested only in the superficial things in life. I was always laughing, never bored, experiencing pleasures without thinking about them. Of course, since the start of the war, I had known fear. In many situations, I bombarded my parents with questions, and they were surprised to see me suddenly anxious, my smile, with the dimple in my left cheek, suddenly frozen. I had been afraid when war had been declared, but I did not react much to the Germans' entrance into Paris.

Since May 1941, I had known we were at great risk. My parents, wanting to protect us from fear, kept us in a state of uncertainty by almost never speaking to us of the persecution that was becoming more and more threatening. The war was the fight between armies that were engaged in killing each other scientifically with increasingly advanced weapons. Only men were involved in this combat, and I was glad I wasn't old enough to take part in the slaughter. I didn't like to hear talk of war— even glorious war—and I had been upset when my father tried to enlist in a foreign regiment in September 1939. When he was declared medically unfit to serve, I was relieved that he was no longer in danger of being killed in the war. Of course, we were all in danger of dying in an air raid, but that was a matter of calculation of probabilities, and the risk seemed higher on the battlefield.

When I thought of my uncles who had been deported after spending over a year at Pithiviers, I feared that my father, who had escaped that first roundup, would also be a victim, especially since the new laws prohibited him from working at the markets. Often, my happy nature would win out over my fears, because, after all, bad things only happen to others. I would go back to playing and laughing, but maybe with less enthusiasm than before. We had become so accustomed to this murky, threatening atmosphere with the possibility of friends being rounded up the next week, the next day, or the next night that we no longer paid attention to the rumors.

July 15 had been a very hot summer day, and the night had been stifling. Around midnight or one in the morning, my father had gotten up, probably to try to get a breath of fresh air. My sister and I heard him at the window murmuring, whether in Yiddish or French I don't remember, "One more night has passed." And a few hours later came the shock of our arrest. We had been conditioned, and we were ready to be snatched away from our home with no reaction, no crying or shouting. The police had a very easy time. We followed them without resisting, almost too quickly, leaving everything behind, without even taking time to look back. I left my trivial treasures: a stamp collection I was very fond of, a few history and science notebooks that were my pride, and—this may seem childish for a boy of fourteen—a many-faceted glass ball that was buried in a jumble of my things and that I never saw again. An ordinary life was ended as if with a snap of the fingers. An unimportant event that didn't stop the world from turning. That day, I think I understood that we counted for very little against the forces at work in the world. When the police made it clear that we were excluded from society, we were so crushed that anything could have happened. We had already been different for the six weeks we had been wearing the yellow star, but it was still possible for us to be with other people—at certain times only, it's true, and not everywhere. We still had the right to come and go, and now, suddenly, it was as if we had been thrown into a dungeon we would never leave.

Being imprisoned is the worst possible feeling, like disappearing into a deep pit while everyone else continues to live as if things are normal. It happened without any fanfare, as if it were a mere formality. The police were there to take away those people society had cast out, and the law must prevail. Were we sheep? I don't think so. We simply had no choice.

They held the power.

Of course, it wasn't really a surprise; we had known that the war being waged against us could not end well. This was something completely unheard-of in France, the land of liberty. The Germans occupied the country, but everything was done in the name of France, although its legality might be dubious. France was in fact betraying the people it had taken in. Its actions were seen as legal and were respected by its people, who accepted everything that was done in their name. How could the foreign Jews have stood firm when the French themselves did not? It was the French police that had been delegated to pick us up, and the few witnesses to the operation in Vincennes had refrained from doing anything, or even thinking about it. The jungle has its rules, and the beasts could play their own game. I know, we could have fought, but not in that minefield.

11

WE WERE PUSHED toward the room on the left, which may have been the bigger one. There were already some twenty people in it, crowded among suitcases and packages, and others came in behind us. We had to get out of the corridor and find some space. With the area along the walls filling up, the people coming in were going to the center. By eight o'clock in the morning, there were already some forty or fifty of us packed into the room. Every generation was represented, from crying babies to dazed elderly people who seemed to have awakened from a long sleep to find themselves reliving a pogrom from their youth in Poland or Russia. The adults in their prime seemed the most deeply affected, their eyes blank, not speaking. A few children, hungry after being woken up so early, were asking their mothers for something to eat. At the mention of food, my own stomach churned, and I clung more closely to my mother, hoping for a smile or a look, the only consolation there could be in this hell from which there was no escape. We couldn't think; we could only submit, which was exactly what our captors intended.

We were pressed together in this room with its empty walls and the traces of its former furniture on the parquet floor that was losing its shine. There was a strong smell of dust and mildew; the house must have been shuttered over the winter and spring. It had essentially been abandoned since its owners had had the good sense to put some distance between themselves and the servants of the Nazi order. It already resembled a prison. From the unsealed chimney of a fireplace came a smell of burned wood along with the heat of the day.

But we weren't paying attention to these squalid surroundings. We were already on the threshhold of the concentration camp. Although we weren't actually in a prison, we were under the control of armed men. What had once been a living room had become a cell at the end of the world, from which nobody would rescue us. Outside, life went on as usual and the residents of the neighborhood were leaving for work, because for most people, nothing had really happened. The motor of the garbage truck was making its familiar noise. In this normally peaceful street, this operation must have been a real revolution, and yet passersby simply moved to the other side of the street so as not to see: "It doesn't concern us!" On one side, the beginning of the horror, the anguish; on the other, indifference, coldness, perhaps tacit consent. The routine of everyday life was going on without us.

After a few disheartening minutes, I looked around me to see if any of my friends or schoolmates were there. My pal Nada, who lived a few buildings down on our street, wasn't there. Looking through the open door to the other side of the corridor, I could see that he and his family must have been spared. They would only be arrested in 1943, because his father had a Spanish passport. Who knows how that could have happened, since he was Egyptian and his wife Lithuanian? I recognized a few people I vaguely remembered seeing in the neighborhood, people we weren't friendly with and didn't really know. We all lived our own lives in isolation from each other, because there was nothing particular to bring us together, certainly not religion.

Among the silhouettes I recognized were Mardoche and his mother. He must have been about ten years old, but he took up enough room for three or four people, constantly gesticulating and rummaging in his mother's shopping basket and taking out candies, chocolate or cakes to stuff into his mouth. The poor woman must have had to carry a supply with her at all times. It was a surprising spectacle to see him gorging himself on sweets in the middle of this tragedy. But Mardoche didn't seem surprised to find himself there. He didn't seem depressed. His consumption of sweets must simply have been the daily ration his mother managed to get for him despite the restrictions. The boy was completely out of touch with reality. He had been taken from the shtetl by people other than his parents, under difficult conditions, and his child's face had the dazed look of someone thrown abruptly into a strange world. Seeing him sometimes walking in the street with his mother, I would imagine the pigsty they must live in, at 18 Rue des Vignerons, in the same group of buildings we lived in. He was always dirty, disheveled, greasy-haired and ill-dressed—like his mother, who wore such awful rags that she was a spectacle when she came down to the street to get the boy, who would be wandering about aimlessly looking in store windows at things he could never have. She didn't even realize the difference that existed between her and the other mothers, and she seemed to live only for her son, because her husband must have fled. She was always looking for the boy, her only reason for living: "Mardoche, you coming do lessons for the school" or "Mardoche, you coming eat." That was how we had learned the boy's first name. He must have had a grandfather named Mordecai whose name he had inherited, turned into French as Mardoche. This was not likely to guarantee his anonymity or allow him to go unnoticed by kids who, like their parents, were always ready to make xenophobic comments. Just try to explain to these French children who were rude to the point of cruelty that Mordecai had been an illustrious person in the court of the Persian King Ahasuerus and had succeeded, because of his intelligence and the charms of his niece Esther, in improving the lot of the Jews in exile in a hostile land. Mardoche's father had vanished a few months earlier, and now the poor kid was alone with his mother in this overcrowded room. After an hour, having gobbled up the supply of chocolate and cake, Mardoche became thirsty. He went to look for a sink, and so was one of the first ones to venture out of the room where we had been confined for hours. There were police officers posted at the door to the corridor, the door to the other room and the door out of the building, plus a fourth one in the corridor to make sure nobody went up to the second floor. Any attempt to escape would have been doomed to failure anyway, because the windows of the upstairs looked out over the little yard in front of the house, where half a dozen policemen were keeping vigilant guard.

After the Mardoche interlude, silence again reigned. People occasionally spoke in low voices, but there were no long conversations. The murmured exchanges seemed banal; there wasn't much to say. All we could do was endure. And the words were always kept within the small circle of the family, as if the groups were total strangers. Indeed, we hardly knew each other, any more than we knew the other residents of the little streets around the Kodak factory near the Bois de Vincennes. Why would we have had a special relationship? We had been living in isolation from each other for years, trying to integrate into our new country, to survive, like the other residents of this suburb. Vincennes was nothing like the neighborhoods of Saint-Paul or Belleville. We lived among the rest of the population, while people in those neighborhoods wished to recreate their own little ghetto. Both were real choices, but they were probably also influenced by circumstances. The fact remains that there were a lot of people who wanted to break with the past. In Vincennes, as in Saint-Mandé or Fontenay-sous-Bois—but not Montreuil, which received the spillover from the 20th district and had a large population of immigrant Jews—there were dozens of Jewish families, mostly from Poland, who had tempted fate by trying to live side-by-side with the native French residents. This was why we didn't necessarily know each other.

These people who had suddenly become pariahs at dawn on that summer day looked at each other as if they were seeing a reflection of their past, of the memories they had thought buried in a bottomless pit. There was indeed something that connected them. It was their accent that was more or less pronounced and their difficulty communicating with the others, the French, but this could only imprison them in the past. What had once brought them together could only separate them here in France, especially if they wished to change their way of life or even their identity. These immigrants from eastern Europe had worked so hard to fit the local model that their children had become replicas of the French people who today were chasing them out of this supposedly welcoming community that had once, ten or twenty years before, opened the door a little for them. The situation was inconceivably tragic, because some of their children considered their own parents foreigners and were ashamed of them.

In this big room that was too small for all of us, it was already very hot and stuffy, and the windows remained hermetically sealed. The police were making sure of that. We were so defeated that nobody complained. To the police who were guarding us with such unfailing zeal, we must have been riffraff, beggars to be sent back to their misery in Poland. It would be good riddance for everyone. It's well known that cops never have any regrets about carrying out their orders, and the ones they were given on July 16, 1942, suited them perfectly. By nature, as good representatives of deep France, they didn't like foreigners, whom they saw as the cause of all the country's woes. They were in fact unaware of the tragedy they were feeding off because they were completely focused on the job. Never had a government placed such trust in its cops, and they must have been flattered, abusing the authority given them. They must have felt that in watching us so vigilantly, they were contributing to the public good. At least, they might perhaps have tried to convince themselves of that when they saw the crying children and their devastated parents.

12

WE WERE UNDER SIEGE from within and outside, but our attackers could rest easy, as we had neither the means nor the intention of defending ourselves, and not even a thought of trying to flee. We just tried to close our eyes and wait for the nightmare to be over. The atmosphere was tense but calm, occasionally broken by the sobbing of the smallest children, who had been awakened at dawn and were terrified. Hours passed. Our stomachs were in knots. My mother had grabbed some food at the house and she tried in vain to make us eat a little, but we couldn't swallow a morsel. Only Mardoche displayed his usual ravenous appetite.

When we needed to go to the toilet, the policemen grumbled and seemed very annoyed. In the little corridor filled with people moving to and from the bathrooms, they acted as if they were directing traffic in the street; the only things missing were the whistle and the baton. While waiting for the next shift, the cops munched happily on the plentiful snacks provided for them. The job they were doing wasn't spoiling their appetite. They weren't asking too many questions; to them, this was an ordinary operation and they weren't about to turn up their noses at the sustenance they were receiving for it.

Nothing was happening. With about a hundred temporary residents in it, the little suburban house was full. We didn't know yet what they were planning to do with us and, surprisingly, there weren't any rumors circulating, not a single piece of false news to make us panic or give us hope. Silence.

The police had been instructed not to engage in discussion with us, and they were obeying their orders, just glaring at us coldly. Their apparent neutrality was contradicted by the weapons they were carrying. Since we were calm, they didn't need to take any action. From time to time, someone would ask a question, but there was never an answer. Did the police themselves have any information? It's possible. At the very least, they must have known the first destination, the Vél d'Hiv, and then the camp at Drancy. But they must have wanted to keep up the suspense that was weighing on people. When you don't know anything, it's still possible to hope. The perpetrators of the roundup knew very well how the people they picked up would feel. Our impromptu community waited without asking any questions, and although we were desperate, we didn't protest. Through the window, we could see commanding officers arrive from time to time, probably to give orders, and then quickly leave again. Apparently, Vincennes police headquarters was on a war footing for this operation, which must have been carefully planned. We kept hoping for information, even while expecting the worst. Anything was possible—internment as in the case of my uncles, banishment to a distant area, being sent to a work camp, being returned to Poland. We didn't even dare express any of these hypotheses. But what was most important was that we had not been separated. My father remained with us, and that was a good sign. All this was going through our minds as the waking nightmare went on.

It must have been three o'clock or a little later when a superior officer with silver braid on his kepi burst into the room to announce briefly that children over fourteen years of age born in France could be released if their parents agreed. This news was greeted with a woman's hysterical scream. It was Mardoche's mother, who grabbed her son, clutched him to her with a strength born of desperation, and cried, "You won't take my son away from me. Never!" The news didn't concern poor Mardoche, because he was too young, but had he been older, he still would have stayed with his mother. Can we judge people's behavior in such tragic situations? Certainly not.

At this unexpected announcement, my mother, without even consulting my father, made it clear that we shouldn't hesitate. In less time than it took to say it, she removed the few thousand-franc notes she had from her bag and handed them to my sister, gave us each a quick kiss and said, "Leave fast!" It is decisions like this, the hardest ones to make, that shape a life. If our parents had asked us to stay with them, things would have been simpler. We would have gone along and thought about it later. That would have been the easy way.

I'm alive today because my mother made that decision without hesitation, realizing that we would have to be separated sooner or later and she had to seize this moment and give us the best chance possible. She had immediately understood that an opportunity like this might never come again.

We had to leave quickly before orders were given canceling this unhoped-for decision. Unlike Mardoche's mother, my parents, in tacit agreement, wanted us to leave without further ado. The meaning of my mother's action in practically pushing my sister and me out of there can only be understood by placing oneself in the context. If there's anything more horrible than a child being torn away from its mother, it must be when a mother herself must decide to cut a child loose in a dangerous situation. My mother's perception of danger, unexplained because it was a matter of sheer instinct, saved my sister's life and mine.

I left at least one friend behind, "Bouboule" Rozenblatt, a fat kid, as his nickname indicated, who was with his mother. He was despondent, and his face had changed. Only days before, he had been fooling around as usual. He was a real joker, not too bright but a good pal who'd always greet you with a funny story. I didn't hear him say a single word that whole day. I'm not even sure we exchanged glances while we were in that room. When afternoon came and they gave him a chance to leave, he stayed there with his mother. The fear of finding himself alone outside won out over the fear of a more uncertain future. In fact, he may not even have considered the question, and because his mother couldn't decide, Bouboule would follow her for the first stage of the journey. Their separation would come a few days later, but without either of them having to make a decision. The essential thing was not to think.

I had searched in vain for some of my schoolmates among the occupants of that temporary prison—Steir and Kuperberg, with whom I had gone to primary school, and Friedmann, who had finished fifth year with me. It appeared that they had been spared in the roundup.

Kuperberg, who had found refuge with some peasants, became a paperhanger in the north of France, and I don't think I've seen him since 1940 or 1941. The building he lived in on Rue des Laitières in Vincennes was the scene of a typical display of initiative by the French police on their mission of repression. After knocking in vain at the Kuperbergs' door, the two officers carrying out the roundup in that neighborhood must have felt very sad and frustrated as they went back down the stairs. Then, a miracle! On the next floor down, they saw a name plate on a door, that of the S. family. Although that name was not on the list of people to be arrested, it had such a Jewish sound that they immediately picked up the family. They had a quota to fill! An unfortunate mistake: the S. family were totally German and not at all Jewish. They were released a few hours later with apologies, but this faux pas revealed certain well-established bad habits on the part of our police.[1]

Friedmann, who also slipped through the net, returned to his studies after the war, pursuing an education in the United States, and then had a fine career in medicine. As for Steir, I didn't hear anything more about him.

All of them were, like me, sons of Polish Jews. We met different fates. The list of our friends and relatives who died at Auschwitz is long. I often think of my young friends who perished in the turmoil and remember how full of life they were, unaware of what awaited them. If they are no longer remembered by those who were their age in that summer of 1942, these few lines represent the trace they left in my memory. Mardoche and Bouboule, René Nada and his sister Maryse, the Rostokers, and so many others whose names I have forgotten were victims of a war in which conventional weapons were not even necessary to annihilate millions of people who could not defend themselves and had probably even lost the will to do so. All of them must have been victims of despair as much as of repression. It is terrible to see their names and their memory used, even anonymously, in the sinister martyrologies good souls consider necessary to throw in the face of a world that has no understanding of that abominable past. The war that ended on May 8, 1945, was supposed to put an end to the totalitarianism that was responsible for such heinous acts. How could anyone seriously make this claim?

---

1. On August 20, 1941, during a roundup in the 11th district of Paris—a prelude to the opening of the camp at Drancy—two policemen came to the home of the Radzynski family to arrest the father, Israël Radzynski. However, the man had been dead since September 2, 1940. "No problem," said the policemen, "that one there will do instead." And that was how the son Samuel was arrested. But this story raises another important question: how could Israël Radzynski's name be on a list of Jews to be rounded up when he could not have registered as a Jew on October 3, 1940, having died a month before? Similarly, Samuel, who was already an underground activist despite his youth, had not obeyed the Nazi ordinance. Are we to conclude that the French police authorities had already set up a file of Jews before the repression of the Jews was planned, or perhaps even before the Nazis invaded France?

13

W HEN I REACHED the street, I was stunned. I didn't understand yet what had happened to me and couldn't imagine what would become of my parents. The separation from them, whether brief or prolonged—and we didn't even dare to consider that it could be permanent—created a situation my sister and I weren't prepared for. I was fourteen years old and she was sixteen. I was an uncouth, boisterous, carefree kid, and I had a difficult relationship with this older sister I saw as bossy and judgmental. In fact, I was hardly capable of living without my parents, especially my mother.

On the sidewalk in front of the house, where curious passersby had been gathering since the morning, I felt lost. My parents were a few yards away, on the other side of a window that was sealed closed. The sun's reflection hid the inside of the house. It was as if a wall had suddenly come up between us. Why stay there any longer watching the police standing guard? And I couldn't bear the sight of the spectators coming and going, among whom I recognized many of the neighborhood gossips. My sister's immediate reaction was to say we should alert the few friends we had in Vincennes but first of all we should probably return home and get the keys back from the concierge. I was afraid to do it, but before I could even react, I was designated for the job. I couldn't bring myself to move, and it was only my sister's repeated orders that made me finally pick up my feet.

At the corner of Rue Louis-Besquel and Rue du Donjon, a police car blocked the way, stopping passersby. There was a huge number of officers for some hundred victims, who weren't putting up the slightest resistance. Did the police fear the local residents more than those poor wretches? If that was the case, they were making a serious error of judgment, because nobody around was very concerned. Although they might have wondered what could be happening in this house, they weren't saying much about it. They looked at it as they went by as you'd glance at a fire or a traffic accident, they exchanged a few words, and they continued on their way. It was only some Jews who were being kept there. Just one more trivial incident.

Having decisively turned my back on that street where my childhood had been destroyed—I felt this very clearly—I took the road leading to our house. It looked as if nothing had happened on Rue de la Villa. The housewives were busy at home. The stores were closed at this hour, and there wasn't much activity. Only a few kids were playing on the sidewalk or in the road; they were on vacation and spent their time playing marbles in the gutter. A few elderly people were sitting on folding chairs in front of their houses just talking. A horse-drawn cart had stopped at the side of the road, and a delivery man was unloading crates of mineral water in front of the wine merchant's shop. Life went on, following its ordinary, even boring course. We were less than a hundred yards from the scene of the crime. Nothing had happened. Nobody looked at me. There wasn't a friend or a relative or a neighbor to say to me, "Maurice, what a joy to see you back! Are your parents also coming back?"

I was still wearing those new clothes that chafed at the armholes, and the shoes that were hurting my feet. I wasn't paying attention to them. As if in a dream, I entered the building whose concierge was also ours. On the door was the customary notice "The concierge is upstairs," with the added information, "I'm at number 32." So it would be in our building that I'd announce to the concierge that my sister and I had been released and that she could return the keys to our apartment. Quickly crossing the courtyard, I climbed the little stone steps up to the building in three strides and went upstairs to find our concierge. On the fourth floor, our floor, the door of our apartment was wide open. I entered in a bound to see a suprising spectacle: the concierge was struggling to open the doors of the Henri II buffet. She blanched when she saw me and then, trying to regain her composure, blurted out "Where's the fruit bowl?" She was referring to the glass bowl where my mother had kept the keys to the cupboards. She had not forgotten what my mother had told her that morning; hence the frantic search that was interrupted by my inopportune entrance. Had I gotten there a little later, perhaps she would have used a crowbar to force open the doors of the buffet, and the cupboards, which surely held some wonderful treasures since they were so carefully locked.

Some thirty years later, I saw the movie *Les Guichets du Louvre* [released in English as *Black Thursday*], which recreates with surprising accuracy some events in the 4th district of Paris during the roundup of July 16, 1942. I relived what I had witnessed in Vincennes: the desire for plunder on the part of some concierges, who shamelessly ransacked the apartments of tenants who had been arrested. In the film, there are a couple of concierges who, right after the roundup, come out of an apartment struggling to carry a sewing machine, the means of subsistence of the tenants who had been taken away to a yet unknown fate. My wife, Marie-Jeanne, cried as we left the theater, and said, "To think that we lived, and still live, surrounded by people who behaved like that or were tempted to. I tremble to think that I could have lived among such vultures."

The concierge and I were face to face, but she barely looked at me. Surprised by my unexpected arrival, she was incapable of forming a coherent sentence, even a lie. She could have made some excuse that she was intending to save anything of value from being seized by the authorities. She could have said she wanted to make sure there was no perishable food in the cupboards. Anything. She might simply have acted on impulse, taking advantage of the situation, and that was why she couldn't justify her actions. She said nothing more after asking that stupid question, "Where's the fruit bowl?" The way she was looking at me, I sensed that she would never forgive me for catching her in the act of looting. My presence must have made her realize how disgraceful her behavior was; if no one had seen her, it would have been as if she hadn't done it. Her gaze was cold and filled with hatred. What business did they have releasing me? What would happen to her reputation if people in the neighborhood found out what she had done? These thoughts must have been going through her head. The atmosphere was unbearably tense. She had a daughter a little younger than I was, with whom I got along well and who had sometimes taken part in our games in the courtyard. Could she be like her mother? The woman was a typical concierge; obese, in her forties, she was watchful, poorly paid and bitter, and she turned her resentment against the tenants instead of the manager or agent in charge. Surprisingly, she wasn't married to a cop. Her husband was a decent working man who was nice to us. The two of them were as different as could be, not at all well matched. Perhaps she had changed as a result of her work as a concierge, so unprofitable and sometimes so disagreeable.

And now the snot-nosed brat she had sworn at and chased with her broom when he made trouble in her courtyard was in a sense holding her to account. Our roles had suddenly been reversed, and now she would have to act nice and try to placate me. Unbelievable. As for me, I was so upset by the morning's events and the separation from my parents that I was almost resigned to this new situation. All I wanted was to be all alone at home to cry. That was what I would have shouted at her if I'd had the strength. She flung the keys at me and stormed out, slamming the door behind her. I was the winner. It was a poor victory. I went into the kitchen for a glass of water. The cupboard was open wide but our grasping visitor had apparently found nothing of interest in it. I collapsed onto a stool. I felt like an old man, my head empty and my knotted stomach refusing even a sip of water.

I was not at the end of my journey. I now had to go warn our friends who lived at the other end of Vincennes. Going down the three flights of stairs was a real ordeal, because my feet, squeezed into the new shoes, were really hurting. It may seem ridiculous that I should remember this so clearly, because the real pain was elsewhere.

14

FOR THE FIRST TIME in my young life, I was apart from my mother. I had never been away from her before except to go to summer camp. The separation bothered me much more than our arrest that morning. It was unbearable no longer to be able to have her hug me, to hold her hands in mine, to see her reassuring smile and hear her laugh answering mine, and instead to find myself alone in a world that was not the same without her. Everything made me think of her, although it was the reflex of a child and I was already fourteen. You couldn't say I was overprotected; I was simply loved. Unconditionally. My parents' love had become part of me, like an essential attitude, and I couldn't imagine being deprived of this presence on which my life seemed to depend. It had always been my father and mother on one side and the rest of the world on the other.

Among my most distant memories is that of the anxiety I felt when my mother went to the hospital for a few days. I must have been four, and the separation seemed endless to me. The emptiness left by my mother's absence could not be filled by my father's presence, though I adored him just as much. It seems to me that I suffered much more as a result of this memory than from the separation itself. After that, I always feared there would be another separation. That possessive desire to have my mother always near became a joke between us. Of course, as a small child, I had wanted to marry my mother—what little boy doesn't? Later on, I was so anxious, I wanted so much to be loved as I myself loved my parents, that I asked a question that made the whole family laugh: I wasn't adopted, was I? Because I was constantly clinging to my mother's skirts, my sister made up a cruel game that involved trying to convince me that I was indeed an adopted child. When we squabbled and she made a comment to that effect, I couldn't stand it and would plead with my parents for hours to say it wasn't true. I would ask them to provide proof, but even then, although they comforted me, I was not at peace, and I would have nightmares of an orphanage where my parents had come and gotten me. I found some consolation in looking at the family photo album. There was no doubt. My resemblance to my mother was obvious. But a boy should look like his father. So I got photographs of my grandfather, my father and me and masked them so that only the eyes were visible. The resemblance was even more striking. I didn't tell anyone about the results of my investigations for fear that they would contradict them. But I didn't need any further confirmation; I was truly the son of my father and mother. The rest was not important. After that, when that bad joke came up in conversation, I would laugh with the others, but it still really made me anxious.

For a very long time, I was subject to bad dreams. I could fall asleep only if there was a light on in the hall, which I must have associated with my parents' presence in their bedroom nearby. Many children are afraid at night, but in my case these fears can't be explained merely by something in my dreams. Since earliest childhood, I had heard so many stories of the pogroms that had occurred in Russia and Poland in the past that I must have been more deeply marked than my parents realized. The fact is that most of the time, I was the one who asked the questions. I'd bother my father for more details, and I wouldn't be satisfied until he told me another story. I would certainly have surprised my primary school teachers and then my history teachers if I had recounted some of the those stories, such as the terrible pogrom in Kishinev in 1903. Maybe I unconsciously fed on those fears, even while rejoicing that my parents had escaped the attacks. I shuddered when I looked back at those events of a bygone era and felt proud to be living at a time when they were over. When my mother told me about the years of starvation they endured in Poland during the First World War under the yoke of the Russians or the Germans, but always under extreme oppression, I would listen to her in amazement that the years of privation had not destroyed her beauty. How could that be? The persecution suffered by the members of my family who had lived there, very far away, were part of my heritage, although I didn't clearly understand the violence that had occurred. When the roundup destroyed the family in which I had been so happy, it was my turn to see the terrible face of discrimination close up. All it took was a highly motivated army of police offiers—seven thousand of them that day in Paris and the suburbs—for the old habits, which had been revived by the Nazis, to be honored in France. Although there was not a history of physical violence, it was proven that you don't need history to find people to do the deed in front of the eyes of a population that is not overly offended by it.

15

I WAS IN THE STREET. The weather was nice. It was hard to believe that the war raging on all fronts had affected this peaceful neighborhood in Vincennes. The heat was beginning to lift, and mothers pushing strollers were leaving for a walk in the Bois. The stores would soon open, and the metal shutters were being unfastened. Clearly, nothing had happened. I must have been the only one who knew of the drama taking place a few steps from here, because nobody seemed upset or worried. In fact, everyone must have known of this morning's roundup, but it didn't concern deep France, which continued taking care of its affairs. However, I wasn't thinking about the attitude of our contemporaries then. I had a mission to carry out: to go and warn friends living on the other side of town. I mustn't think of anything else. Walk, warn. I looked at the people I passed on the way. They seemed almost about to stop me and say, "Young man, it's such a nice day. Now that the holidays have begun, you should be enjoying them instead of hanging around in the street." My ears were ringing. I had to walk, to walk and to warn.

I didn't want to think about my feet, which were very painful because of the new shoes. I had broken blisters on both heels, but I quickened my pace. At the corner of Avenue de Paris, the traffic policeman gave me a look that was far from reassuring, that seemed to say, "What's that one doing still at large?" And how could you go around with a yellow star on your chest on a day like this? It was sheer provocation. I was indeed the only person walking around with this ornament, like an actor in costume sleepwalking out of a theater.

The path was familiar. The primary school I had attended for years was not far from the neighborhood I was going to. I went along Rue du Moulin, where before the war there was still a small farm with horses. I was stumbling over the bumpy cobblestones, and the pain from the blisters, which must have been completely raw, kept getting worse. I probably looked like a crazy person, because my mind was elsewhere. In fact, my head was as empty as my stomach, which was beginning to gnaw, because I had eaten nothing since the night before and it was the time of the all-important after-school snack. I felt hot, then cold, I wanted to vomit, and my head was spinning, but I had to keep walking, to go faster, to warn them. I took the footbridge over the Bastille-Boissy-Saint-Léger rail line. When we were very young, it used to be a special treat on the way to school, if we got there early enough, to wait on the footbridge for the train to come and to stand enveloped in its acrid white smoke.

At the end of the footbridge were Rue Auber and the school on Rue de l'Égalité. That was where I learned to read and write. That was where the son of the Foreigner had become a little Frenchman. To what good? I still had several dozen yards to go before I could fulfill my terrible mission. I would have to recount and explain what had happened, while controlling my emotions and having to deal with their exclamations and maybe tears. I got to the home of my sister's best friend, on the border between Vincennes and Montreuil. They weren't expecting me, obviously, and they were very surprised. The roundup had been carried out so quietly that news of it had not yet reached the distant neighborhoods. There was nothing to be done. Nothing but to give the horrible news. When I had done so, the girl I had been sent to tell was in a state of shock. Now I just had to go back, to endure the same ordeal with these shoes I wished I could take off.

When I got to Rue Louis-Besquel again, there was still a group of people from the street standing around, with new ones replacing those who had satisfied their curiosity and gone on their way. Still the little group of watchful cops. It was impossible to know what was going on in the house, because the windows were still closed. My sister hadn't moved since I'd left more than an hour ago. She seemed frozen in place, completely focused on this ordinary house that had witnessed the destruction of our family. I couldn't bear the waiting, the unhealthy atmosphere of these voyeurs who had come to feed on this tragedy as if it were a show. I couldn't bear the children playing on the street where my parents were being held, while nobody knew what was in store for them. I left and went back home, the only place I could find some peace.

In the tiny apartment, I kept going from room to room. I had a headache, and the need to vomit became stronger and stronger as my stomach protested. I could only drink some water. And then the apartment itself became unbearable to me and I ran outside again, taking the stairs four at a time. I had to go see what was happening there. Maybe they would open the doors to the house. Maybe at the end of the day the cops would release the elderly people and mothers of young children. Maybe this ordeal would be over.

Alas! When I got to Rue Louis-Besquel, two buses had already come, and the people from the house were being pushed into them. I didn't get a chance to see my parents on either bus. They must also have been looking for me, but there were cops everywhere—in the street, in front of the buses, on the platforms, keeping close guard. The police wanted this operation that had been so orderly to go smoothly right to the end. The motors roared and the buses pulled away. Where were they going? We would know only the next day that some of the people had been taken to the Vél d'Hiv and the others, directly to the camp at Drancy, which had been functioning for nearly a year.

Around October 1942, when a semblance of everyday life had returned, we received from the dead letter department of the postal service a note scribbled in pencil, probably in an uncomfortable position, because it was barely legible, but that we were able to recognize as my father's writing. On the same scrap of paper was our name and address, which must have taken some effort to decipher, and a short sentence, whose terseness did not bode well: "We are leaving for Germany." This bit of paper must have been slipped between two slats of wood in the wagon carrying my parents, and as chance would have it, some anonymous person must have picked it up and given it to the postal service.

Between May 1941 and the summer of 1944, some twenty people from the two working-class streets that made up our neighborhood were arrested and deported to Auschwitz. To my knowledge, not one of them returned. I didn't know most of these neighbors. Their disappearance, like that of over a hundred Vincennes residents arrested on July 16, 1942, went practically unnoticed.

PART TWO

No Witnesses, No Crime!

1

LOCAL AMNESIA

ALTHOUGH SOME MAY FIND this shocking, I have always felt that the French were largely indifferent to our tragedy. It's true that after the roundup—long after—some people woke up. It took until August 1942 for the Protestant church federation of France to react. The same was true for part of the Catholic hierarchy, which reacted to racial discrimination only after the roundup, having loudly supported Pétain and his gang when they came to power in 1940. How could one expect more Christian charity from the French in general than from their official Christian representatives?

It's true that the information did not spread quickly. In Paris, apart from the areas where there were a lot of Jewish immigrants—where it was said that there was "running water and Jews on every floor"—people did not learn of the roundup until the next day, or even several days later. Curiously, the Nazi-supported papers in the northern zone and those in the southern zone, which (with the exception of *La Croix*) were pro-Vichy, did not print a word on the subject. As for the underground press, several papers, such as *Franc-Tireur*, *L'Humanité* and *Défense de la France*, harshly condemned the roundup, but their distribution was limited despite the courage of the members of the resistance networks, which were still very few in July 1942.

The fact remains that in certain parts of Paris, people had been impressed by the police action and were careful to avoid reacting. In such troubled times, it wasn't a good idea to get mixed up in these matters. And in the past two years, the French had gradually become accustomed to the persecution of Jews. It is not my intention here to point a finger at anyone—except the police, of course. It is not my intention to assign guilt, but that should not prevent me from giving my impression of my compatriots who could witness such horrible events without a shudder because they felt these things didn't concern them. They were ill-informed, it's true, but they often did not try to learn more. And one cannot compare the effects in a little suburb like Vincennes with those in Paris. Immigrant Jews were far less numerous in Vincennes than in some streets of the capital, but on the other hand, people usually knew each other better. Although foreigners were not under constant watch, they were identifiable by their neighbors. So if we were to give the people of Vincennes the benefit of the doubt, we could say they might have been unaware of the roundup. The problem, however, is that the lack of information is too glaring. Even if the police could have forgotten the actions of their senior members, it's hard to believe that the city hall did not know of them and that it was unaware of this part of the city's history. Rather than a mystery, this is intentional concealment of the past.

In trying to find the causes of the general amnesia, I was taking on a task I suspected would be difficult. Field investigations have many drawbacks, especially when they deal with sensitive issues that go beyond politics to racism and its effects. Several decades after the war, people clearly wished to avoid this kind of discussion by claiming ignorance. Anyone who questions contemporary French people should know that while the French are not racists—no more so today than in the past—they especially dislike reminders of recent history that appear to incriminate them.

Having worked professionally with public opinion surveys, I know very well how fragile a statistical sample is, especially when it is limited, and even more so when politics are involved. In addition, I was not trying to discover anything, but rather to verify what I felt I knew intuitively. Despite the amnesia that was evident so many years afterward, I wanted to find traces of the big roundup in Vincennes, the city that was once so dear to me but now seemed to have forgotten its tragic past. In the course of my investigation, I would finally understand why the 1972 documentary film *The Sorrow and the Pity*, which has little violence and is actually quite inoffensive, upset deep France as well as many people in government for such a long time. You were not supposed to remind France of its past. But I refused to obey that injunction; the people of Vincennes would be the subjects of an experiment that went beyond simply questioning them. What was involved was a reminder, not of some feat of arms or a victory or defeat, but one of the darkest pages in the history of a country, of a city, of an entire people, an event that became increasingly shameful with the desire to ignore it. I was looking for the stages leading to acquiescence or indifference, the refusal to see what was happening to the neighbors in order not to risk becoming involved in it or troubled by it.

For the average resident of Vincennes, the event was buried in a general amnesia about local history. Little information traveled from one neighborhood to another, from one street to another, from one house to another, from one floor to another. People knew nothing about their next-door neighbors who seemed different from them, and they were certainly not going to get upset over their disappearance. With the foreigners gone, they mainly continued to worry about the all-important question of getting food. Besides, there were two million actual French prisoners of war in the stalags. People moved on to other things so quickly that it might have seemed as if nothing had happened on July 16, 1942.

After the war, all that had been forgotten. Praise had been heaped on the police, and new faces had appeared at city hall—people who had been involved in the Resistance and did not want to bring back the sad stories of the occupation. The residents of Vincennes continued to worry about what was in their cooking pots, because problems with the food supply lasted for a long time. Years went by, and the hundred or so Vincennes residents—immigrant Jews—who had perished in the turmoil didn't stop the city's citizens from envisioning a pleasant, tranquil future. The memory of the war had been erased, buried under the advantages of the consumer society. It was to this well-organized ant colony that I delivered a hard kick, to the surprise of its members.

2

THE POLICE HAVE FORGOTTEN

THE POLICEMAN ORDERED TO ARREST US, that man who had picked us up in the early hours of the morning as if we were common criminals, died in December 1987, a few weeks before the publication of the first edition of this book. He lived at least forty-five years longer than my parents! Marcel Mulot spent his retirement in Vincennes, the city where he had applied his talent for dirty work under the Nazi occupation. If circumstances had been different, this ordinary cop might have had an innocuous career apprehending offenders, moving his arms at the traffic in an intersection, doing his shifts on duty at his police station, wielding his billy club during a banned march or workers' demonstration. That's all—a banal cop's life without having to think about too many problems. He was a cop like the others, with his kepi at eyebrow level so he could avoid revealing his low forehead.

Without the war and his country's defeat, Mulot's fate would just have been life as a hard-working cop: not thinking, following orders, playing cards with his workmates, going for a drink from time to time. Dullness guaranteed, but a very simple working life, with perhaps the prospect of one day becoming a sergeant or even precinct captain. But Mulot was one of those cops for whom the job would be, not a political revelation—a cop doesn't understand political nuances, he doesn't make political distinctions, he's simply loyal to the established order, whatever it is—but a discovery of the power a representative of the fascist order could wield. Like his Paris colleagues, he had been disarmed on June 14, 1940, on the arrival of the Germans in Paris. However, his service weapon had been returned to him a few days later when the Nazis realized what an asset this police force was, which was so compliant and had remained in the capital under prefect of police Langeron, since the fleeing government felt that order must continue to be maintained in Paris.

In this new situation, Mulot was typical of the police breed. Regardless of where the orders came from, it was imperative to follow them, head lowered, billy club raised, ready for action. Meanwhile, the population had become aware of the importance of the police's role, and people behaved themselves in their presence. During this period, when the German-Soviet Nonaggression Pact was still in force, the Gestapo was not—yet—hunting Communists, but that didn't matter, because the stalwart French police had already taken on the task. Respectful of their superiors' orders, they punished any breach of the new laws harshly. What counted for them was no longer protecting property and persons— their primary mission—but going after small dealers in the black market and mercilessly hunting down illegals with false papers. As for crooks, they hardly bothered with them anymore since important underworld figures were working for the Gestapo in the infamous Carlingue, known as the "French Gestapo," which was run by a former high-powered police officer, Bonny, and a pimp, Lafont. The role of the police was finally respected. People trembled as never before when they saw a kepi.

Beginning in the spring of 1941, hunting down Jews became one of the missions of these upstanding citizens. They practiced by circling the 11th district of Paris on August 20, 1941, and taking in all the foreigners, who were put behind barbed wire in the newly inaugurated French concentration camp of Drancy, which would quickly become notorious. When going through the streets of the area, they arrested people whose sinister look could only mean that they were Jews, to be gotten rid of as quickly as possible. Did these policemen have any qualms about applying in Paris the racial laws decreed in Nuremberg in 1935 by Hitler? Certainly not. They only knew the *Statute on the Jews*, a law of the Vichy government, and that was all they needed to know. Racial profiling had begun. Some police officers had left their original positions to work for the Police for Jewish Affairs, which had been set up by the Commissariat-General for Jewish Affairs, a temporary reassignment but with a bonus, of course.

Marcel Mulot had been a zealous police officer, an indispensible link in the chain maintaining the Nazi order. He must long ago have forgotten that black Thursday, which was just one of many similar missions. He had a clear conscience. You didn't discuss the validity of an order, you carried it out after saluting the superior officer who had transmitted it from the higher-ups, who knew what they were doing.

Although I never got over the arrest and its tragic consequences for my parents, I wanted to see Mulot again. When I was writing this book, it suddenly struck me as essential. I felt that even after more than forty years, this man's testimony could be an important part of my difficult, and possibly vain, search for the past. While I hadn't forgiven or forgotten anything, I felt the time had come for me to face the man who, by acting as a stooge of the Nazi order, had destroyed my family.

All I had to do to find his telephone number was open the Val-de-Marne directory at the Vincennes section. Before picking up the receiver, I needed to get control over my feelings. I had to stay calm and avoid attacking him, while at the same time making myself clear. Not an easy task. This man of more than seventy years of age must, like his surviving colleagues in the mobile guard and the gendarmerie, have cleared his memory of his police force's past. Throwing my painful recollections in his face could not serve my purpose, which was to have him recount his own experience of the night of July 15 to 16, 1942. I hadn't gauged the shock that might entail for a respectable old retired policeman. His wife, who answered the phone, told me, "You know, my husband has just been very sick. I'm not sure I should disturb him." The woman didn't know who I was; I had that advantage over her. I explained my reason for calling: a research project involving history, I said to impress her, adding that I was interested in the period of the German occupation. I went into greater detail: her husband and I had some shared memories and I wanted to compare them, and so on. After a few moments of hesitation, she finally said what I was hoping to hear: "I'll let you talk to my husband."

I immediately became very cold and almost unfeeling, adopting the attitude of a journalist requesting an appointment with a source who should have no reason to refuse. "Hello, is this Monsieur Mulot, the former police officer?" I was respecting the conventions, and my tone of voice was firm but not harsh. The terse reply came quickly: "Who are you?" I stated my last name and a few details to give him an idea of my purpose and the events involved: "You know, during the war we were neighbors in Vincennes, on the fourth floor at 32 Rue de la Villa, which today is Avenue Franklin-Roosevelt." There was a silence, whose length forced me to say more: "On July 16, 1942, I was arrested by two police officers, the senior one of whom was you. Time has passed and passions have cooled, and I would like to try to talk about it calmly with you. Would you grant me an interview?"

The answer was a flat refusal, stupid and contemptuous: "I'm not interested!" I imagined the gesture of the hand that would have accompanied the words. With that, his door was closed to me, and there was nothing I could do. This man I could have slaughtered with impunity at Liberation was very lucky I don't have the temperament of a murderer or avenger. This cop who, objectively, had been an accomplice of the Nazi executioners, who had killed my parents, and whom I could easily have eliminated if it would have assuaged my grief, allowed himself the luxury of spitting in my face at the end of his life. It's true I had sought him out, but it was so important to me to talk to him. Despite my horror, I had wanted to contact this cop, who, like his colleagues, had become a fighter for the liberation of Paris at the very last minute. This model cop, who likely had been given a good evaluation by his superiors and had never balked at a mission, had won his stripes by cheerfully subsisting on very little while playing the less and less dangerous game of resistance when the end of the German occupation was in sight. He might have been a fellow traveler or even a member of the Communist Party, but his past activities weren't held against him. Under the new laws, it was possible for him to rise in the hierarchy of underlings to the point where he worked in plainclothes, in a sense incognito, and was thus more dangerous.

What could a nuisance like me, long ago driven from his memory, have to say to him? What was I doing in this former cop's life that was nearing its end? Did I want to cause nightmares for this man who hardly ever dreamed, and certainly not about his past? "I'm not interested!" It was the kind of answer you give a door-to-door salesman of useless encyclopedias or life insurance policies. Of course, the prospect of talking about our shared memories did not interest Mulot, with his sordid past as a little cop playing both sides of the fence while watching his back, and my own interest counted for little with him.

"I'm not interested!" Mulot's rejection meant he had once and for all erased our shared past, the past that continued to haunt me. Nothing had happened in the life of this model public servant. The deaths of other people weren't his problem. A policeman didn't need to know if the person he was sent to arrest was guilty or innocent of a crime; he didn't need to know if the person was a criminal or someone who was being unjustly persecuted: thieves, criminals, small-time crooks and pimps would fit in well with people who had questionable political opinions, skin of a different color from that of their contemporaries, or a nose a little more curved than those of respectable people. It was up to the judge to sort them out and decide who was guilty and who was not. The important thing was to follow orders, or else there would be no more police, and the public peace would suffer. A policeman shouldn't wallow in sentiment. He had to arrest men, women, old people, children. Why should he need to know if they were innocent of any crime? Give him an order to bring in a certain number of Jews, he carried it out. Ask him to club some Arabs, he clubbed them. Happily, even.

If a colleague or even a superior had asked Mulot in July 1942 what he thought of those arbitrary arrests, he probably would have answered just as impatiently, "I'm not interested!" A good cop didn't question his mission. In fact, if he had agreed to talk to me, what would he have told me? Probably he would have spoken of having been in the Resistance, of the need to keep up appearances in order to deceive the occupiers, of his ignorance of the fate awaiting the victims of the roundups, which he would have assured me he thought were harmless. This cop who was "not interested" in his past would have reeled off the whole litany of made-up arguments used by those Johnny-come-latelies who were crooked collaborators and then became resisters in one night, the night of August 18 to 19, 1944. If he had agreed to see me, maybe he would have put on a good show, and I would have felt a certain pity for an old man who at the end of his life had found the courage to explain the deep motivations of his attitude, why he had followed the orders he was given, perhaps adding that he had done so against his will. Having regained a sense of conviviality, he might have offered me a coffee or a drink. I feel a pang at the mere thought. How could I have had a drink with that murderer?

With his cynical "I'm not interested!" things were crystal clear. He had forgotten nothing and regretted nothing—other than my late intrusion into his monotonous existence as a retired cop who expected nothing more from life than his public servant's pension, regularly increased as a result of the demands of the policemen's unions—some of which claim to be on the left. How can a person be a cop and a leftist? That's one of those impenetrable mysteries for which I'm still awaiting an explanation. "I'm not interested!" could also mean "I'm no longer interested!"

Nothing happened between 1940 and 1944. Nothing except the German occupation, that is, but during that period, the police did their duty, all of their duty and nothing but their duty, even making a point of taking part in an insurrection when the occupiers were on the verge of leaving. Nothing happened. Nothing, at any rate, that could justify, if not remorse, at least a slight regret expressed to that child, now a man with graying hair, whose life he had ruined and who was asking him to tell his story.

Of course, I was not so naive as to believe it would be easy. I had envisaged a refusal, but not in this way. A brutal rejection like "Stop bothering me, I have nothing to say to you," or even "Fuck off!" wouldn't have surprised me. It would have shown the enduring feelings of a public servant who didn't have to judge his past or that of his administration. But this expression of annoyance was much worse in my view. It showed a profound indifference to human misery. "I'm not interested!" Are cops today any different?—the ones responsible for maintaining order in the subways, who target Arabs, Blacks and, in general, anyone who doesn't fit the established norms?

When I pass a building in Paris bearing a plaque commemorating the death of a policeman who died in the fighting during Liberation, I'm so filled with ambivalence that I don't feel any special emotion. Maybe—certainly!—that cop had taken part in the roundup of July 16, 1942. Perhaps he was hit by a stray bullet, while others may have been killed by genuine resisters taking advantage of the fact that bullets were flying from all directions to settle their accounts with these guardian angels of the dark years who were finally vulnerable. If I had killed Mulot in August 1944 in Vincennes, maybe he would have had a little plaque with a tricolor border on a building in Vincennes, or maybe even a street named after him? Who can know? When I contemplate one of those plaques, I obviously think of the thirteen thousand foreign Jews arrested on July 16, 1942, some of them by those same police. If there were plaques on the buildings of Paris and its close suburbs for the tens of thousands of Jews arrested and deported between 1941 and 1944, the workers would have been guaranteed jobs for a long time after the war. It would have been pathetic. And the proximity of all the plaques commemorating the heros who died in police uniform would not be very pleasant. The few cops who were shot died in the line of duty, so to speak, and they were accordingly decorated posthumously. Their victims received only collective incineration, without fanfare. As for Mulot, who was courageous but not rash, he must not have taken any great risks in the fighting of August 1944, adopting the prudent wait-and-see attitude that was customary for public servants, zealously respecting the need for discretion.

My memories and my feelings did not interest Mulot. Faced with this predictable, indeed inevitable, attitude, I was filled with rage and a desire to shout every curse in my vocabulary in his face. I could easily have become obscene and turned the insults heard in police stations back against him with impunity. I could have allowed myself to do anything to Mulot, but he had taken the liberty of turning his back on me, saying, "I'm not interested!" It would have been a poor revenge, since my rage and curses would have just bounced off him.

He had sent me packing with his contemptuous "I'm not interested!" but I could imagine the marks of recent illness and the passing of time on that face I had known when he was still young. I saw him sprawled in a fake antique armchair with a blanket on his knees, his hand trembling with Parkinson's. I wished this imagined invalid a long life of harsh physical suffering, because he would never be tormented by remorse. I had a sudden desire to go knock on his door to hear him tell me to my face, "I'm not interested!" and to answer that I was extremely interested in seeing his pathetic carcass. I entertained these absurd thoughts, surprised that his refusal to see me—which was quite normal, after all—had plunged me into such a rage. Indeed, I was reacting mentally like a primitive sorcerer sticking needles in a doll or effigy of an enemy in order to cause them a painful death. This man had without doubt shortened my father's life by some twenty years, and my mother's by more than thirty. All it had taken was for a policeman who was no different from others of his ilk to unquestioningly obey his disgraceful orders. At that precise moment on July 16, 1942, Mulot and his peers had the power of life and death over some people whose names were on a list. They had chosen death at the risk of their own peace of mind. They had chosen death because the matter wasn't especially important to them. And to think that these cops who fueled the extermination camps turned out to be exemplary fighters in the Liberation! And that in their honor, on ceremonial occasions, the Paris police proudly wear the Fourragère Rouge, a decoration red with the blood of those tens of thousands of foreign Jews they obediently sent to their deaths. On July 16, 1942, there were seven thousand murderers in police uniforms, all of them French. All of them covered in glory. All of them base. Go-betweens for the Gestapo, draped in respect for the law, confirmed haters of foreigners, agents of repression, they paved the way on that dawning day of summer for genocide in France. And in my eyes, they bear the largest share of responsibility for that. Much more than the Nazis! Mulot was in good company, and he put his heart into his work, as did all the policemen who without hesitation answered the call to serve that day. Only a single one, an officer at the Nogent-sur-Marne police station, resigned the next day.

I wanted to find out if any trace of the roundup remained at the police station in Vincennes, and I wrote to the captain, the "boss," as his subordinates called him, to ask for an interview. That was in mid-May 1985. I had called beforehand and had been advised to request an appointment in writing. I didn't want to risk a refusal so I did not give any details about my research, saying only that I was working on a book on Vincennes under German occupation. After a month passed without a reply, I decided to go to the police station. From the reception desk, I was taken to a man who seemed to be the assistant to the "boss." My letter was there in full view at the top of a pile of papers waiting to be dealt with. After a cursory greeting, a brief question: "What's your problem? We were just about to write to you."

Had they done research on me? I had stated in my letter that I was a former resident of Vincennes. So my answer and my interest in the roundup of July 16, 1942, should not have surprised him. Despite his impassive manner, he did not seem completely at ease. His immediate response was to send me elsewhere: "You should consult the archives of the prefecture of police. Perhaps they will be able to provide you with information. Look at the department's archives as well." From behind his desk, the senior officer scrutinized me as he spoke, a natural effect of years as a policeman. Maybe he was trying to recognize me (you never know). And he continued his monologue: "You know, every ten years, we get rid of our accumulated papers. So after forty years, how can you know what happened? The men also leave." Curiously, he kept mentioning the names of police officers who had been victims of the enemy, especially one: Charles Silvestri, a Vincennes policeman who had been shot in August 1944. I at least learned that if the "papers" of possible interest to civilians who had been victims of the police had disappeared, the officers' exploits had not been consigned to the dustbin of local history.

In spite of the fact that he had closed the door on my inquiries—albeit politely—I kept trying. He was respecting the conventions and showing surprising courtesy. I asked, "There must still be records of the people detained at the police station?" The answer was the same: "I'm sorry, Sir, not even that." Then he added, "Only the Germans kept those records." That was astounding. Did this policeman know nothing about the past of his predecessors? I explained briefly that the occupiers had carefully refrained from taking part in the actual roundups, and had only given essential directives to the higher-ups of the prefecture of police after agreement with the Vichy authorities. The chief inspector made another sad comment: "But our police were surely commandeered to accompany the German Feldgendarmes who were making the arrests."

He had probably never imagined himself in a situation like this, forced to stay calm with a lunatic throwing in his face the exploits of the officers who had gone before him in this station. I played the expert, citing every detail, speaking quickly to give him a maximum of information: "You know, on July 16, 1942 (he seemed unfamiliar with the date), as in the other roundups, the French police operated alone," adding for good measure the fact that until July 1943, it was the French police and the Gendarmerie that were in charge of managing the camp at Drancy. I took advantage of the opportunity to say to this very embarrassed police officer, "You're lucky to be doing this job today, because back then, you would have had to do that dirty work just like the others."

A new reaction, a very natural one from a policeman: "How can you disobey your orders when you're commandeered for a mission?" I didn't want to get into that discussion. I reminded him that I had come to him for information, and not to trouble him with my past misfortunes or be given excuses or futile explanations. It's extraordinary how bold you can be when speaking to the police, even verging on impertinence, without risking a charge of contempt for insulting an officer, when you remind them of the Nazi occupation and the role the police played during that time.

I was dealing with one of those public servants who feel they have an obligation to preserve the honor of the force. Hence the obligatory reminder of some of his predecessors' opposition to the occupiers. Those ones, of course, had been shot. As for the others, I knew the refrain, having heard it before. The newer generations of policemen could even say with a straight face, "July 16, 1942? Don't know anything about it!" The rest was equally familiar: "You know, we had our heros and our dead." So this policeman without a memory, born in 1939, had to be told that it is always more gratifying to speak of the victims among your own than of those who are unknown, of whom there is no trace. Clearly, he needed to understand that I was as concerned for the police force's martyrs as for the size of the clubs used by the thugs on duty at demonstrations.

For the ten minutes of our conversation, this officer's behavior toward me was impeccable, and he listened to the information I gave him without raising an eyebrow. Before leaving, I remarked that the new police station in Vincennes had been built in the former red light district of the city, opposite the offices of the French Communist Party. That led to the response, "Yes, we're right across from the Bolshoi." Did I need to explain to this gray-haired policeman that the Bolshoi was a Soviet theater with no connection to the Bolsheviks?

On July 16, 1942, in an instant, everything changed, everything exploded. My familiar world disappeared with a policeman's sudden knock on our door. That's how it must have been sixty years before when a pogrom broke out in a town in the south of Russia. At the beginning, people's lives were not threatened, only their possessions, because the czar had said, it was suggested, that Jews could be robbed with impunity. So there was systematic looting of the little shops, then the houses, and then the synagogue, which probably contained some valuables. The looting and fires inflamed people's spirits and, with the help of alcohol, they went on to tear out men's beards, rape women and even little girls, and slaughter young boys in the streets and the schools. The right to loot became the right to murder, always under the protection of the czar, who was seen as practically divine, and who must be protected by brutalizing the Jews, who were a constant threat to him. In the streets, the Cossacks waited with their weapons at the ready for the order to restore calm. The order never came. As for the police, the higher ranks of which secretly organized these riots, they contemplated the violence that was unleashed with a smile on their lips, content to arrest any Jews who tried to resist, especially the courageous—or reckless—ones who organized self-defense.
These stories I had heard dozens of times suddenly came back to me. This time, however, it wasn't the populace, the drunken peasants and wretches from the poor neighborhoods, who were leading the attack. The police had come out from behind the scenes to take part in the hunt for Jews. The police had been given orders as if for an important mission entrusted to experts. People no longer threw themselves unthinkingly on the Jewish neighborhoods, they no longer attacked people they easily recognized from their dress or sidelocks. Those were the practices of a bygone day, and the Jews living in France increasingly looked like the natives. No need to settle for hunting people down in the streets as they had in some neighborhoods of Paris in August 1941; in July 1942, the files

were complete, and they only needed to go to the homes of the victims in the early morning and snatch them from their nests without any resistance. Sometimes the victims had even been warned and were waiting for the police, because it would have been pointless to try to escape. The police, sure of their actions, triumphant, quickly occupied a territory that had already been conquered, simply comparing the file given to them with the people in the home in a sort of roll call. Everyone present? Please follow us. Sometimes, these policemen were even capable of showing initiative, because they didn't hesitate to take in people who weren't on their list but who "looked the type."

These officers, who would say after the war that they were only following orders, did not worry about the disasters they caused, did not hear the crying of the mothers and children, did not see the glazed eyes of the fathers unable to defend their families. "Hurry up" were the only words in their limited vocabulary. They had to move quickly and efficiently. When the door closed on a home with a few pieces of furniture acquired at some sacrifice, a whole life with its memories of happy days was spirited away. What could that matter to those policemen who were only doing their job, following to the letter an order that they couldn't discuss?

Like a Jesuit, the policeman is as obedient as a corpse[1]—but not as intelligent, of course.

Since the 1960s, the Vél d'Hiv roundup has been recounted in a few books, and only very recently, a small number of history textbooks. Never has a policeman felt the need to explain how he experienced his part in the action of that terrible day. I think I'm the only person who has been able to present the testimony of actors in that brilliant demonstration of police work,[2] but only of "resisters." Some forty-five hundred policemen were purged in 1944. These temporarily black sheep were taken back into the force through the efforts of the "socialist" prefect Baylot; their careers were reestablished and most of them received compensation for the harm they had suffered in the form of more rapid advancement than their peers who had not been purged after Liberation.

On every anniversary, the roundup of July 16, 1942, is mentioned. It's part of History, they say, but they avoid saying too much about the role of the French police in it. This is especially perverse because, aside from

1. The Constitution of the Jesuit order stresses that the Jesuit must be "as a dead man's corpse without will or judgment" in the service of the order. [PA]
2. Maurice Rajsfus, *Quand j'étais juif* (Paris: Mégrelis, 1982), pp. 159–205; Maurice Rajsfus and Jean-Luc Einaudi, *Les Silences de la police* (Paris: L'Esprit frappeur, 2001), pp. 34–70.

government employees—sometimes accompanied by thugs from the gangs around the fascist politicians Doriot and Bucard—nobody else appears to have taken part, that day or the following day, when they finished the job. It was all under French authority, from those who gave the orders to those who carried them out. The French had learned to persecute for themselves. *Not a single German police officer or soldier participated in the operation.*

Furthermore, it should be stressed that this monstrous roundup was never considered a criminal act when, after the war, the authorities listed the misdeeds of active collaborators. None of the organizers and, even less, the participants in Operation Spring Breeze were judged for it. The secretary-general to the Vichy police, Bousquet, who had negotiated the roundup with Dannecker's anti-Jewish section of the Gestapo, was never judged for the approximately thirteen thousand legal kidnappings committed that day. His assistant, Leguay, had been ordered personally by Pierre Laval to suggest to the Nazis that children be arrested as well as adults, which the Gestapo had not even envisaged at the outset. Leguay died unpunished in 1989. The French police had to exert pressure on the Nazis to have some children deported to Auschwitz and certain death.

If I had coldly decided to kill Bousquet, who was the main person responsible for the deportation of my little cousin Denise, then eleven years old, I would have been judged and probably condemned, as was Christian Didier, who did exactly that in June 1993.

3

THE BUS DRIVERS DID THEIR JOB

O N JULY 13, 1942, circular no. 173/42 of the prefecture of police announced to the administration of the CMP (Compagnie du Métropolitain; Paris metro company) that the surface bus network was to be placed at the disposal of the police for the transport of persons arrested. This was a requisition order.

For years I tried in vain find one of the drivers of the buses requisitioned at dawn on July 16, 1942, to transport thousands of Jews to the Vél d'Hiv or the camp at Drancy. I made many inquiries to both the RATP and the unions. After a lot of back-and-forth and quibbling about changes in the administration of the Paris transit system, the fact that the unions were underground organizations during this period, the need to respect the confidentiality of the personnel, who had been forced to obey, I was, for all intents and purposes, turned down by everyone. I was unable to find even one of the drivers, who would have been retired by then.[1]

What did they imagine? The simple research I was carrying out had taken on on a suspicious aspect because "the workers" might be criticized for what they had been forced to do under the requisition order. Did they want to make people forget something that could be considered shameful? In fact, these actions had already been forgotten, and nobody was interested anymore. Did those things really happen? "It's not possible that

---

1. The CMP had recently absorbed the Société des transports en commun de la région parisienne (STCRP). The administration of the RATP (Régie autonome des transports parisiens; Paris public transit company) told me that the files of the STCRP and the CMP had disappeared.

our coworkers could have carried out such missions," one bus driver who was still on the job said to me. All this was the past, and since everyone took care not to mention the events, any questions asked were seen as provocation. They maintained a wall of silence, afraid that something might get out. That past must be buried. The *de facto* cooperation with the occupiers—forced or passive—by the French population must be hidden. The arrest and deportation of tens of thousands of poor souls was now part of ancient history. Without equating the two situations, let us recall that in 1945, the residents of towns near the concentration camps in Hitler's Germany claimed they knew nothing about the camps. No witnesses, no crime.

It's easy to understand the "thinking" of the trade unions: even under duress, "the workers" could not possibly have collaborated with the occupiers. The attitude of the RATP is more difficult to fathom; its refusal to acknowledge a part of its past is surprising. A high-level manager of the surface network told me he was sorry but he hadn't found anything to do with the requisition order from the prefecture of police, such as lists of the drivers on the night of July 15 to 16, 1942, that would have been compiled by the managers of the depots. I said, "Since there are no written traces, it must be that the order was never officially given or transmitted." After an embarrassed silence, he was forced to conclude, "That must be it."

This operation was clearly not as flattering as that of the taxis [that delivered soldiers to the front line] in the Battle of the Marne, which in their time were also requisitioned, but perhaps the one explains the other. Of course, there is no question of equating the role played by the bus drivers with anything like active collaboration. In retrospect, these men could perhaps have decided not to do the work, reporting in sick with a medical note, or refusing en bloc, because the drivers in that company have always shown solidarity. It would not have been possible, even under the German occupation, to lock out a whole occupational group. It's true that in 1942, all of France was commandeered, often for tasks that were even more ignoble. And it is likely that when the requisition order arrived, nobody would yet have known what the mission involved. Even the managers of the depots, who were responsible for designating the men to take part in the operation, may not have been entrusted with the information. Why, then, this systematic refusal? All I was asking was to meet with witnesses. Some fifty drivers must have been commandeered that night, and I was not able to meet with a single one of them.

I obtained the beginning of an answer upon rereading *Betrayal at the*

Vél d'Hiv, by Claude Lévy and Paul Tillard. The eyewitness accounts in that book make it clear that the drivers quickly realized what was expected of them, especially when the order was given to some of them to gather in the courtyard of the prefecture of police. It was obviously a mission in support of a police operation. At the same hour, in other neighborhoods of Paris and the suburbs, the buses left the depots with police officers already in place on the platforms. This is what the authors of *Betrayal at the Vél d'Hiv* have to say:

> Now the sinister carrousel of buses began moving from the initial centers to the Vél d'Hiv, where families with children were detained, and to Drancy, where adults without children were held, and back again. There were buses crammed full of people lined up in front of the Vél d'Hiv, the drivers waiting patiently in their seats while the passengers filed off. The drivers were doing their job as if they were merely bringing spectators to a sports event. When one bus was empty, it would leave again, and another would take its place. This would continue with perfect regularity until evening.[2]

Roger Boussinot, an eyewitness, gives the following account: "When I got out of the metro, I stopped walking. In front of me, pulled up at the corner of the street, was a Paris city bus, green and white, with a platform. At the other corner, in front of the building opposite me, which looked like a school, a blue police car."[3]

It appears that some fifty buses were requisitioned for Operation Spring Breeze by the prefecture of police. Since more than thirteen thousand immigrant Jews were arrested and one bus could not carry more than fifty people with their baggage, we can reasonably estimate that each bus must have made a minimum of five trips that day. That proves at least that if the drivers did not know at night what was expected of them, by the time they had made the first trip, they would have to have been aware of the reason they had been commandeered. Since the operation was carried out to its conclusion, it is clear that the drivers were not put off by either the mission itself or the repetitiveness of the task. Nor did they refuse to obey the next day, July 17, when the job begun the night before had to be finished. How many of them failed to heed the call, citing medical or other reasons? History does not tell us. Nor does history tell

---

2. Claude Lévy and Paul Tillard, *La Grande rafle du Vél d'Hiv 16 juillet 1942*, (Paris: Éditions J'ai lu, 1968), p. 68.
3. Roger Boussinot, *Les Guichets du Louvre*, translation.

us if their managers congratulated these drivers or gave them a special bonus for working at night and doing overtime. What were the reasons that I was not able to meet with any of these men, who were no more guilty than others in their attitude to the common enemy, but finally, just as indifferent to the fate of the victims?

At the risk of boring the reader, I want to make it clear that my investigation was as exhaustive as possible. In 1986, I more than once contacted the administration of the RATP and that of the surface network, the central file service, and the RATP's press service and public relations department. I approached the health insurance company for the RATP and two retirement residences it ran. I asked four trade unions, including two that ran groups for retirees from the RATP.[4] I wanted to leave no stone unturned, so I also questioned the Fédération des anciens combattants (veterans' organization) of the RATP and the joint committee of veterans' associations of the RATP. Finally, I went to the Musée des Transports urbains (Museum of urban transportation) in Saint-Mandé. Why not?

Nothing!

Curiously, the central file service of the RATP was able to provide the names of CMP drivers who were ordered to drive soldiers to the front in 1939 and 1940, and those who took part in the evacuation of children from Paris to the provinces in the spring of 1940. The names of those who were deported for acts of resistance were also known. But there was no trace of those who were commandeered on the night of July 15 to 16, 1942. So nothing special happened that night in the bus depots, and one has to conclude that the drivers who went back and forth between the primary assembly centres, the Vél d'Hiv and Drancy were only carrying out an everyday task— as would later be the case—which did not raise any questions.

At the outset, my intention was simple: to find one of the former drivers and ask him about his experience that night and the following day. Yet, it seemed impossible to have a relaxed meeting that wouldn't result in unpleasantness. Perhaps I could have met with one of those former drivers—some were surely still alive—but their successors apparently did not see fit to put me in contact with any. Should I conclude from the unanimous negative response at every level of the RATP—executives, managers, workers—that the action of July 16, 1942, was highly reprehensible and the new employees were covering up for the old ones?

---

4. The four trade unions were the Confédération française démocratique du travail (CFDT; democratic French confederation of labor), the Confédération française des travailleurs chrétiens (CFTC; French confederation of Christian workers), the Confédération générale du travail (CGT; general confederation of labor) and Force Ouvrière (FO; workers' force). The CGT and FO ran groups for retirees from the RATP. [PA]

This behavior, this refusal to furnish even the slightest detail or allow me to obtain what could be new information, leads me to certain negative ideas about those who try to conceal, not the truth, because it is known, but a whole portion of the history of their company during a period when the whole of France was under the yoke of the Nazis. The mechanisms of the drivers' participation in Operation Spring Breeze are known. The requisition order from the prefecture of police was transmitted to the administration of the surface network of the CMP, and the administration had to tell the managers of the depots to designate the men who would carry out the transportation that night. Will history tell us if the depot managers called for volunteers before drawing up the lists? Had there actually been any volunteers? This possibility should not be dismissed. Some might have wanted a positive evaluation with the threat of compulsory work service in Germany looming. None of these possibilities should be overlooked, but I might not have formulated them if I had been able to talk to one of the drivers commandeered on that night of horror.

It should be pointed out that the operation of July 16 and 17 was not the only one of its kind; the drivers would be pressed into service on numerous occasions. Every convoy of some thousand deportees that left Drancy for Auschwitz was boarded onto public transit vehicles, which in most cases were the buses that were so familiar to Parisians, to go to Le Bourget station.[5] That meant twenty buses per convoy, with as many drivers. From March 27, 1942—it started before the Vél d'Hiv roundup— to mid-August 1944, a total of sixty-seven convoys would leave Drancy. How many drivers, commandeered or not, participated in these operations that had over the years become routine? Certainly a lot more than the fifty for the roundup of July 16 and 17, 1942.

According to some of the retirees from the RATP who worked on the Paris surface network during the Nazi occupation, there were angry protests against the successive requisition orders for drivers. They were marked by drivers speaking up in the depots and distributing leaflets, a former union official recalled over the telephone. I would have been glad to hear of these angry protests, but I didn't see anything of them, and nobody offered to show me a single document or put me in touch with a single witness. Should I conclude that there were none? If any such demonstrations against the horror had occurred, we would surely have been told of them after the war. Having never been informed of these generous actions, I must conclude that they never occurred![6]

5. This is confirmed by Henri Amouroux in *Les passions et les haines*, vol. 5 of *La Grande Histoire des Français sous l'Occupation* (Paris: Robert Laffont, 1981).
6. Thousands of political prisoners detained at La Santé or Fresnes were deported between 1942 and 1944. Paris buses were also used to transport these men and women to the stations they left from.

Terrified, fearing for their freedom, the CMP drivers obeyed the requisition order from the police hierarchy, itself under orders from the Nazis. After that dark period of our history, things changed, and one could imagine that never again—especially not under a democratic regime—would there be such deplorable behavior. Alas!

During the Algerian War, the prefect of police of Paris was Maurice Papon, who as secretary-general of the prefecture of Gironde had been responsible for the deportations of Jews from Bordeaux in 1942. On October 17, 1961, Papon sent his men to suppress a large demonstration of Algerians that included women and children, and he requisitioned RATP buses. Old repressive habits die hard. Papon was repeating the actions of his colleague Bussières, who in July 1942 took his orders from the Gestapo. But Maurice Papon did not need a political order.

As in the years from 1942 to 1944, not a single driver balked at the order. Throughout the night of October 17 to 18, 1961, RATP buses took Algerians from the demonstration to the Palais des Sports de la Porte de Versailles, the Stade de Coubertin and a center on the edge of the Bois de Vincennes. There were almost as many rotations of buses as in July 16 and 17, 1942, because more than ten thousand Algerians were transported.[7]

Every single employee of the RATP who was commandeered on October 17, 1961, obeyed his orders. Was their behavior as serious as that of the drivers of 1942? I have two answers. First, with less than twenty years separating the two operations, it is quite possible that some drivers participated without qualms in both of them. Second, while a refusal could have negative consequences under the Nazi occupation (dismissal, arrest, and after 1943, perhaps forced labor in Germany), that was no longer the case in October 1961. The unions could have urged their members to refuse to support that repressive action. Once again, there is no trace of intervention by any union official, although every depot had its delegates, who were very active in other circumstances. There is no trace of a leaflet of protest afterwards. There would have been no risk in refusing this dishonorable job, especially if all the employees of the corporation had supported the call for a strike—but no call was ever given. And individually, the drivers could have said no to their superiors without jeopardizing their jobs.

It is thus possible to say that the RATP drivers' participation in the roundup of October 17, 1961, was even more wrong than the obedience of their elders of the CMP under the Nazi occupation. In a democratic regime, it

---

7. For further information, see Michel Lévine, *Les Ratonnades d'octobre* (Paris: Ramsay, 1985); Jean-Luc Einaudi, *La Bataille de Paris* (Paris: Seuil, 1991); and Anne Tristan, *Le Silence du fleuve* (Bezons, France: Au nom de la mémoire, 1991).

clearly showed their lack of interest in any action that did not concern bread-and-butter issues.

How did the RATP drivers, who made several trips back and forth that terrible night, feel when they saw the Algerians being clubbed after getting off their buses, particularly at the entrance to the Palais des Sports de la Porte de Versailles, where six thousand Algerians were brutally beaten. These well-placed eyewitnesses apparently saw nothing—or perhaps they turned their heads at that exact moment to make sure there was nobody left on the bus. And one last question: how many veterans of Algeria were there among these drivers who were numb to the horror before them?

An account by the journalist René Dazy, who was then writing for *Libération*, describes these loathsome acts: "A bus with the number 27 drove into the crowd. An Algerian man grabbed my arm and said, 'Did you see that? Did you see that?' I learned later that many of the bus drivers at the site of the demonstration used their headlights to signal to the cops that they were carrying Algerians. And the drivers who were then commandeered to pick up the arrested Algerians agreed to do the work without any discussion, as in the roundups under the occupation."[8] Several hundred Algerians were murdered that night; one hundred and fifty bodies were pulled from the Seine between Paris and Rouen.[9] Between 1942 and 1944, the Jews were killed only after they got to Auschwitz.

---

8. Account by René Dazy in Lévine, *Les Ratonnades d'octobre*.
9. These numbers represent estimates made by eyewitnesses. Since the records of that day were later destroyed under orders from Papon (which came to light in 1998 when he was convicted of crimes against humanity for deporting hundreds of Jews to German concentration camps during the Second World War), the exact numbers remain unconfirmed to this day. Papon persisted in his testimony that there were only three Algerians killed that day. [PA]

4

VINCENNES CITY HALL HAS NO INFORMATION

WHEN I TRIED to find significant documents in the archives of the city of Vincennes, I had no illusions. I was hoping, perhaps, for a record of some action taken by the mayor or his assistants after the roundup. At any rate, I had to look; you never know what you might find, and it was important to search, even if it was chancy. What could be found in official documents written or published during the occupation? Perhaps some information had been gathered after the war. Anonymous acts of generosity—who knows?—might have been noted in these offices I was entering for the first time.

In the record of the city council's deliberations for July 1942, there was nothing. This logbook of the municipality, which was referred to regularly by the services of the Seine prefecture, did not contain what I was looking for. If the mayor or members of the city council had any qualms at the time, it did not show up in this record, which was produced under the gaze of the occupiers. Thoughts or perhaps even acts of solidarity would have had to remain secret. The silence on the roundup was thus natural. What is certain is that the city council, which was elected before the war but remained in place under Nazi jurisdiction, was condemned to silence and had to limit its work strictly to the administration of the commune.

The *Bulletin municipal officiel* (BMO; official municipal newsletter) was equally mute regarding the roundup. Some hundred inhabitants of Vincennes, maybe more, had disappeared from one day to the next, and the people of Vincennes could not learn of it from the local newsletter. Those who hadn't been neighbors of some of these dispossessed people would not be informed of what had happened nearby. Lying by omission is a time-honored practice: no information, no problems, no waves. Nobody will be upset. Silence was the rule on the violence of the Nazis and their French accomplices; the newsletter mainly offered trivial news items, announcements of validated ration coupons and discussions of problems related to crime.

Its monthly publication schedule made it hard to keep pace with events. When something occurred immediately after an issue had been put out, it was simply not reported. Sometimes information would come out at the wrong time. Thus, in the issue of August 10, 1942, the newsletter published an item entitled "Notice to Hungarian Jews," which came rather late:[1] "Jews of Hungarian nationality are obliged to wear the *special badge*[2] starting at the age of six. In the Seine department, the badge must be obtained on presentation of the identity card for a clothing ration coupon for each person. Those who do not comply with this measure within the deadline will be subject to severe punishment."

This notice published by the Vincennes city hall is interesting for several reasons. First, it was too late for people who wanted to respect this Nazi law in the guise of French law, because the Hungarian Jews who were being addressed would have had to comply before August 4, 1942, that is, before its publication. Second, the order was addressed to a category of immigrants that was very small, especially in Vincennes. But what was most cynical, and most hypocritical, about it was that it used the words "special badge" for the yellow star, because it would have been disturbing to speak of it openly. It was not the requirement to wear the yellow star that was considered disturbing, but rather its description. They marked the Jews and deported them—so be it, but why should they have to talk about it?

What I found most sinister about the newsletters of the summer of 1942 were the quotations from letters written to Marshal Pétain by children. I do not recall being subjected to this exercise, but it appears that children in the early grades of primary school were often asked to write in praise of the man who had given himself for France. Among the quotations from these letters published in the newsletter that summer was one that particularly caught my attention, written by a student in second grade whose name was Rostoker: "I am glad to know that you are the leader of our country. I

1. See pp. 54–55, *Operation Yellow Star*: the 8th Nazi ordinance went into effect for Jews from Nazi-allied countries on July 25, 1942. Moreover, the previous requirement of June 7, 1942, for all Jews except those from Nazi-allied countries to wear the yellow star, had also not been announced in a timely fashion. [PA]
2. My emphasis.

embrace you with all my heart." I should add that the letters were written before July 14, 1942, and that the Rostoker family was taken in two days later.

Was that all I was able to find? No. It would be unfair not to mention a document whose existence I learned of in the Vincennes archives. It was a memoir written in December 1944 by a man named Montgermont, the secretary-general of city hall, who was dismissed from his position at Liberation. In this account, entitled "Memories of the Occupation of Vincennes by the German Army," Montgermont sought essentially to show the human face of the mayor—a Vincennes industrialist named Bonvoisin, whose salt-and-pepper beard I remember scratching my face during a prize-giving ceremony before the war—and some of the mayor's assistants. His aim was to show how many of the local elected officials had "effectively contributed to maintaining social peace during the occupation." We know very well what that means.

At Liberation, then, Montgermont was given an important mission by the mayor: to inform the population that its elected officials, who had remained in their positions during the occupation, had behaved well under the Nazis. The intention was sincere, because they wanted at all costs to guarantee their immediate future at a time when purges were widespread. The following points make for astounding reading:

"Three unexpected events marked 1942:
– the first bombing of the Paris region, in March;
– the death of Dr. Boyé, a major figure in Vincennes, in June;
– an event of major social significance, the opening of a cafeteria by the factory-owners of Vincennes, in June."

Of course, they also had to mention the actions of the elected officials of Vincennes on behalf of the persecuted "Israelites," although they were not among the "unexpected events that marked 1942," because even four months after the liberation of Paris, there was no mention of the roundup of July 16, 1942. You'd think this police exploit had gone unnoticed by Vincennes city hall and that the mayor himself had only been informed of it much later, perhaps without ever knowing the exact date of the operation. In principle, mayors have police powers, but even if they were not consulted by the local police captains, who were expressly responsible for the arrests, they could not have been unaware of what was happening in their cities. But never mind that. The extract from the Montgermont memoir on the "poor Israelites" is worth quoting in full:

During 1942, the battle against the Israelites changed drastically. Many Jewish families were deported, leaving young children in the care of neighbors. Monsieur Bonvoisin decided to place the young Israelite children who had been separated from their parents under the protection of city hall. Quietly but effectively, with the help of a UGIF social worker, Mademoiselle C., we found places for them, and every month I would bring what was needed to provide for them.

For the fourth or fifth time in two months, I received a visit from young Jeannette R., eighteen years of age, the eldest of four siblings. She was an Israelite. Her parents had been deported and she was being pursued by the Gestapo, to which I had been denounced for having many times protected her. The unfortunate young woman had just had her parents' apartment and its furnishings taken from her. She was being sought by the Gestapo, who wanted to arrest her. So despondent that she wanted to kill herself, she sought refuge in my office. I comforted her and, using false papers authorized by Monsieur Bonvoisin, helped her find a place to hide in a religious institution in the 12th district in Paris, which generously took her in with three of her sisters, despite the risks. The two brothers were placed elsewhere. As the justice official had designated me to receive the military allowance for these minors—as well as for some ten others—we would meet every month, at night so as not to arouse suspicion, in a busy spot in Paris, always a different place, and I would give her the allowance so that she could pay for her room and board and that of her brothers and sisters.

Needless to say, this young girl, whose morale I tried to bolster each time we met, today feels much gratitude, which I must share with Monsieur Bonvoisin and the head of the institution that took in her and her sisters.

A little later, another Israelite woman, Madame P., the wife of a prisoner of war, sought refuge in my office, saying she and her nine-year-old daughter were being pursued by the Gestapo, which wanted to deport them. Since she had family and friends in a remote place in the Massif central, I took off her Jewish badge and gave her another name and papers to cross the line of demarcation and arranged for her to leave that night from the Gare d'Austerlitz. For two years, I received her military allowance under the Germans' noses, and every month I sent it to her under the false name I had given her when she left Vincennes. When she came back to our city a few days after liberation, she didn't know how to express her gratitude.

This text obviously calls for a certain number of comments, the first one being that methinks he doth protest too much. First of all, Monsieur Montgermont's memoir ignores the roundup of July 16, 1942, and subsequent roundups, as well as the arrests of people belonging to specific categories of immigrants. Nor is there a word on the actions of the officers from the Vincennes police station, of which he, as secretary-general of city hall could not have been unaware. Only the Gestapo is mentioned, several times. Yet, with rare exceptions, the Nazi political police never pursued Jews in the Paris region; the French police carried out this task quite capably, and the Nazis only got involved when the prey was more important than those poor souls who could be arrested without difficulty, often without even any resistance. What is certain, to my knowledge, is that the Gestapo never intervened in Vincennes for those reasons.

There's another interesting aspect: this document remained in the archives without ever being taken out, without anyone trying to use it to clear the name of the former mayor of Vincennes. It's true that this laborious apologia is hardly credible. Monsieur Montgermont had indeed taken on a tough job: to rehabilitate a municipality that had fulfilled its responsibilities in a garrison town where several thousand German soldiers lived during the occupation. At no time were the local authorities challenged by Vichy, nor by the Germans. Only a person considered trustworthy would have been allowed to manage such a commune of the size of Vincennes.

In addition to the absence of the French police from Monsieur Montgermont's memoir, there are a number of other implausible elements. What were the "military allowances" paid to Mademoiselle R. and some ten other minors, whose names are not even given? And I can't help questioning the generosity of the religious institution that asked Mademoiselle R. and her sister to pay a monthly fee for room and board. The good works of the Vincennes city hall deserve no fanfare, despite the former secretary-general's assertion that "Monsieur Bonvoisin decided to place the young Israelite children who had been separated from their parents under the protection of city hall." That, it seems to me, is patently false. After my parents' arrest, I was never contacted by any department of Vincennes city hall.[3] We had been attending the local secular schools for more than ten years, and we were not unknown. The city hall must have had the list of all persons of Jewish origin arrested in Vincennes, as well as the children released in the evening on July 16, 1942, of whom there were not many. So it should have been possible for this discreet agent of city hall to give us the extremely effective support described by Monsieur Montgermont. On the other hand, if they did not have such a list at their disposal, they could only have helped those who came to them and asked directly. The latter case is completely different, because it would have taken unshakable optimism to beg for help from a local elected official who everyone said was hand in glove with the Germans and regularly hosted the senior officers of the garrison at his table.[4] Since the mayor certainly did not sort people into those he wanted to help and the others, it must be admitted that he too must have had a few "good Jews," an investment in the future, so to speak. He thus killed two birds with one stone, because at the same time he was practicing Christian charity.

His cooperation with the social services of the UGIF seems quite plausible, however. That organization, which was created on the orders of the Nazis and led by some important people from the Jewish community of France, was responsible in 1943 and 1944 for the arrest and deportation of hundreds of children entrusted to it by gullible people. It seems that Monsieur Montgermont was one of the gullible ones; even if he was unaware of the exact role of the UGIF, he knew it was an institution created under French law by the Vichy government and controlled by the Commissariat-General for Jewish Affairs. As for the specific cases he described, apart from the fact that they are relatively anonymous, there is no reason to deny what he says. Once again, a "good Jew" might prove useful in the future. You never knew how things could turn out in a war! I myself was saved in July 1944 by an associate of the Gestapo[5] who was not a particular friend of persecuted Jews.

It is clear that Vincennes city hall, showing little originality, behaved as most municipalities did in this period. It does seem, however, that Monsieur Bonvoisin went to the Vél d'Hiv on July 16, 1942, to have one of his citizens released. I never heard the name of that fortunate person, and after Liberation, the former mayor—he was quickly put on the sidelines—

---

3. Although I have no memory of this, my elder sister tells me that after our parents' arrest and deportation, we did receive help from Vincennes city hall, several times. The amounts were always insignificant.
4. Rumors circulated about the mayor's role in relation to the local German authorities. It was said that some Communist militants had been handed over to the Gestapo.
5. I described these events in *Quand j'étais juif.* In general, it is only after the danger is over that one realizes one has been the "good Jew" for someone who probably has a lot to answer for.

never boasted of this great achievement, which probably owed a lot to the imagination of one of his most ardent supporters.

In reality, Vincennes—like all municipalities—could do nothing in this situation without contravening the law, but had it done so, there would be evidence to that effect. The fact remains that if one digs a little, one can find in every city hall some good deed done by the mayor or one of his assistants. A person could be a collaborator by conviction or by opportunism without being anti-Semitic, and could witness the persecution with indifference while not agreeing with the racial laws. There is no known example of a mayor being removed from office by Vichy for helping abandoned Jewish children—and by helping, I mean something completely different from the pittance from the city hall's secret fund that salved the giver's conscience without compromising him. There is no known example of a mayor being removed from office for opposing the roundup while the police were preparing to carry out the orders from the prefecture.

In my case, I can say that during the two years following my parents' arrest—from July 16, 1942, to Liberation—I never received a visit from a local social worker wanting to relieve our misery nor was I ever summoned to meet with one. And the few francs we may have been given won't change my view today. People say you have to remember how difficult the situation was in those times. I know, it was more than difficult, it was dire, but it was worst for those who were being persecuted. Those who were afraid of losing their revenue, or simply their peace of mind, wanted to forget the difficulties caused by the occupation and continue to manage the city while "remaining neutral." These good folks figured that when the inevitable day of reckoning came, nobody could blame the local elected officials, who had done their duty as best they could in delicate circumstances. They had to survive in order to be of service, because we all know that mayors and councillors are there to serve the local people's interests. Some of those mayors did not understand that with liberation, their citizens could hold them to account or even remove them.

Just as I had visited the captain of the police, I felt it was important to meet with the mayor of Vincennes. Perhaps, beyond the archives—which were necessarily mute on certain subjects—there was information he had personally received on events in his city under the occupation. His office gave me an appointment with no problems, and I felt that augured well for my research.

I met with the mayor in 1985. He was a long-time resident of Vincennes and had even been a teacher in the schools I had attended. Give or take a few years and I could have been his student. His reception was warm and without formalities, and he invited me into the office with a sweeping gesture. This was a man who had attended the ENA (École nationale d'administration; national school of administration) before joining the prefecture, and was accustomed to people coming to him with requests or grievances. He must have had a knack for getting rid of those for whom he couldn't or wouldn't do anything—gently, with just a hint of unctuousness in his gestures and his gaze. Like the police captain, he knew nothing about me at the outset other than that I was a former resident of Vincennes and I was doing research on the period of the occupation.

I very quickly gave him more details, reminding him that I knew Vincennes well, having lived there for thirty-five years. I immediately told him the purpose of my visit, and said how disappointed I had been to find nothing significant in the city hall's archives. I said I knew that there was probably nothing in the archives that would have displeased the occupiers, and I therefore needed to try to get eye-witness accounts. Perhaps the mayor of Vincennes could put me in touch with a few well-informed people. The mayor listened in silence to these introductory remarks, as if I were telling him a story that was completely new to him. That led me to question him directly. After asking his age, I inquired about his own memories of the occupation, particularly the roundups of Jews carried out in Vincennes, and more particularly, the roundup of July 16, 1942. I was not asking him to defend himself, because my question was not intended to trap him. However, his first answer was curious, to say the least: "I wasn't in Vincennes at that time." Then, correcting himself, he added, "Oh, no, I left Vincennes in 1943 to avoid compulsory work service in Germany."

For a few minutes, it was no longer the mayor I was interviewing, but the citizen, the young teacher who was working at his first job in the city of his birth. My next question was simple, and it concerned the purpose of my interview: how did you feel about the roundup of July 16, 1942? The answer was as simple as the question: "I never knew there had been a roundup in Vincennes, this is the first I've heard of it." That did not surprise me; it was typical of the memory of the city's residents. The people of Vincennes didn't know anything forty-three years after the events, nor did their mayor. Of course, he had heard that some Jews had been deported, but he knew nothing of the roundup or its size in Vincennes. More than a hundred residents out of some fifty thousand is not insignificant. While he had heard of the Vél d'Hiv roundup, he couldn't place it in time. It was one among many tragedies, one of the numerous events that had marked the four years of German occupation.

The mayor was not sitting behind his desk, but close to me, informally, as if we were having a conversation in a living room in front of a fire. We could even have been drinking tea together, talking about various events, because history is full of unexpected incidents. Our interview was so relaxed at that point that I wouldn't have been surprised to hear him say, "Have another one of these little cakes, they're so delicious." In fact, the mayor didn't have much to tell me, and it was probably just out of politeness that he was listening to me relate a part of his city's past that he had been unaware of. A person can't know everything! I don't think he was feigning ignorance. It was simply that the tragedy I had experienced was not part of his local history as he had learned it since taking office.

What could he have told me? Like the policeman who had been shocked by what I'd recounted, he said, "Look in the archives of the department." Or like a passerby you ask to show you the way and who advises you to inquire at the local bistro or newspaper stand. The city hall would also give me contact information for the president of the association of friends of Vincennes, which it would be interesting to consult. In fact, I was sent on my way gently, smoothly, with a smile, a bit like the nuisance who gets escorted out and told to come back... sometime.

We were already standing, but the door was far from his desk, and we exchanged a few more banalities as we moved toward it. So much had happened in Vincennes during the occupation. "Did you know...?" "Do you remember...?" The polite chatter continued for a few minutes. "Do you remember when the Germans blew up the monument to the dead the day after they arrived in Vincennes?" Yes, I remembered the monument, of course. I still have a photograph taken under the statue of the glorious victorious French soldier of 1918 crushing the German imperial eagle under his boot. The whole family had posed under this symbol of France triumphant a few years before the war. And the mayor added, "You understand, the Germans couldn't tolerate that. The night before, they had asked Monsieur Bonvoisin to cover the monument with a tarp, and it was only after he refused that they decided to dynamite it." I hadn't known of this act of "resistance" by the former mayor. But the fact remains that this difficulty communicating with the conquerors in the first days did not cost him his position as mayor, which he would hold until August 1944, occasionally providing guarantees to the occupiers, and not only as mayor, because Monsieur Bonvoisin was also an industrialist whose good offices were of economic value.

I recalled all this as my interview with the mayor was coming to an end because we didn't have much left to say to each other. As he spoke, the mayor was gently pushing me toward the door. There were probably other visitors waiting their turn. He would surely be just as polite to them, just as attentive to their concerns. "It's been a great pleasure talking to you." We hadn't said much to each other; he had mainly listened to me. He had no information to give me. I found myself standing a bit foolishly at the bottom of the grand staicase of the city hall, below the great hall where one of the mayor's predecessors had performed my marriage in 1954.

A mayor often reflects his city. Like most of his citizens that I had met in the course of my research, it had taken the mayor of Vincennes more than forty years to find out what had happened beneath his windows at the dawn of one summer day.

5

WHAT ABOUT THE CHURCHES?

A S ORGANIZATIONS involved in charitable activities, the churches had to show solidarity with the Jews rounded up on July 16, 1942. How could it have been otherwise? In the Catholic church, although the priests did not commit themselves publicly, some prelates denounced the heinous crime from the pulpit.[1]

There were two parishes in Vincennes, Notre-Dame and Saint-Louis, the latter located in a neighborhood where there were more immigrant Jews than in other parts of the city. Did one of the two priests speak up that day or the following days? Did a priest mention the roundup that the residents of those working-class streets must have been aware of? I had to ask these questions in order for my investigation to be as complete as possible. But it is certain that positions were taken, albeit very quietly. Thus, Mgr Suhard, the very collaborationist cardinal-archbishop of Paris, expressed to Vichy the "profound emotion" he felt at the treatment of mothers and children at the Vél d'Hiv. Was this reaction, which followed the assembly of cardinals and archbishops of the occupied zone, echoed

---

1. At the end of August 1942, Mgr Salièges, the archbishop of Toulouse, joined by Mgr Théas, the bishop of Montauban, had a text read in the churches stating that "the present anti-Semitic measures show contempt for human dignity and are a violation of the most sacred rights of the person and the family." However, until the end of 1941, there were many French prelates who justified the French racial laws against the Jews. I need only cite Mgr Caillot, the bishop of Grenoble, or Mgr Delay, the archbishop of Marseille. Certain high dignitaries went even further. On December 31, 1941, Cardinal Beaudrillart said, "Against the demonic powers, the archangel Gabriel brandishes his avenging sword, shining and invisible. With him march united the civilized Christian peoples who are defending their homeland and their future at the side of the German armies." Cardinals Gerlier, of Lyon, and Salièges, of Toulouse, said nothing when the *Statute on the Jews* was decreed. It is true that in September 1941, the Vatican had informed the Vichy government that it would not take any action against the *Statute on the Jews*, as Léon Bérard, Pétain's ambassador to the Holy See made clear.

in the two churches of Vincennes? When they learned of this statement, did the priests and any of their flock in Vincennes come to the aid of those who might have evaded the roundup, particularly the children? If the average Vincennes resident had forgotten this episode of the Nazi occupation, the Catholic church and its faithful would surely have remembered it, especially if there had been recognized acts of charity to assist those who were most threatened. Was that the case?

Although the highest levels of the Protestant churches tended, like the Catholic church, to suppport Pétain at the beginning of the occupation, they had expressed indignation when Jews in the occupied zone were made to wear the yellow star, and they could not fail to react after the big roundup. The fact remains that their official reaction was also extremely quiet and it was not expressed until August 6, 1942. In a document limited to three copies, signed by the Conseil de la fédération protestante (council of the Protestant federation) of France and addressed to Pétain, Pastor Marc Boegner asked that "entirely different methods be used in the treatment of foreign Jews." Although this demand was somewhat ambiguous, it showed that they would no longer accept the arbitrary measures that increasingly threatened a part of the population. Did the little Protestant temple in Vincennes get wind of Pastor Boegner's document? Did the faithful of the Protestant community have an opportunity to put these discreet words into practice? It is certain that many Protestants became involved—sometimes risking their lives—in saving families in distress and particularly, children who had been abandoned in the turmoil. Was this the case in Vincennes?

There remained the synagogue. The problem here was very different, because rabbis, like other Jews, were at the centre of the storm throughout the occupation. In spite of everything, I felt I had to contact the synagogue on Rue Céline-Robert. I spoke on the telephone with a person who seemed extremely annoyed by my call; he must have been the janitor. But my question about the roundup of July 16, 1942, surprised him. He had not known that the operation had also taken place in Vincennes. In any case, he said there was no trace of it in the archives of that little synagogue, which was attended mainly by Jews from North Africa. I do not want to make any judgments about their ignorance concerning a painful event that had taken place some twenty years before the arrival of Jewish *pieds-noirs*[2] in Vincennes. I simply want to observe that this religious

---

2. The term *pieds-noirs* (literally "black feet") refers to people of European Christian or Jewish ancestry expelled from North Africa at the end of French rule, many of whom had been living there for generations. More specifically, the term is used for those who "returned" to mainland France when Algeria gained independence. [PA]

community did not have the same memories as I did. But I am surprised that my "coreligionists" could deliberately overlook a local tragedy that should concern them most of all. If they really did, then we indeed do not share the same history.[3]

The Protestant pastor, who had only been in Vincennes for a few months, had never heard of the effects of the big roundup in this suburb. He said there was nothing in the archives of the local church about what had happened on July 16, 1942, in the shadow of the Château de Vincennes. The members of this little community whom I reached by telephone at the pastor's suggestion stated that they hadn't heard anything after Boegner's discreet protest in August 1942. Two of them made a point of telling me that they and their families had belonged to a resistance group and had sometimes taken in "illegals" in their homes. They also said they had been of common mind with the Protestants of Chambon-sur-Lignon who had set up a network to protect Jews who were on the run.

There have never been more than a small number of Protestants in Vincennes, and I don't remember hearing much about them as a child. Once in primary school, I had seen one of my schoolmates point at another one, saying, "He's a Protestant!" At that time, most of my fellow students at that secular school were excitedly preparing for their first communion. This meant they had to go to catechism class after school. There were only three or four of us who did not have to do so, including the one I mentioned, who was the first Protestant I ever knew. Later, I would sometimes pass the Protestant church in Vincennes, and I was always surprised at how few people there were and how discreet they were.

I later had many occasions to meet Protestants, who are more concerned with temporal matters than Catholics. During the Algerian War, they provided space for risky semi-clandestine meetings. It seemed natural that Protestants who had been that involved between 1955 and 1962 would also have been active twenty years before, helping immigrant Jewish families in distress. Yet in Vincennes itself, initiatives by Protestants following July 16, 1942, were nonexistent, or so secret that no trace remains of them. Other than the pastor, the three people I had the opportunity to speak with by telephone lived in Vincennes or Fontenay-sous-Bois at that time. None of them—including a former member of the local

---

3. I am all the more surprised because in recent years, Jewish religious institutions have criticized the content of the school history textbooks with regard to the Jews during the Second World War, and Chief Rabbi Sirat has encouraged the publication of a textbook specifically on the subject.

church council—remembered hearing of the effects of the Vél d'Hiv roundup in those communes although they had been hard hit by it. However, in my quest for information among Protestants, I was never met with the coldness, surprise or annoyance I encountered elsewhere. They simply hadn't known. Perhaps they regretted it.

I was apprehensive about contacting the priests of the two Catholic parishes in Vincennes. I felt a certain unease at the idea of talking to those champions of Christian charity. I am quite familiar with the Catholic church's ability to adapt to the most contradictory situations and turn them to its advantage. With its heritage of the Inquisition, the Church for centuries stigmatized the "perfidious Jews," "murderers of Christ." It did not find the first anti-Semitic measures of the fascist Vichy government disgraceful. Of course, after the roundup of July 1942, the Catholic community began to be moved, and it agreed to hide endangered children in its institutions or in people's homes. I knew they had indeed hidden children—in return for fees paid regularly—but very often they were not disinterested, because there was a constant desire to convert those children. There were so many flagrant cases that the Church did not deny the facts. The best-known example was that of the Finaly brothers, who were hidden from 1942 to 1944 by a pious person who, when the war ended, would not return them, and went so far as to send them to Spain so that these souls that had been won over to the true faith would not be able to leave the path that had been decided for them. This matter was all over the newspapers until the early 1950s, and it took years and a vigorous public opinion campaign for the Finaly children to be returned to their family.

It doesn't matter that parents sometimes agreed to what was actually moral blackmail, presented to them in the following terms: the best way to save your children we are hiding is to have them live like the others, therefore to make them Catholic, so that they will go unnoticed. In baptizing these children, who were often eager to believe in miracles and the supernatural, they mortgaged their future.

It seems that most of the children who were hidden in convents were subjected to the same kind of proselytizing. Certainly, all the children I knew after the war who had been given refuge in Catholic institutions had been, if not baptized, at least solicited, and not always gently. The fact remains that this enabled children to be saved, and we shouldn't forget that. As for the attempts to seduce innocent children who are weak and defenseless against the arguments of adults, especially those who are giving them charity, they should be chalked up to the bad habits of a church once accustomed to converting by fire and sword. Under the occupation, persuasion was sufficient, because the times were hard enough and usually the main concern was to save the children.[4]

The Catholic church as such never organized any networks to save children. There were only individual Catholic activists, sometimes battling their hierarchy, such as those with *Témoignage chrétien* ["Christian witnessing"; a newspaper founded by a group belonging to the Resistance], whereas the Catholic church as a whole could have demonstrated the power of that much-vaunted Christian charity. Certain institutions would take in children whose families sought refuge for them in return for hard cash. This paid off doubly for them, because they were also able to win souls, and what could be more satisfying than converting Jews? These were my thoughts as I prepared to meet with the representatives of the Catholic religion in Vincennes.

I arrived a little early for my appointment at Saint-Louis de Vincennes Church. That allowed me to try my chances again at the synagogue, which was located across the street, at 30 Rue Céline-Robert, while the church was at number 23. I pressed the button for the intercom. A few minutes later, without anyone even asking the reason for my visit, a head appeared over the metal grillwork and a pair of eyes scrutinized me. A voice asked, "Are you Jewish?" (Did that mean they wouldn't answer people who were not?) Once again, my reception by the observant Jewish community was negative, confirming the response to my telephone call. But at least I had discovered this synagogue, which had been unknown to me when I lived in Vincennes.

At the time of my appointment, I presented myself at the presbytery of Saint-Louis de Vincennes Church, where, after a few minutes' wait, I was greeted by Father A.—a decent fellow, I'm sure, as they're trained today, able to melt into the crowd in ordinary garb. He had nothing to tell me, however, having exercised his calling in the city for too short a time. He added, "You know, we don't keep any archives." He listened to me without comment and advised me to go to his colleague at Notre-Dame de Vincennes Church, who might have more information. I insisted: "Hadn't they read one of the messages of protest by an anti-establishment prelate from the pulpit?" The same answer again: "We don't have any

---

4. On this subject, see my *N'oublie pas le petit Jésus!* (Paris: Manya, 1994).

archives." We had nothing more to say to each other, and I left after we shook hands—somewhat insistently on his part, it seemed to me.

Unlike his colleague at Saint-Louis, the priest at Notre-Dame seemed to have some knowledge of the history of his parish, although he knew nothing about the dark day I had come to discuss. Actually, he knew of the Vél d'Hiv roundup, but was not aware that its effects had been felt in the communes in the suburbs of Paris, Vincennes among them. Had the faithful of Notre-Dame felt a shock wave that threatened their faith? Were there any traces of charitable acts carried out as a result? Had he heard of any denunciations of anti-Semitic measures like that of Mgr Théas in Montauban? Under the onslaught of my questions, his silence had nothing hostile about it, and I was grateful to him for not putting on the look of commiseration so beloved of charitable priests. There was nothing unctuous in his gaze or his gestures. He was shocked by the information I gave him, and even more by the forgetting of it by both the individuals and the archives of institutions. Our meeting lasted only some ten minutes, but every sentence of our dialogue was meaningful. Almost immediately, he proposed that he consult the old archives in the basement and promised to let me know if anything he discovered could be useful to my investigation. He said that history should not be covered up, that it was a shared heritage we had to make known. He also expressed agreement with me regarding the danger of racial persecution of North Africans, Blacks or Asians without the general population reacting any more than they had to the Vél d'Hiv roundup, and without it leaving any trace in people's memories.

After that meeting, I never got a phone call from the presbytery of Notre-Dame de Vincennes, probably because there was nothing in the church archives that might have shown Vincennes residents in July 1942 as caring people. At least, I had tried everything to convince myself of that possibility, and I am certain that Father Ch. would have been glad to tell me if one of his predecessors and a few of his parishioners had braved the prohibitions to come to the aid of those people Vichy France had made outcasts.

6

A S CHILDREN, we were very lucky in that History was present everywhere in Vincennes: the royal city, Saint Louis rendering judgment under an oak tree, the Château de Vincennes with its inner tower that had housed many famous prisoners. Vincennes was a garrison city, with regiments of dragoons that would parade on Sundays during the warm part of the year. We were proud of Vincennes, with its wooded park designed by Haussmann, its racetrack, its Pershing Stadium, its airfield that was the site of some unforgettable maneuvers, its lakes and the redoubt of Gravelle. There was no place like it, thought the kids, who would be reminded at school that we should take pride in the memory of General Daumesnil, the military governor, a glorious soldier of the Empire who, during the siege of the city in 1814, told the Prussians—or was it the Cossacks?—"I'll surrender Vincennes to you when you give me back my leg!" The things we'd heard about our city! Our teachers talked constantly about it, and we enjoyed listening, because History was right on our doorstep. They also taught us the basics of economics in relation to the city and its château. Later, as a journalist, I would learn that Napoleon III had set up his experimental farm within the walls of the château, and that a chemist there had developed the formula for margarine "for the poorer classes who do not have the means to buy butter."

We were taught all this in primary school, but why didn't they teach us that, in the Middle Ages, the royal city did not yet exist and the first château was built in a place called La Pissote? It's true that was not as glorious. Our teachers told us of Saint Louis and Charles V, who had both lived there, and Louis XIV, who had renovated the château in the style of his time with a beautiful colonnade, of the Musée de la Grande Guerre (Museum of the Great War) and the chapel, which was contemporary with the Sainte-Chapelle on Île de la Cité. They only told us about the wonderful things. Indeed, why tell us about the Kodak factory, which was right nearby, where workers of both sexes toiled, usually in darkness and damp and even with their feet in water? What would be the point, since many of our parents spent most of their time there? It was no pleasure, but there was the satisfaction of having a job. At Kodak, before 1936, merely joining a union, or even being suspected of it, was sufficient for a nasty little low-level manager to send you packing.

It's hard to blame a city for losing its memory, especially when there has been a lot of turnover in the population. Yet Vincennes has remained a small provincial city despite its proximity to the capital. The housing has hardly changed, and the residents of Vincennes's neighborhoods still know each other, which is not the case in new towns or neighborhoods on the periphery of cities.

Although the events of July 16, 1942, in Vincennes were less intense than those in Paris, they were far from ordinary. There are many reasons why they have been forgotten. The population has aged. The young people do not know, and the older ones no longer know. There remains the group that was between the ages of fifteen and twenty-five years old when they witnessed the roundup, who should have had a memory of the event when I carried out my inquiry into (or against) the past. It is also true that the city has changed in spite of everything, and many residents have gone to live elsewhere, while new residents have arrived. That is true for the city as a whole, and for my neighborhood, my street, and even the building we lived in with our parents, as well as for that calm street where we were detained for a whole day that never ended.

What were you doing on July 16, 1942, at five o'clock in the morning? What were you doing at six o'clock, at eight o'clock, at ten o'clock in the morning, or at four o'clock in the afternoon? If a policeman asked questions like these to an adult who was already old, but still in full possession of his or her faculties, it's not certain he would get an answer. I am surely one of the rare Vincennes residents who is able to answer that question in detail. It's true that I would be unable to say what I was doing on

September 22, 1957, to choose a date at random. There should be more answers if the question were formulated as follows: what happened on July 16, 1942? Well, maybe. To whom could I have addressed that question? Certainly, to the policeman who arrested us. I did that. To the current police captain, in order to verify his information on the activities of the Vincennes brigade under the occupation, particularly on that day. To the city hall—the mayor himself never knew anything about that tragedy—to try to find traces of the attitude of the local elected officials or the actions they might have carried out once the roundup started. I could have gone to the elderly people who still lived in the buildings around the courtyard where my childhood was spent. To the people living on the streets nearby. To the neighbors of the little house that would be the antechamber of the death camps for my parents. To any man in the street in the city, at random.

Memories are fleeting, but a dramatic event like the roundup can remain fixed in the minds not only of highly emotional people but also those who watched it without emotion or even, for the most hate-filled, with satisfaction. I should have been able to find witnesses without having to take out a classified ad, which would have trivialized the matter.

While writing the preceding pages, trying to go beyond my memories, which at that time were over forty years old, I accused my city of being cold and indifferent in general. I did not want to hear about the possible warm aspects of it or the indignant reactions of a small number of individuals. In my memory when I began to write, Vincennes had betrayed me. The city where I had already spent twelve years of my childhood when the storm broke over our heads had not cooperated with my parents' executioners, but—much worse in my eyes—had averted its gaze from the actions of those who were supposed to be our common enemies. Yet Vincennes was my city. For a long time, I had thought I was at home there, warm and cozy. The war and the Nazi occupation would make an orphan of me, but they would also exclude me from the city. I was cast out, and for a long time, I believed my city had been complicit in this, and that I could accuse it of failing to help a person in danger. I did not want to look coldly at the situation of those who, not being involved, had remained prudently on the sidelines. The reasons for my distress were indivisible, and I had no desire to accept the apologies or regrets of those who had deliberately ignored my suffering.

My city had taught me everything that my parents had been unable to teach me, not only the language of the country, but the art of being a little Frenchman. For a long time, that is what I had been, relatively ignorant of my difference from others. I was thus tormented by a sense of betrayal. My bond with my city did not allow any breach of the unwritten code guaranteeing that my loyalty would be returned.

After the war, I had a wound in my heart, but not an open wound—not yet, in any case, because at an age when I could have been doing other things, I threw myself into politics the way others take refuge in holy orders, perhaps hoping to find a new family. Forty years later, however, I decided to return to my memories of the city in spite of the necessarily subjective aspect of the process. I knew intuitively that while the past was darkened for me by my recollections, it would inevitably be brighter for other people. I therefore was wary of the answers I would be given to my questions. I would have to stir up the embers of the past and force others to remember.

In turning my back on that street near the Bois de Vincennes and leaving the city that had seen me grow up and become a man, and that had ignored me when I was a desperate adolescent, I had abandoned part of myself. It's been a very long time since I lived there, but Vincennes is a constant presence, as if my steps could take me there blindly, automatically, knowing every street, every house, every path in the park. What was I hoping to find there? I knew instinctively that it isn't good to go back to your past; there's nothing to be found there but regrets. Yet I couldn't resist the urge. I had put it off for years, but the time had come.

There was no question of doing a traditional statistical study, especially since I had chosen to question men and women I knew as well as certain possible witnesses, which would limit the scope of my investigation. It's true this approach ran the risk of presenting a distorted image insofar as the answers I received might reflect nothing more than my own concerns. What I would be told would not be neutral, especially if childhood friends wished to please me, or at least, not to displease me. This fear turned out to be unfounded, because while memory is a distorting mirror, what I encountered was a slippage of memory, or more often a glossing over, as if nothing had happened on July 16, 1942, even if the event was still in their memories without their being able to place it in time. In the case of my former schoolmates, that was perfectly natural: they, like me, were fourteen years old at the time of the roundup, and many of them had left on vacation a few days before. Several said they had only heard about the arrests in October, when it was no longer anything more than one piece of news among many, an old story they didn't talk about at school or in their families, almost a nonevent.

Finally, I did not want to know if the residents of Vincennes at the time were angry, favorable or indifferent with regard to the roundup. What was important to me was to verify what remained of this tragic event in the memories of those who were my neighbors when I suddenly became a lost child.

One thing quickly became clear: the majority of the people I knew had forgotten it. Others were not even aware that on July 16, 1942, before dawn, the French police had taken away some one hundred residents of the commune. This memory loss did not only involve men and women my age—the adolescents of 1942. Their parents expressed the same ignorance. I do not question the good faith of the people I interviewed, but it is obvious that their forgetting confirmed that the police operation had little impact in the city of Vincennes, where the immigrant Jews did not live in concentrated groups. These people were certainly aware—knowing me— that my parents had been arrested and deported, but they had no memory of the roundup. It had happened so quickly that summer morning before the men had even left for work or the mothers had begun their chores, while the children—my schoolmates—were still sound asleep. At that early morning hour, the people of Vincennes could not have suspected the horror that was occurring, in many cases on their very doorsteps.

On my street, there must have been some fifteen people arrested, many of them in the building next to ours, whose tenants told me in 1985 that they hadn't been aware of what happened that night. Other people even said that until I questioned them, they hadn't known that there had been any arrests so near them. What is clear is that they all seemed to live in their own little world, and when they no longer saw any sign of some of their neighbors, they simply forgot about them. There was already such a vaccuum around us: first of all, there were the prisoners who had been absent since the summer of 1940, and then, little by little, some people had left for the southern zone and others had gone away for various reasons. Nobody asked any questions. They had to keep on living while Nazism under the French banner was still triumphant, and their primary concern was to find food, clothes and heat for the winter. The newspapers provided a certain amount of information, but aside from the section of local news, they mainly devoted their pages to stories of great German victories. There was nothing in these papers about the roundup of July 16, 1942. So it is quite possible that some people in Vincennes only learned of it later, even after the end of the war. A person would have had to be particularly inattentive to what was happening to be unaware of it, but I accept that it is not impossible.

In the course of my search for witnesses among the Vincennes residents I had known some forty years earlier, I had a number of surprises. I spent a lot of time studying the Vincennes section of the Val-de-Marne telephone directory, hoping to find familiar names, especially those of my classmates, who had seen me come to school with my yellow star on June 8, 1942. They were witnesses of my last year of school. One name particularly drew my attention: that of a boy who openly expressed collaborationist views, even in school, behaving as his elders must have taught him. He and one of his friends would look for classmates who should have been wearing the yellow star but were not, in contravention of the law. I was not especially happy to see his name in the directory, but I felt it was important to find out how the little Nazi of 1942 had turned out and whether he still remembered me and the events that had no doubt delighted him while plunging me into despair. I called the number and his father answered, informing me that the son had died a "hero" in the climactic losing battle of Dien Bien Phu that ended the Indochina war in 1954. I refrained from telling the old man the reason for my call, and so as not to seem impolite, allowed him go on about the virtues of the young man who had died serving his country. To each his dead! Peace to the ashes of the little fascist who became a soldier, whom I don't need to name here, even if his name does figure on a monument to those who died for France. The only other memory I have of him is that in 1942 he belonged to Jeunes du Maréchal [the marshal's young people; a collaborationist organization for youth], or more likely, a group close to the fascist thugs of Doriot or Déat. In class and during recreation period, he behaved like a member of the master race, arrogant and contemptuous of those he considered his inferiors. He was a little fascist at fifteen, destined to become one of what General Bigeard [a commander at Dien Bien Phu] called his "boys" ten years later. We were all good little Frenchmen, as the expression has it. He must have been a better one than I was, because he gloated while I cried.

I didn't have much to show for my scrutiny of the telephone directory. The research was difficult. There were few witnesses remaining. So I decided to meet with all those who were willing to talk to me about that day, whoever they were. There were not many. And they were not very talkative—a few empty phrases masking embarrassment at this reminder of a rather awkward past. When they were pushed to say more, they came up with evasive replies:

"It wasn't my problem."

"There wasn't much we could do."

"It was every man for himself."

"We didn't realize what would happen."

"We didn't know."

"It's very unfortunate, but we had our own worries and our own children to protect."

Every time the memory of these tragic events was addressed, there was a defensive reaction, a reflex of self-protection against a possible accusation of complicity.[1] It was as if the shame of having passively accepted what happened on July 16, 1942, had to be hidden under other difficulties. As if all that was very sad, but after all, they were foreigners. It's true that the slogan "France first" was being trumpeted from all sides by the nascent Resistance. Collaborationists, active or passive, either closed their eyes to the roundups or applauded them as public hygiene measures. They were ridding France of its Jews. So what? Good riddance. But the majority were simply indifferent, coldly indifferent.

I am not going to set myself up as judge, and even less as prosecutor; I merely had the "privilege" of being a first-hand witness. And I have a terrible observation to make: deep France had other things to do than worry about its Jews. "France first"—which bore a strange resemblance to the slogan of the ultra-conservative writer Charles Maurras, "France, France alone"—could concern only French nationals; the Resistance would not begin to worry about the repression of the Jews until well after the roundup of July 16, 1942. "We couldn't know" was the usual leitmotif, but such operations had been increasing since the summer of 1940.

One has to look closely at the stages of the conditioning that worked effectively to put people to sleep. Deep France had accepted everything—how could it do otherwise?—without any moral problem. It is important to point some things out again, even at the risk of repetition. It all started in August 1940 with a review of naturalizations acquired since 1936. Later, there was a proposal to revoke the citizenship of those who had been naturalized after fighting under the French flag in the First World War.

---

1. Taking part in a radio program on the France Culture network on the subject of concentration camps in France on May 10, 1985, I was surprised to hear residents of Drancy who lived on the site of the former camp explain, "We were not there at that time, so, you know, we don't have much to say."

Then the *Statute on the Jews* was decreed in the southern zone by Pétain on October 3, 1940, immediately followed by the requirement for Jews to register. Arrests quickly followed. From the beginning of 1941, some forty thousand foreign Jews were interned in the southern zone, the so-called free zone. In the occupied zone, the arrest of four thousand Polish Jews in Paris on May 14, 1941, was only a prelude to the August roundup of nearly four thousand more in the 11th district, which was in a state of siege by the French police. These actions should have served as clear warnings of the intentions of the Nazis and their helpers, the French cops. But even the most clear-sighted did not see them as signs of the New Order. After the big roundup, networks were organized for people to escape to the southern zone, and a bit of money and a few places of refuge were found for the survivors, but the harm was done. Passivity combined with indifference had helped to realize the aims of Hitler's followers in France. Although the uniforms were French, the process was the same, and our guardians of law and order carried out the arrests of foreign Jews in 1942 and of Algerians in 1961 with the same enthusiasm. They were often the same men, with the same respect for orders and the same hatred of immigrants. As I have tried to show elsewhere,[2] even when the Resistance dealt with the problem of protecting persecuted Jews, it asked the immigrants themselves to see to the logistics, as if to say, "Save yourselves, we're behind you all the way!"

Among the Vincennes residents I met with, there were some who had suffered persecution but whom I never considered actual informants. Their memories, like mine, were too selective, and putting their accounts on par with mine would only further distort my research. We were a minority, and we could not be representative of the collective memory. On the other hand, there was no question of ignoring any person's memories, and I was able to gather some amazing information. One example is the story of an elderly spinster, the daughter of Russian Jewish immigrants who had come to France before the First World War. Her parents had registered as Jews in October 1940 without including their two children. So in June 1942, the father and mother wore the yellow star while the children did not. On July 16, 1942, the police came to pick up the parents (they found only the mother) and didn't bother with the children, who were not on their list. It is hard to know if this was a unique or unusual situation. It is also interesting to observe how distorted memories can be, because this

<hr />

2. *L'An prochain, la révolution* (Paris: Mazarine, 1985).

same person told me that her family had known that a roundup was imminent because "it was announced on the radio the night before." How could
I upset that charming lady by contradicting her? How could I explain to
her that even the radio in London had only announced the event a few
days later? To each his or her memories, to each his or her truth. Am I
myself certain that I am not distorting this past whose traces we must
leave for future generations?

Aside from a small community of religious Jews that my parents did
not associate with or even know, the Jews in Vincennes were relatively
dispersed, with no contact among them. This is why, on that day when we
were detained in the little house on Rue Louis-Besquel, we were total
strangers to each other. If my memory is correct, I did not see a man or
boy wearing a skullcap there. I do not recall any men forming a group to
pray or anyone taking a prayer book out of his pocket and chanting by
himself. We were as much strangers to each other as we were to the
French—apart from their contempt for us. Without being absolutely certain, I have the impression that the people assembled in that little house
were poor or at least of modest means. There were certainly bourgeois
Jews in Vincennes, well-off families. But they were not there among us.
This is merely an observation, and as I have already said, those who had
the money had every reason to get out while there was still time.

Although I did not discover the collective memory of Vincennes
residents, I did not become discouraged. I had expected this concealment
of the unpleasant event. I would have to go back and investigate the
details, particularly Rue Louis-Besquel, where we had spent the day of
July 16, 1942, in detention until the Paris buses came to load their cargo
to go to Drancy or, for families with children, to the the Vél d'Hiv. It was
a very quiet street, with plain, unembellished brick buildings on one side,
except at the end of the street nearer to the park, where there were a few
affluent buildings dating from the beginning of the century. On the other
side, there were detached houses and taller buildings. I wanted to focus
on the buildings across from the house where we had been detained. I
went to number 4, directly opposite, whose residents had spent all day at
their windows on July 16. There must still be someone there from that
time, tenant or owner, whose memory was not failing. Despite that fact
that the front door had a lock requiring a code, I hoped I would be able to
get in. I waited like a door-to-door salesman, a beggar or a petty thief,
determined to enter. I was in luck; in a few minutes, I was able to walk in
after a tenant, who obligingly held the door for me. In the vestibule, I

found myself facing an elderly man who was about to leave. Perhaps he would be the one, the first of the witnesses who would allow me to reconstruct that terrible day as seen from the exterior. When I was explaining my purpose, the man immediately stopped me, saying, "First of all, I didn't live here at that time," and adding, "Ah, the Jews, it was their affair. It didn't concern the French. Don't ask me anything about it. If you want to know more, go to the synagogue on Rue Céline-Robert." The thing that struck me most in the two or three sentences from this very average Frenchman was that to him Jews were clearly foreigners, certainly not French.

At number 6, the door was opened by a janitor. He greeted me equally coldly, but without any comment on the purpose of my visit. No, he didn't know the people in the building, he had only been there a short time. He said few of the old tenants still lived there, especially since the apartments had been put up for sale around 1960. Most of the tenants had been workers at the Kodak factory nearby, and they hadn't had the means to buy and had left. "There may be a former tenant at number 8," he told me. I asked what floor the tenant lived on and what his name was. "I can't tell you." Not very promising, especially since I was stopped by a lock with a code at number 8. The same was true all the way to the end of the street.

Forgetting, indifference, doors guarded even in daytime by those codes that foil a person trying to retrieve the traces of his past—with all these obstacles, how could I not get discouraged? I decided to try the other side of the street. At number 1, the janitor told me there were two couples who had already been living there in 1940. I knocked on their doors and went back several times, but they never opened the door at either apartment. I found the telephone number of one of the couples in the directory and called, but I was met with the same refusal, that cement wall barring access to the past: "I don't have time to answer you, I have other things to worry about." I couldn't insist. One last chance presented itself in the same building; the janitor suggested that I knock on a journalist's door on the ground floor. Perhaps she would know people in the area. It was a good idea, because she indeed knew some people who had lived on the street during the war and had moved two streets away. This was a new trail I would have to explore.

I paced up and down Rue Louis-Besquel as if I were discovering it for the first time, although it was familiar to me. I again passed the little house that had held a good hundred people crammed into two rooms for the ten or eleven hours of our detention. I had seen it often after the war, but had never stopped there. I had even pointed it out to my wife or my children when we still lived in Vincennes. Years had gone by, and although I didn't try to forget the past, I also didn't want to be trapped in it. Little by little, I even tried to stop giving any special notice to this small house, which was not properly maintained and seemed uninhabited. I did not want to place too much importance on it. There was no point shedding tears in front of every house filled with old memories or wringing my hands at the sight of every old stone wall. Memories should be happy or moving, and going back to the places of your childhood should not give rise to melancholy and despair. I was especially fond of Rue Louis-Besquel for its peace and quiet, and I remembered endless races on roller skates in the evenings after I'd done my homework. You could play ball or marbles there without being bothered by cars. There was even a courtyard behind a garage where we'd have snowball fights in winter.

I had been away from Vincennes for twenty years, other than when I happened to pass through it, before I decided to confront Rue Louis-Besquel to continue the research that had thus far been essentially unsuccessful. As I have said, Vincennes residents in general could have been unaware of the roundup of July 16, 1942, because it was dawn when we were kidnapped. But that was not the case for the people who lived on Rue Louis-Besquel. Many of them had spent the whole day at their windows, watching, and many had remained crowded in the street like onlookers to an assault or an accident who don't lift a finger to help the victims. Of course, I am not accusing these eyewitnesses of refusing to help people in danger. But just as serious, most of them were cold and uncaring.

After several vain attempts, because only the cleaner was there, I finally found someone who opened the door to the little house for me. It was a young boy, who was a bit nervous with this stranger. Then his older brother, who was about sixteen, came to the door, and I told him in a few words the reason for my presence there. The sight of my journalist's ID reassured him, and he agreed to let me in. I climbed the few steps in front, from which I could already glimpse the two rooms that had been our prison. One look convinced me that it was the place where I had been forty-three years earlier. The older boy went over to the telephone, and I realized that he had been talking to his mother when I rang the bell. He mentioned me in their conversation, and after a few moments, he handed me the phone; his mother wanted to talk to me, perhaps to make sure I was not some hoodlum who was using this ploy to get into the house. I told my story again, with some details, even asking if the lady herself

240

knew what had happened in her house many years ago. From where I was sitting, I could see the other room, the one that had been the antechamber of death for my parents. The woman asked me some questions, showing genuine interest and warmth, and I sensed her stupefaction.

These walls, these doors, these stairs seemed not to have changed over all those years. Was it the conversation with this woman who seemed so gentle, the children looking at me, the living room with its bookshelves, the family atmosphere that was apparent in every detail, in this house where my parents' journey to the extermination camps had begun? It all became unbearable, and I suddenly lost control of myself, sobbing, hiccuping, unable to excuse myself to the woman at the other end of the line, who must have been very uncomfortable.

You don't take on the past with impunity. It is not possible to intervene coldly in a history most of whose witnesses have disappeared. How can a person be comfortably ensconced in the present and forget those whose long road to horror began in this place?

The weather outside was lovely. The passersby turned around to look at me, like the old ladies who were surely watching from behind their curtains. It was a bit like the country here, and the trees at the edge of the Bois de Vincennes some hundred and fifty yards away contributed to the feeling of tranquility you don't find in the city anymore. Who could this man be who was prowling the street? I kept questioning passersby, coming up against closed doors or slipping into buildings just before the doors could shut. Nobody recognized me as someone who had spent thirty-five years living in this part of Vincennes. How many residents of Rue Louis-Besquel could there still be who, without knowing me, had witnessed that extraordinary gathering of terrified people crammed into a house built for a single family?

Through a few encounters on that street, I was given some names, which allowed me to get further in my quest for the past, using the directory and then the telephone. There was no longer any question of stopping my investigation, no matter what the results. The first interesting reponse, finally, came from the husband of a woman—aged twenty in 1942—who had lived on Rue Louis-Besquel; it gave me some valuable information. I had met the man on a street nearby. The next day, on the telephone, he told me he had spoken to his wife about the event, which she had not forgotten although she wasn't able to place it in time. She had witnessed part of the operation. Leaving for work at seven in the morning, she had seen families being brought to the street by policemen, and police

241

cars filled with women, children and old people. Although she had to hurry to get to work on time, she was curious about what she saw. When she came back home in the evening, her mother, crying, had given her the details. What she had found the hardest to accept was the sight of all the children surrounded by police as if they were criminals.

I sensed genuine emotion in the man, who had not known about this event although he remembered the Vél d'Hiv roundup. His wife hadn't thought about the drama she had glimpsed from a distance for a long time, and my questions had upset her. Before hanging up, he gave me an unexpected piece of information: he had found out that I had the wrong house. It was not number 3b on Rue Louis-Besquel, as I had thought, but number 5. Did this really matter? To me, it certainly did. How had I made such a mistake, knowing the area, and especially that little house, so well? The reason was simple: the two houses had once been perfectly identical, but the one I was interested in had been extended and renovated, as had the railing around the little garden bordering the street. My attention had been drawn to the house that still looked as it had when I first saw it. Before hanging up, I asked my informant to tell his wife that she was the first person I'd found in the neighborhood who remembered that terrible day and that I was truly grateful. A few days later, I went back to Vincennes. The owner of 5 Rue Louis-Besquel was willing to talk to me for a few minutes across the railing, but he did not invite me inside that house where I had parted from my parents forever. The man seemed ill-at-ease, and by way of a goodbye, he said, "During the war, I got involved— for all the good it did!"

I was moved by this. So not everybody was indifferent. Even if this case turned out to be the only one, it allowed me to view my contemporaries a little less harshly, and at least to soften the judgment I had made of the Vincennes residents who had concealed their embarrassing past. One last detail: the same lady who recalled the events on the street also remembered the name of the people who had lived in the little house that had been requisitioned for officers' quarters at the beginning of the occupation. This information made my investigation more demanding, because I had to research the members of the family who had survived the war, but all trace of them had been lost. Their daughter had lived on Rue Louis-Besquel for a few years and then moved elsewhere.

I also visited the apartment where I lived with my parents until July 16, 1942. Although I had continued to live there until 1965, I wanted to see it one last time. I knocked, and the door was opened a crack by a faceless person who at least was able to speak, but who didn't have time to talk to me and in any case was not interested in doing so. Always the same refrain: "I'm not interested!" There are a thousand ways to refuse to answer, but "I'm not interested!" is a really horrible one. Those four words express the same attitude the people of this country could adopt if there was a roundup of North Africans, Turks or Malians tomorrow. As with famine in the third world, they are not interested! Three million unemployed: "I'm not interested!" War in the Middle East: "I'm not interested!" Afghanistan: "I'm not interested!" There are millions of people in peril amid general indifference, so why should anyone be interested in something that happened decades ago?

Almost nothing had changed about Rue Louis-Besquel apart from the trees planted a few years earlier and the parked cars lining the sidewalks. Aside from a few new houses, it seemed as if the place had withdrawn from the world and fallen asleep. There must have been some three hundred dwellings on this street, and perhaps five hundred people living in them, but those who remembered what happened here one day in July 1942 were rare. Of course, there were not very many people left from that time. But the oldest ones no longer knew—or maybe they didn't want to know—and the young ones were never told. I continued to come up against the locked doors of buildings that were defended like fortresses, and the closed faces of people who could have remembered. What was this survivor doing there?

For a day, there had been a miniature concentration camp there. All that had been forgotten. Not a trace left. Not a nightmare. And forty-three years later, an intruder had disturbed the peace and quiet, stirring up that past nobody was interested in anymore. Yes, that old fool at number 4 Rue Louis-Besquel had been right: "It was the Jews' affair. It didn't concern us!" Behind this incredible statement, there was without doubt an even harsher thought, more disdainful, perhaps more full of hate: the French had nothing to reproach themselves for, in what was only a settling of accounts between the Germans and the Jews. Does anyone still remember, so many years later, the nomads chased from a vacant lot where they were living, where they were tolerated until being asked to go live elsewhere? The Jews had come from elsewhere. So it hardly mattered where the Germans sent them. You say they were massacred? Well, others say that isn't so. In Vincennes, we don't have this kind of conflict. Besides, the mayor is a friend of the Jews. You know, it's thanks to him that a

Jewish school was set up last year right nearby on Rue Anatole-France.

Of course, there were also other reactions. Ah, yes, those Jews were very unfortunate and the Germans put them through hell, but do you think there were any in Vincennes, in this neighborhood? Are you sure?

Apart from the Vincennes residents who didn't know, those who didn't remember, those who didn't want to know and those who weren't interested, I found a few witnesses whose memories would have satisfied me completely if it weren't for the fact that they totally contradicted my own. It's true that my account is not neutral, that it is far from impartial. I only saw one side of the situation, and it's hard for me to refute certain statements. The fact remains that logic can only correct some exaggerations, no matter how pure and uncalculated one's intentions are. So I met with some friends from my adolescence, hoping to reconstruct this page of our city's history from their point of view. Yes, they had witnessed that base act of aggression. Yes, they had come to the aid of the poor defenseless victims. How? It was very simple. *People* had alerted the neighbors who might be in danger. Throughout that day, *people* had gone to the house on Rue Louis-Besquel to comfort the detainees and give them food and drink. It seems—although I have no recollection of this—that someone did indeed bring clothing to those who had been taken there without any baggage because the police who arrested them had been in such a rush. *People* supposedly gave us food and drink. *People* had even gone to the exit of the metro to warn the father of a family that had been picked up, who was coming home from work, not to go to his house because the police were waiting for him there. This story, which was the only one of its kind, might have been plausible, because it was told to me by a friend. But unless I am mistaken, the onslaught of generosity reconstructed after the fact cannot be believed in its entirety. First of all, the door and the windows of our prison were sealed closed and none of us were able to communicate with the outside. The police kept close watch to prevent any contact. People warned the neighbors? That was possible. But at five in the morning, few people in the neighborhood knew what was going on. As for the story about the father, it is totally unbelievable. Jews had to wear the yellow star and they were under a curfew from 8 p.m. to 6 a.m., which meant that they were not permitted to work at night. A person who had not registered as a Jew, and thus did not wear the "special badge," would not be on the list of people to be arrested, nor would that person's family. There are so many inconsistencies in this attempt to present

France as having resisted the occupation as early as 1942. It is far from the truth. Still worse, simple solidarity was very rare, let alone direct opposition to the occupier. It's true that some witnesses spoke of women crying in the street, and even after all these years, that gives me great comfort.

For some people—very few—the attempt to reconstruct history involves, perhaps unconsciously, the escape from a responsibility that cannot be attributed to a single individual, and retrospective remorse for having allowed these things to happen, while the idealized image of France portrays the country as standing up in resistance to Nazism. At best, we were still in the time of "sorrow and pity." It was only when the effects of the roundup of July 16, 1942, were made known by the MNCR [Mouvement national contre le racisme; national movement against racism]—which was formed by immigrant Jewish Communists—that new organizations were created that worked with Dr. Eugène Minkowski's OSE [Oeuvre de Secours aux Enfants; Children's Aid Society] and a few private initiatives to save Jewish children.

Although it took a lot out of me, I went back to Vincennes several times. I finally succeeded in meeting with a few people who had been in the neighborhood on July 16, 1942. These witnesses had not forgotten, and even better, they did not try to avoid talking to me about that day, which seemed to have marked them. Among them was a lady in her eighties whose testimony touched me deeply, although it was brief: "On July 16, 1942, I saw the arrival of the first people arrested, because I lived on the corner of Rue Louis-Besquel and Rue du Donjon. I clearly remember Monsieur and Madame Treish's house, where the police brought them. There were some men, but mainly women and children. That I remember with certainty. I also saw them boarding the buses a little later. I had thought it was in 1943."

I was eager to meet with my childhood friend Yves. We had so many shared memories of that time, and I thought he would associate July 16, 1942, with those particular events. In 1943, there was more solidarity, although it was still too rare. Yves' parents could not tolerate the persecution we were experiencing. They invited my sister and me to spend the month of July 1943 with their family. We went to the department of Aube, without our yellow stars, of course, because travel outside the Seine department was prohibited for us. His parents were running a considerable risk, but they accepted it. Would that have been the case in 1942? It is impossible to know. The fact remains that this act of solidarity never had the slightest aura of charity. A year later, when the Allied landing allowed us to glimpse the end of the nightmare, the threat suddenly became greater, and at the end of June 1944, I was once again welcomed by this family, before leaving for a safer place in a village in the Vexin region. All that was still very present in my memory, and I thought Yves—who was a little older than I—would have the same memories since he knew my story. He was a little embarrassed when he had to admit he had forgotten the actual roundup that had led to his parents taking me in.

A lady who lived in the building next to ours had witnessed the roundup. She and her husband were themselves Jewish, but they were both naturalized French citizens, so they were not on the list of people to be arrested that day. "On July 16 at sunrise, we heard some noise that attracted our attention. On the third floor, on our landing, there was someone knocking on a door, and then shouts of people arguing and refusing to be taken away. At times, there was screaming that reached all the way to the stairs. Then, looking out the window, we saw them pass by, with other people who had children with them. It was about five in the morning. That was when I realized it must be a roundup. A little later, we saw police cars. There were heartbreaking scenes in the street.

"It's all still very vivid in my memory. A little later, there were people bustling around and running over to Rue Louis-Besquel with packages of clothing. During the day, I went over to that street, where we had heard the people who were arrested had been taken. I was wearing the star on my clothes, but you couldn't see it because I put on a scarf to hide it and I was carrying my little girl in my arms. I wanted to see what was really happening. I saw the house packed with all the people who were detained, but I didn't imagine what was in store for them.

"Of course, there were crowds in the street in front of the house, but I had the impression they were hardly more concerned than the usual curious onlookers who congregate whenever something out of the ordinary attracts their attention. It's true that in 1942 nobody was aware of the danger facing the Jews. Maybe if people had known what was going to happen in the concentration camps, their attitude would have been different. The things people in the street were saying were along the lines of 'Those poor people,' and 'What are they going to do with them?' Some people were saying they were going to put them in a work camp.

"What struck me most, finally, was the old couple who lived on our landing and had tried to refuse to go with the police. They were intellectuals who lived only for their books. I can still hear their shouting. They had to drag them down the stairs. Until the roundup, I hadn't known they

246

were Jewish. I knew very few Jews in the neighborhood. It was only after June 1942, when we were forced to wear the badges, that we recognized each other as Jews. That was when I learned that your parents were Jewish.

"The night of the roundup, I left my apartment, and I didn't go back until the end of the war, except occasionally to pick up a thing or two. I left with my daughter, because I couldn't live in that atmosphere anymore. And the next day it could have been our turn. The few times I went back, I was terrified. I was still sick over the spectacle we had witnessed.

"How naive we were. We could never have imagined what was going to happen. On the eve of the roundup, a policeman had warned some friends where my husband was spending the night for safety. So I can say that there was at least one policeman in Vincennes who warned people.

"I have another memory, from farther back; when we went to the police station to have our identity cards stamped with the word *Jew*, the policeman who did it looked at us as if to say 'How foolish you are, children.' We were very young then. We had registered as Jews in October 1940, so we had already fallen into their trap."

In the same building, I was delighted to find a childhood friend I had been out of touch with since the war. He almost had tears in his eyes when I told him about the book I had decided to write. He still remembered everything, unlike other primary school classmates I had approached. "These events are part of the distant past, but they had an impact on me. I don't really remember your parents leaving, except for our talking about them after that roundup. If we didn't know anything that night, I remember perfectly that during the day, we went down to the street while the arrests were still going on. I think I even saw that cop you told me about, who I knew from seeing him in the neighborhood. I later saw him in civilian clothes.

"What stayed in my memory of that day is when some friends from Rue des Vignerons, the Rozenblatts, who had two sons, one our age[3] and another about ten, were arrested. I think I recall that some people wanted to take the younger one with them. It was all pretty confused, but I haven't forgotten it. I also remember all the people brought to Rue Louis-Besquel. During the day, I went there several times. Frankly, I had a lot of questions; I was fifteen, and I wondered what would happen to them. They said the buses were going to Drancy, but when I think about it, we never imagined that they would be taken from there to some unknown destination.

---

3. That was Bouboule, whom I wrote about above.

"I knew they had been picked up because they were Jewish, and I sensed an uneasiness in the people around me. My parents were kind of embarrassed and were wondering what they could do. Of course, they wanted to help, but how? I don't think there was any contact between the families who were detained and those in the streets, who were just watching. After that, I don't really know what happened. What I remember is mainly the Rozenblatt family with the young boy. Someone wanted to take him with them, and I have the impression that would have been possible. It was all happening right in front of my house, on Rue de la Villa, where a number of people had been brought before being taken to the house on Rue Louis-Besquel. It must have been eight or nine in the morning.

"Almost immediately, the question arose of what would happen to them. I'm sure you remember our friend Friedmann. Until the spring of 1944, he continued attending school, and then some friends undertook to find a refuge for him. It was around the time of the [Allied] landing. After Liberation, I saw him again, and then he managed to leave for the United States with a scholarship and studied medicine.

"I have another very clear memory. There were two brothers at school in 1939, German Jewish refugees, who told us about the camps that already existed in Germany. We didn't pay attention, because none of us could imagine that concentration camps could really exist. After Liberation, when the Americans went into Germany, we started to hear about the camps that were liberated. To be honest, I could hardly imagine such horrors. I'll always remember an exhibition at the Grand Palais in May or June 1945, where they showed a film, a real horror movie. It was very hot that day, and I fainted. It was unbelievable. I always knew war was awful, but that was something different. I hadn't thought it was possible, on a human level, to be so base. I had wanted to see it, to try to understand; I found it hard to believe what had happened.

"I wondered if the French realized things like that could happen. Had the collaborators envisioned such violent acts? It's a problem I wonder about. In 1950, I took a trip in Germany with my younger brother. We went down the Rhine Valley and near Munich, because we were going to Austria. Since our route took us near Dachau, we went to see the camp, and I was really upset: there were all those barracks still practically intact, where so many people had suffered. The smell of death was everywhere. And that wasn't the worst place.

"All that is to say these effects of racism marked me deeply as a Frenchman. Now, whatever happens, I don't think I could allow these things to occur again. I have some Morroccan friends, and I'm embarrassed to see the problems people from North Africa have here. I went to Morrocco recently, and what I'd really like now would be to go to Israel. I want to understand the reasons for so many hatreds. We're living in a strange time in France, and people seem to have forgotten a lot of things. It's not that we should cry over the past, but it's essential that we not forget it.

"Today when I think back to that tragic time, I wonder if there could have been more human caring. Maybe we could have reacted more quickly, tried to do something instead of just standing by passively. We could have tried to hide the children if we couldn't save the parents. Of course, most people were indifferent, but you have to look at things in context and remember that there was already a form of racism, a rejection of foreigners. That's why I'm afraid that today, again, French people in general are so focused on getting by from day to day that they don't realize what could happen."

This discussion with my childhood friend Jean d'Yturbide comforted me and in a sense reconciled me with my city. Leaving him, I once again crossed that courtyard where there were still traces of the kid I had been. The painful past receded, but when I got to the street, I found myself in front of some billboards for an upcoming special election in Vincennes. Among the candidates was one supported by Jean-Marie Le Pen, who was campaigning in favor of a harsher policy on immigration. The past immediately came back to me.

PART THREE

Survivor of the Absurd

1

MEMORIES, A USER'S GUIDE

J ULY 16, 1942, and its never-ending anniversaries. At the beginning, we counted the weeks and the months in the unlikely event that our loved ones would return. After a year had passed, there was nothing left to hope for. All that remained was the memory, which our contemporaries no longer even shared. In 1945 and the years immediately after, what did they count for, those thirteen thousand foreign Jews who were arrested in Paris and its suburbs on July 16 and 17, 1942, and then deported? There were the "seventy-five thousand shot" among Communists, according to the claim by the Communist Party, and the twenty million dead of the "glorious Soviet Union." Above all, there was the victory of the democracies over fascism, which was supposed to assuage our pain.

Then came the celebration of the fifth, the tenth, the twentieth and the fortieth anniversaries. And then the seventieth, when I am rereading these words. Even if they had come back, they would be long dead now. Hence the attitude of resignation of those who carry the banners at the commemorative ceremonies. Yet, each year that passes since my parents' deportation and my own arrest, I get upset at the fact that another form of racism has become established in France in recent years. The baseness of the past has now given way to a present that is equally worrying. There has not really been any anti-Semitism in this country for a long time. Deep France is no longer racist. No, it just doesn't like dark-skinned people in general and Arabs in particular.

When I was a child, my parents were known as foreigners, and I was called a "dirty Polack" and accused of taking the bread from the mouths of French people. All that has changed, and Portuguese kids, for example, are not treated quite as badly. Only Arabs are targeted by the good French people. The fact that millions of young Frenchmen were sent to Algeria to "beat up on Arab rats" between 1955 and 1962 was not without consequences in France.

When I was in the line of fire on July 16, 1942, I have to say at the risk of offending some people that I did not encounter the generous France that is extolled in so many glorious stories and legends. While the average French citizen did not approve of the persecution, it was seen as a settling of accounts between Germans and Jews, and something that didn't concern French people. It may seem spiteful, but I have neither forgiven nor forgotten the actions of the French police that made me an orphan for the rest of my days. I know that those police forces that were accomplices of the Nazi criminals were ready and willing to serve the forces of oppression, as they have been throughout their contemporary history. The men of law and order never miss an opportunity to become a criminal army. They don't just carry out their initial mission; they quickly turn into legalized murderers. This is what we saw during the entire period of the occupation.

What happened on July 16, 1942, was only one episode, and you cannot blame the police for the thirteen thousand arrests that fueled the crematoria of Auschwitz without also holding them responsible for other misdeeds in their long history of persecution. Every anniversary of my parents' arrest brings these thoughts, and I think my father would be happy to see that I have not retreated into the parochialism that makes people deaf and blind to the suffering of others.

I think I never really grew up. On July 16, 1942, I didn't understand that my life had, if not stopped, at least become somewhat petrified. It was only much later, looking into the mirror, that I had to admit the obvious: time had stood still for me while my life passed. The child of war remained an adolescent, even when appearences conspired against him and he found himself having to live a man's life. Despite my salt-and-pepper hair, my face has remained youthful enough, and it appears that my smile is still just as mischievous. I haven't aged, and my mother is still forty-two, the age she was in 1942. She would no longer age, which certainly kept me from changing. I never became the mature man who would have made her proud in her old age. The perennial adolescent puts on an act as an adult, but his bluff only fools others. Or so I believe.

Since my mother's tragic death, I have lived much more than the forty-two years of her lifetime. I couldn't reconcile myself to that when, still haunted by memories of my childhood, I didn't feel old—yet. Whenever I hear a familiar feminine footstep in the corridor, I still always expect to see her. For all these years, I have had a recurring dream of a single person on a desolate plain in a country ravaged by war. It's my mother, wandering in the deserted countryside with no concept of time, going from village to village in search of her children. She is endlessly calling her Moishele—my Yiddish childhood name, derived from Moishe, which means Moses. My mother liked to call me by all those diminutives people would give their children—Bubbele (little father), Ketzele (little cat), Golem, Tim-Tam (untranslatable) and other affectionate nicknames—but when she was angry, which was rare, she would let herself go and call me Merder (murderer) and Lobous (rascal), and her harshest comments were usually made in Polish rather than Yiddish. There was nothing extreme about her language, because the words were used with tenderness.

On Sunday mornings, when my mother didn't work, I would crawl into bed between her and my father, and hug and kiss and tickle her. I would find my way back to the breasts that had once fed me. I would only leave her alone when she finally got annoyed and pushed me away. I loved to breathe in the smell of her hair, of her underarms. I would study her gentle face, the long eyelashes and the cheeks that had never known makeup. She would respond to my ardor by speaking Polish, often repeating a word I didn't understand and that my father found especially funny: *kobietach.* A lot later, I learned the meaning of this mysterious word. In Polish, *kobieta* meant woman, and the adjective could mean "lover of women" or even "skirt-chaser" or "fondler." Since I was only about ten, it was funny.

July 16, 1942, was a complete breakdown, a plunge into emptiness. The little apartment in Vincennes was like a desert. The two-rooms-with-kitchen had been small for the four of us, but there was no television, radio, refrigerator or washing machine, and not even a vaccuum cleaner— just a space in which to talk, listen or say nothing and look at each other. Every word, every silence, had a meaning. There were no barriers between the Polish parents and their French children. Perhaps we lived in a world apart, ignoring our neighbors, who in turn ignored us. After nearly twenty years in an environment that was relatively hostile, my parents had apparently adapted to the new situation resulting from the war and then the Nazi occupation.

There were a lot of Germans in Vincennes; it was traditionally a garrison town. There were so many of them around the Château, which was only about two hundred yards away, that we couldn't fail to notice them as soon as we left the house. They were not frightening and did not seem interested in what was around them. When we had to start wearing the yellow star, we would avoid getting too close to them, but they mainly seemed embarrassed—especially the older ones—or looked away. It's true that the German soldiers based in Vincennes were mostly veterans; the others were defending Aryan civilization on the Russian front.

At the same time, the arrogance of the French police knew no bounds. You could sense in their attitude the zeal they would show in carrying out the orders that came more or less directly from the Gestapo. Our six-pointed black-bordered yellow stars marked us. Our being Jews created disorder, and our badges gave us away as foreigners (how could a Jew be French?). We had everything to fear from those cops, who were well-fed, well-dressed and, increasingly, well-paid.

My father preferred to just smile when he saw the French police serving the Nazis. Before the war, as law enforcement officers in the Republic (the Third), they had the exact same attitude, and their contempt for foreigners was already very obvious. Except that their coercive power was relatively limited, because their harshest actions could only lead to expulsion, even though they sometimes allowed themselves to beat people up just to maintain authority. In 1942, they realized that they had the power of life and death over these people whose yellow stars marked them as different from other foreigners. The prefecture of police had a list of these undesirables, and they were to go and pick them up at dawn. It was done with no difficulty. The Nazis knew they could count on these mercenaries, who were armed to the teeth, and even had submachine guns, to see that the New Order and the racial laws were respected.

On July 16, 1942, like the day before, like almost every day, the atmosphere was morose. It was a time of daily horror, for Jews much more than for other people, because in addition to the constraints resulting from the occupation, Jews were specifically targeted and persecuted. Adults had to have an ironclad morale not to succumb to fear. The bad news every day brought only intensified the next day's fear.

For two years, my father had worn a mask of optimism so as not to show his children the worry that must have been gnawing at him. He probably stopped smiling only when we were not with him. I loved his laugh, a full-throated laugh that showed his gold teeth (the only luxury he had ever allowed himself). Until the dawn of July 16, 1942, I never saw him afraid, or at least showing fear. This was not just an act; it was an expression of his determination to continue to live joyfully, at least within the family.

My father was not merely a good man, he was the very image of goodness. It wasn't in his nature to unquestioningly accept dogma, obligations or prohibitions, and he was uncomfortable in Poland, but he seemed happy living in France. At least, he strived to believe that his children had been born in the land of liberty, and he felt we were lucky. As for him, he had done what he could. There was a joyful closeness between us, and he was delighted to see my sister and me playing the role of little French kids. He knew very well, however, that it wouldn't be that easy, but the integration he had hoped for in France after having missed it in Poland would finally come about, respite from a hellish flight that had gone on for centuries. Having children who were apparently accepted in the country of exile he had chosen was already success to him. His stories of Poland at war, Palestine, Egypt and Italy revealed him to me not as a fugitive but as a true hero. I admired him. What I knew of his life seemed like an amazing adventure. He was an intellectual educated in the schools of Poland, and he spoke Polish fluently—which wasn't always the case for Polish Jews—as well as Russian, and he was also studying Hebrew; in addition, he spoke German as easily as he did Yiddish. His height impressed me. To me, he was the most fabulous father. I was not ashamed to climb into his lap, without saying anything, without asking for anything, content just to stare at him and run my hands through his already graying hair. He was so myopic that he had trouble shaving, and often on Sundays I would watch my mother give him a shave, a ritual that showed the natural cooperation between these two perfectly matched individuals.

My mother was all calm and possibility, while my father was essentially happiness, despite the difficulties he had faced over the nearly twenty years he had lived in France. Our lives were tough, and more so when new worries were added to that of hard, poorly paid work. But we always had enough to eat, because my mother did everything to make us children feel we were living in reasonable affluence. We didn't realize what sacrifices our parents had made, but later, we remembered many little things that had gone unnoticed at the time and understood how difficult it had been. Other than on Sunday, which was almost always a special day in our house, we did not know what our parents ate. During the week, my sister and I had lunch in the school cafeteria, which meant that we didn't eat with them. At the markets, they usually just ate a sandwich while selling their wares. In the evening, with the four of us crammed into our little kitchen, my parents ate from the same plate, explaining that this was the custom in Poland between married couples, and that, besides, the table was too small for four plates. We found that logical, and since our parents always seemed like a pair of lovers, it never occurred to us to question what they said. In 1942, my father was fifty and my mother forty-two, but they were an amazingly close couple. That gave us peace of mind during a time when we had everything to fear, when adversity was more common than good luck.

How could we imagine it would all end with the country losing its self-respect and embracing absolute evil? Some thirteen thousand people suddenly found themselves excluded from the community, and there was no reaction. After all, it was only Jews, and it was wartime, and deep France had a lot of other things to worry about. People had to keep living, without asking themselves questions, without looking back at those who had disappeared along the way. It was every man for himself and the devil take the hindmost. That expression had never seemed truer in this cruel situation in which people who wished to live freely could not worry about those who had been plunged into uncertainty. As long as everything was fine for those who felt they had nothing to feel guilty about, their neighbors' future didn't matter to them.

Since May 1941, we had been hearing vague rumors of an imminent roundup. On the eve of July 16, 1942, that information had circulated more emphatically. A few police officers had even—it appears—warned their Jewish friends. Did immigrant Jews really have friends who were policemen? My parents did not so much disregard these warnings as disbelieve them; in fact, I could say they were no longer frightened by them. The threat of a roundup became a reasonable possibility, one they had finally resigned themselves to. A fate it was no longer possible to escape. A necessary stage before the end of the turmoil.

During the first mass arrests, in 1941, women had not been arrested, nor had children. The men would stay at home so as not to endanger their families in the event of reprisals. There was nothing to be done but wait until political prospects might suggest a different attitude. Usually we awaited the next day in uncertainty, hoping for reassuring news, which never came. In any case, things couldn't be worse than in Russia sixty years earlier. Jews were being arrested and put in camps outside Paris, but the prospect of deportations was completely unforeseeable. The outcome, though inevitable, was unbelievable, because it was something that had never occurred, and to escape it would have required not having fallen into the trap of registering as Jews in 1940. We had a perfect Polack family name, and according to the racist definition, we didn't "look Jewish," so the bluff would certainly have worked. But things weren't that simple. We also would have had to leave the neighborhood or even the city, and my parents would have had to change their work. Leaving for the southern zone was impossible, because my parents didn't have enough money and didn't know anyone there, and they would still have been foreigners. Staying in Vincennes without registering would have guaranteed their being denounced, and in 1940, it seemed there was nothing worse than disobeying the law. To us as foreigners, there was little difference between the law of Pétain's Vichy regime and that of Daladier, who, from 1938 until the war, had already enacted decree-laws against foreigners. After the declaration of war, many foreigners had been interned, particularly German anti-fascists, Jews among them, who had sought refuge in France between 1933 and 1939.

For lack of other prospects, we had to resign ourselves to waiting. Anxiety reigned, but we tried not to think too much about the future. We became accustomed to living in this atmosphere without obsessing, without even questioning the inevitability of the constant persecution, as a long time had passed since the last acts of violence. Those conducting the racial war were different and had different methods, but from generation to generation, new tormentors arose in the war against the Jews: the Russians before the First World War, then the Poles and the Romanians, and since Hitler had come to power, the Germans. Each time, the Jews had had to submit, to wait for the next pogrom, the next limitation of their rights, the next prohibitions and obligations—and flee a little further. This time, we had our backs to the wall, waiting for the next stage, not knowing what it would be. Perhaps my father sensed in a confused way that there was no longer a way out. Without talking to us (except maybe to my mother), he was clearly preparing himself for the separation he felt was near ever since he had stopped hearing from his two brothers who had been interned in Pithiviers in May 1941. In June 1942, they had already been deported, but we didn't know that yet. The virtual certainty of joining his brothers in a detention whose end was unknown to him must have, if not tempered his dread, then at least allowed him to await his arrest without too much anxiety. At any rate, he never broached the subject with his children or spoke to us of the fears he may have felt, and until the end, until that evening of July 15, 1942, he kept his unfailing smile and the steadfast good humor that was no mere facade.

Although he tried as best he could to keep his morale up, my father was often silent. In the evening, back home from his job as a laborer on a public works site, where he had been working since being banned from plying his trade at the markets, he was exhausted and spoke less. We attributed his silence to fatigue, and then the approaching summer vacation made us oblivious, even though there was no question of our leaving Paris. Most evenings, we went to the Bois de Vincennes, where my father would join us later. He would sit with his back against a tree, holding a newspaper, seemingly absorbed in his reading, and we didn't know how preoccupied he might be. He had long ago stopped talking about Poland, his adventurous youth, that family in Radom that we didn't know and that he hadn't had any word from in a long time.[1] He had also stopped telling the stories of pogroms that made me tremble, stories of drunken Cossacks coming into little towns on horseback, slashing, looting, burning houses, tearing out old men's beards. "Run, Abrashka, or watch out for your side-curls!" That was well before the war. I always wanted to know how my father had lived when he was my age, especially because he was a good storyteller. And I was a good audience. The stories of the persecutions interested me as much as those about the wars in my books on the history of France. I would listen, divided between horror and the satisfaction that my parents had managed to escape the violence. It's true my father didn't have a beard; this simplistic explanation constructed by my child's mind was enough for me.

---

1. Thus he never knew that his brother who had remained in Poland and was a Communist leader in Radom had been shot in September 1939 when the Germans arrived in the city.

2

LOST CHILDREN

IN FRANCE, there were no undisciplined Cossacks, only disciplined German soldiers who obeyed the laws of war. The best evidence of this was that in two years of occupation, nothing very serious had happened to us, aside from the word *Jew* on our identity cards and the lovely decoration displayed on our chests for all to see. We did not yet know it was from the French police that we ultimately would have the most to fear. We did not know that they would anticipate the demands of the Nazis. How could we have imagined that the heads of the French police would suggest to the Gestapo that not only should women be arrested, but also children? It was unthinkable.

Frenzied accomplices of the executioners—as if they were taking advantage of the German occupation to settle their own scores—those in charge of the French police did not want to leave any trace of their misdeeds. There must be no survivors to remember the racial violence committed in France by Frenchmen. If the occupation had lasted a few years, or even a few months longer, we would all have taken our final voyage, along with the Jews of French lineage, who had been relatively protected until then. Children must not be allowed to bear witness to the murder of their parents. Into the ovens with them. Infants still in the cradle would have gone with their mothers on their first and last voyage. Even people who were bedridden would not have been spared. No more Jews, and no trace of them. France would be as *Judenrein* as Nazi Germany. As for the

French from France, they would have been so happy to have a new lease on life that they would hardly have paid attention to the disappearance of some three hundred and fifty thousand people. The investigation I carried out in Vincennes clearly shows that it would all have been quicky forgotten.

It is indeed extraordinary that the mayor of Vincennes, or at least his administration, should be unable to say how many Jews were arrested in the city on July 16, 1942. It's a wretched task, a sad calculation. There were survivors, and a certain number of children—including myself—miraculously escaped the massacre when they were practically on the verge of boarding the train for deportation. We are still here, but the misdeeds of the police have never really been exposed to the light of day, let alone punished.

As long as the police administration—under whatever regime—does not condemn the roundup of July 16, 1942, and express its regret, we can conclude that it does not consider that action reprehensible, despite the fact that it exemplifies the most despicable Nazi perversion. The silence that has lasted so long shows that the police want to hide their odious past as mercenaries. This is understandable, since the police regularly make major blunders; in fact, it is a habit of theirs. How important were a few more or a few less Jews yesterday; and how important are a few Arabs roughed up today or brutally repressed tomorrow?

The day must come when a minister of the interior will remind the French in general and the cops in particular that certain actions should be added to the list of police misdeeds. Why, when the justice system deals so readily with petty criminals, were those who delivered thousands of children into the hands of the Gestapo not dragged before the courts?

To my last breath, I will bear witness against that institution of law enforcement that never recoiled before the most heinous acts. How could I not demand justice for the police officials of Vichy, who showed themselves to be even more base than their bosses in the Gestapo? And to think that the likes of Bousquet, Leguay and prefects such as Papon had supposedly been honest public servants before June 1940. They no doubt did their duty—or so we are told—during the "phoney war."[1] Then, becoming leaders of legal gangs, suppliers to the extermination camps, channels of communication for the anti-Jewish section of the Gestapo, they gave orders to tens of thousands of cops, who followed them faith-

---

1. The "phoney war" refers to a period of eight months at the start of the Second World War during which there were no major hostilites on the western front; it began when the invasion of Poland impelled the United Kingdom and France to declare war on Germany on September 3, 1939, and ended in the spring of 1940 with the Germany invasion of France and the Low Countries. [PA]

fully. I can only repeat once again: *these men, like the Nazi torturers, were murderers, and, like the Nazi torturers, they were guilty of crimes against humanity.* Unlike their German counterparts, they did not require long years under the Nazi regime to learn to become executioners; it took them only a few months.

I consider this charge against the French police a necessary act of public hygiene. French people who do not know (as well as those who do not want to know) and those who believe that the Nazis alone were responsible for the racial persecution perpetrated in France between 1941 and 1944 must be made aware of the role that can be played by a police force recruited not only from the rural population but also from the dregs of society.

How many of us are there who were rounded up and then released a few hours later? How many of us are there who were lost children, abandoned by mistake on the orders and counter-orders and interpretations of some police official? How many of us are there who have been ageless since the legalized murderers of Vichy and Berlin decided that we would no longer have parents? How many of our playmates, especially the youngest of them, never had the luck we did of escaping detention that day in spite of everything, and thus being saved? We are survivors of the absurd, and since 1942, after two years of horrible uncertainty, we have been taking the trains with everyone else, pretending to live as other people do, with the same concerns and the same passions. We had to put up a front, constantly pretending, and finally, we came to believe in the spectacle, rejoicing at the liberation of Paris, shouting our joy in victory in unison, while hiding our pain so as not to spoil other people's pleasure.

Most of the children of the deportees integrated very well into society, and even held what were considered prestigious positions. Among them were doctors, lawyers and businessmen, but also painters, writers and journalists, not to mention—of course—those who followed in their parents' footsteps and worked in the *shmate*[2] trade and did well in it. I don't think the survivors have any concerns in common—we share only the memory of those who died prematurely. But we must not join together under any banner or in the name of any ideology.[3]

---

2. Yiddish word meaning rag. Working in the *shmate* trade can involve manufacturing or selling textiles or clothing.
3. Remembering does not necessarily mean commemorating, especially not with a lot of fanfare. Moreover, I cannot discuss the victims of July 16, 1942, and all those who were to follow, with anyone who can stand by and witness the slow death of an oppressed people. Of course, I am referring here to the Palestinians. It is not on the battlefield or in cemeteries that the victims of barbarism should be honored, but by fighting to make sure that these things never happen again. Never again.

July 16, 1942, made orphans of us for the rest of our days. Not being able to see our parents grow old blocked our own aging. We had to learn very early to live without relying on a father or mother, but this premature responsibility, which should have hardened us, had a different result. Perhaps we became old children, like the aged and wizened dwarves people treat like adolescents.

I occasionally meet one of these eternal children, and their behavior, everything else being equal, is essentially the same as other people's. This is perfectly natural, but the fact remains that they all have something youthful in their gaze, in their tired smiles. They have rubbed shoulders with messengers from hell. For these lost children, abandoned to the unknown, uncared for by society, hell was Hitler and the Nazis, and most of all, it was the French cops, it was the indifference and the coldness of the population, it was the empty house and the fear of tomorrow. It was the obsession with the end of the war and the desperate need to survive until then, to be there for the return of our parents, because we didn't yet know that they had already gone up in smoke.

Having been removed from our natural setting, separated from our parents, plunged into uncertainty, cold and hunger, we had little in common with other children our age. Later, when the time came for us to settle into adult life, there was always an emptiness. Our children would not have grandparents. They would not know those touching old Polish Jews with their accent from far away, who had become French from force of habit, who would have loved them. Our children too were no doubt traumatized by that absence, those roots torn from their own memory.

Interview with Maurice Rajsfus

APRIL 11, 2016
CAFÉ LE ROSTAND | 6TH ARRONDISSEMENT, PARIS

S ITTING IN A CLASSIC Parisian café, Maurice Rajsfus speaks candidly in an interview with publisher Carrie Paterson and filmmaker Justine Malle to fill in some of the aspects of his work, political motivations, his family, and his life after the war. Many of these subjects have been covered in his dozens of previously published books, none of which are available to date in English. We order coffee, for it is pouring rain and cold, and sit outside under the awning where we are allowed to film and record. Maurice Rajsfus and his wife, Marie-Jeanne, together for over sixty years of marriage, sit together facing the Luxembourg Gardens.

Maurice Rajsfus' experience is unusual, and his attitude even more so. There is an ironic tone to his stories, but no bitterness. Before the questions begin, he pulls out a folder of photographs and documents, as well as the yellow star he once wore. It is sheathed in plastic and has darkened with time. "I wore it for two years, so that's why it's dirty," he says. His face takes on a somber expression as we take turns holding it. He explains that his mother sewed the star to another piece of fabric and reinforced the edges. She made a concerted effort because she said it had to last, he explains. "After all, I was a fourteen-year-old boy." We snap a photo of his hand holding the star, which appears on the cover of this book, and start recording.

Q: What did you bring for us?

I'd like to show you two documents that will help explain my work.

This picture, a very tragic one, was taken in 1921 in Radom, in the south of Poland: [on the bottom row] my father, Nahum, and his fiancée, Rivka, my mother; my father's brother, and one of his sisters. The tragedy of this photo is that nearly everyone here was killed. My uncle Yechiel was shot by the Germans when they came into Radom in September 1939. [In the top row,] these two are twins, Aron and Faivel, who were arrested in Paris during the first roundups on May 14, 1941, and deported one year later to Auschwitz. And David, the older brother of my father who in 1920, after the Red Army was defeated outside Warsaw, went back to the Soviet Union with them. But during Stalin's purges between '36–'38 he disappeared in Ukraine. So he was the victim of another repression.

These are my parents. My mother was about twenty years old, my father thirty. We were arrested together on July 16, 1942, in Paris, and they were deported to Auschwitz on July 27.

And among all my uncles, Pinchas is the only one who survived. Well, it's a long story... When Poland was invaded in 1939, a temporary Polish government was established in Paris. All Polish men from France were called up to join the newly created Polish army in France. And the twins didn't want to go, but he went. He became a prisoner of war in 1940, and he was the only one who came back in 1945. The Germans, the Nazis, didn't harm the Jewish prisoners of war. They were sometimes isolated, but never persecuted as Jews.

The Plocki siblings: Top row, left to right: Faivel, David, Pinchas, Aron. Bottom row, left, Yechiel; in the center, Rivka Rajsfus, the author's mother whose maiden name he has kept as a memorial, and his father Nahum. The author's aunt Ruchela is on the right. Not pictured are aunts Chanah and Zlata (both of whom disappeared from the Radom ghetto in 1942–43) and the author's grandparents, Avrum Plocki and Gita Rajsfus. Radom, Poland. 1921.

266

Q: How did your mother and father come to live in France?

I have something else to show you, a letter, which will answer that question indirectly. My father was part of a left-wing Zionist movement in his youth. He wanted to go to Palestine in 1912, but the Zionists who went there didn't know that Palestinians actually lived there! Maybe just some Bedouins with sheep... The Turks didn't allow him entry because they were allied with Austria and Germany against Russia, France, Germany and England, so they didn't recognize Russian subjects and Russian Poland.

In 1922 he wanted to try again. He had been in Vienna. He was teaching Hebrew at a high school, and he couldn't get a visa for Palestine. There was the famous [British] "White Paper," [an interpretation of the Balfour Declaration], which restricted the immigration of Jews to Palestine to keep a [population] balance with Arabs. He took a boat anyway. But as he didn't have a visa, he wasn't allowed to disembark. After a few months of traveling, he wrote this letter. We know he arrived in Haifa, then part of Greece, on December 21. He went all around the Mediterranean Sea, and the boat brought him back to Trieste where he had started. Trieste was more or less Austrian—Austria was fighting against Italy there. He asked to be repatriated. But he was stuck on the boat because he didn't have a visa. I don't know if you know the book *Planète sans visa* [a novel by Jean Malaquais published in 1947]? Well it was a little like that, because he couldn't leave the ship.

He wrote to the French consul in Trieste from the ship, the *Dalmatian*, in 1923—I suppose that's how he got a visa to France. He probably came to Paris at the end of January 1923.

This is how we became French. My mother arrived one year later. They were already engaged.

Q: You mention the pogroms in the East in your book. They were one reason that your family left Poland?

I think it is important to note that the repression of Jews was not limited by borders, that it existed throughout Europe, for different reasons.

Q: What was France like for you and your family, as Jews?

France was still the land of Freedom when I was young, and I always considered myself a good French patriot. I was the best student in French history at school. It's often the case with immigrants' children. The best student with me in History class was named Borghi, the son of an Italian immigrant who was an anti-fascist and immigrated to Paris. He was the one who taught me about French history.

We had a laid-back life until the war, except that my parents petitioned for French nationality three times and never obtained it. Perhaps it would have saved their lives, although all the Jews who were nationalized after 1936 were denationalized under Pétain and arrested afterwards... [In my early years] it was a very liberal period, in a positive way. The foreigners' children became French with a simple declaration. I petitioned [for citizenship] on April 9th, 1928, and on the 10th I was French. It was *droit du sol* [birthright citizenship]. Notwithstanding, the mayor of the town I was born in was named Pierre Laval![1] He was a socialist at that time.

And to think, he officiated at the marriage of my parents.

Q: What did you do after the roundups?

After the roundups, when my sister and I were set free by chance, we moved into my parents' small apartment of three hundred square feet. My sister kept going to high school. And people forgot about us, even with us wearing the star. The people who had seen us with it would have informed the police if we weren't wearing it. Denouncement was a favorite pastime during the Occupation—there were roughly five million denunciation letters. When I was fourteen years old, a friend of my mother wanted me to learn a trade, so I learned jewel setting. That's what I did during the war.

Q: And you were still living in your parents' flat?

Yes, but it was terrible! Even the war prisoners' children all had their mothers, but we had no one.

When my parents were deported, my sister explained our situation to our flat's owner, that we were out of money. And this man, an Italian immigrant, told her no law anticipated this. We asked for a rent reduction. It was still hell.

Then, at the end of the Occupation there was a rumor saying there would be a new roundup. It was at the start of June 1944. My sister hid at a friend's, and I hid at the house of my boss' friends in the Vexin [region] in Normandy. I stayed there until the Liberation. Nobody knew where I was.

Q: Was there a network of Resistance fighters in the Vexin?

There were a lot of "Resistance fighters," but they only appeared the day of the Liberation. The day the Americans arrived, the so-called

---

1. The same collaborationist Pierre Laval who became the head of the Vichy government from 1942–1944 and was later executed under de Gaulle for "high treason" and collaboration with the Nazis.

Maurice Rajsfus, April 11, 2016.

Resistance fighters wore armbands. Then "France Libération" was every-where. In reality, there was no Resistance in the Vexin. The Resistance existed, but it wasn't what people were talking about—the "Resistance" grew very strong when Germany enacted forced labor laws in 1943. According to de Gaulle, all of France had been resistant. This was a com-plete lie. I don't have to tell you that, do I? Commonly speaking the gen-eral state of mind and mood of the French in 1943–1944 was to hope that the Americans would come soon, but also stop dropping bombs.

Q: What did you do after the Liberation?
I went back to Paris. I continued my apprenticeship without any joy or commitment to the profession. The next seven to eight years I lived a half-bohemian life. I worked in a factory, in vacations camps, theater—I was an actor, a lot of things… I worked as a docker. But I didn't have the body of a docker. I did anything to survive, but I didn't want to have a boss, and least of all to be a soldier. It was a hard time; I was struggling. Then I did a degree program to become a holiday camps supervisor. And at my first holiday camp in 1953, I met a young woman who was a teacher. *Looks to his wife, seated on his left.* The next year, I went back to this holiday camp. With she being the supervisor's wife! We got married. She was only eighteen, so we needed her mother's consent. Soon we had children, and I had to stop this bohemian life.

Q: How many children?
Two. But four grandchildren and three great-grandchildren.

Q: And then what did you do?
I started to work as a printer. I did final copy corrections. I quickly advanced and became an editor. It was a big publishing group that disappeared, called *La Vie des Métiers*, and then I worked as an editor and journalist at *Le Monde*.
At the same time I never stopped being politically active.

Q: Within the Communist Party?
At the beginning, yes.

Q: How did you get involved with the Communist Party?
Like many children of immigrants who were deported, I wanted to be part of the revolution. Just after the Liberation, I had gone to the Communist Party and the "Jeunesse communiste" [Mouvement Jeunesse Communistes de France, or MJCF, a political youth organization]. There I happened to meet again the policeman who had arrested us! In the Communist Party in Vincennes. Mulot was his name. They were extremely nationalist at the Communist Party, no one could criticize French people or institutions. I didn't leave the Communist Party, but I was kicked out in 1946. I was a bad asset.

Q: But you continued as an activist in 1946?
Yes, as an agitator against the police.

Q: Why didn't they want an agitator?
At that time, when the Party was still part of the government, all the opponents—like [Communist] André Marty—were police informants. I had this double charge against me when I was eighteen years old—police agitator and "*hitléro-trotskiste*" in the jargon of Moscow, a pro-Trotskyist agent. The Trotskyists were extraordinary (compared to the Stalinists), very interesting and cultured people.

Q: In what organization?
The International Communist Party. But I quickly understood that I couldn't work within their authoritarianism. I left the 4th International in 1949. And I left with someone you must be familiar with, [Cornelius]

Castoriadis. An economist, a philosopher. And with friends we created a commission against the deployment of soldiers to Algeria. During this campaign, we made a lot of trouble. I found myself working again with many people formerly from the Communist Party and and the PSU [Parti Socialiste Unifé; United Socialist Party].

Throughout the war in Algeria this developed a lot, the second left.

Q: And the United Socialist Party?

It disappeared. [Politicians] Édouard Depreux and [Michel] Rocard arrived then, unfortunately.

When I left the United Socialist Party in May 1968, I was very politically active. Meanwhile I had made a professional career at *Le Monde* where I started as an editor, when they fired me because I was an activist.

I worked as a journalist, and when I retired I started to write books.

Q: How long were you a journalist?

Thirty years. From 1958 to 1988. The last ten years of my career I was a freelance journalist. I had made a good living as a journalist, so I had the time afterward to write.

Q: Is this how you came to write your book Les Juifs dans la Collaboration [Jews in the Collaboration], *about the role of the UGIF in the deportations?*

At the end of the '70s, I started to develop a personal interest in the history of war. That's how I discovered this institution of French Jews

Maurice Rajsfus' journalist identification card with his *nom de plume* "Michel Marc."

collaborating during the war. My book is now out of print. Maybe you could find it; someone made a pirate copy. It is online.

You have to understand that those people weren't the usual political collaborators, but long-time French Jews, including old war soldiers with medals from 1914, who thought they wouldn't have any trouble [with the Nazis] if they had control over the mass of immigrants in France... They contributed not directly, but indirectly to their arrest.

Q: It's a Marxist point of view. Were their actions motivated by class difference?
This is what Hannah Arendt says.
But this isn't the problem. It is that long-time French Jews absolutely hated the Jews who came from Poland.

Q: Where did you get this information?
Well, from everywhere.
There was a saying: "Just because we have welcomed them here, doesn't mean they are allowed to break the dishes."

Q: So, in your view, how did the UGIF collaborate?
I'm going to give you a horrible example from the roundups that took place on July 16, 1942. The night before, at the UGIF's office on Rue de la Bienfaisance, they prepared labels to put around the necks of children who were to be separated from their parents. So they knew about it. It wasn't innocent.

This organization was huge and [worked] between Paris and other big French cities. There were 1800 employees. The terrible ending to the story was that once the Nazis didn't need them anymore... They were eradicated too, even the French.

I met some survivors, but it was very hard to get them to speak...

Also, the narrow-minded people of the UGIF felt that children had to continue living in Jewish surroundings. Some of those children's households were rounded up for deportation in 1943–1944. Have you heard about the "Houses of Isieux"? It's a place were they put children, and they were snatched by [Klaus] Barbie in 1944. The Resistance had told the UGIF to spread out the children, but they didn't want to. This communitarianism was a very tribal phenomena.

So *Les Juifs dans la Collaboration* was my first book in 1980. I worked on it at the Archives in Paris.

Q: The Archives in the 4th arrondissement?

Yes. But they didn't know what I was doing. They understood later on. The feeling was that you shouldn't talk about those things, because it was within the community. I wrote a book about the camps in Drancy. I said there were just as many as Jewish kapos there. It was a horror. In times of trouble, humanity disappears.

Q: Are you considered an enemy by the Jewish community?

There's a distinguished historian who wrote in one of his books that my books should be looked at with caution. I wouldn't say I had an obsession, but I did have to settle some personal scores... Yet, I've also written many books about the Second World War that weren't related to the Jewish question. I wrote about the censorship during the 1914 war, the French Resistance, the liberation of Paris, much more about the police, almost twenty books. I cannot be considered as an anti-Semite. How do you say that in German?

Q: Selbsthasser? [A self-hating person.]

A *"Selbsthasser"* to me is a troublemaker, someone who is an agitator.

Q: One might say that is exactly what's interesting about you, that you are an agitator. On the Internet it says that a bomb was thrown through the window of the publisher of Les Juifs dans la Collaboration?

Not a bomb. The place was destroyed! It used to be here, in this neighborhood. After *Les Juifs dans la Collaboration*, I published a book called *Sois Juif et tais-toi!* [Be a Jew and Shut Up!], telling the story of the Jews in the Consistoire in 1930–1940, which explained their behavior during the Occupation. After that, I believe integrists [reactionary conservative Jews] set the publishing house on fire.

Q: So, the fire was due to the second book?

Yes.

Q: Were you afraid?

No. At that time several bookshops had been set on fire in Paris. And a bookseller named Jonas, who was in the 13th at that time, after a fire had been set in his store, sent all the damaged, burned books to the authors, and I have a copy of mine.

Q: But the culprits were conservative Jews?

We have no proof, but those people really didn't like me. That was clear with my third book *Quand j'étais Juif* [When I Was a Jew]. When I was a guest on a TV-show, I was asked why I called it "When I Was a Jew"—I couldn't make the title "People Know That I'm a Jew Because I'm Wearing a Star," so I had a shorter title.

Next I wrote *L'An prochain, la révolution* [Next Year, The Revolution], relating the fate of the Jewish communist immigrants in France between 1930–1945. Then I wrote about the Palestinian problem. In 1984, for the first time, I traveled to Palestine and the occupied territories, as my father had done. I went to see what's going on in Israel, and it was worse than what I had imagined. I published four books about that.

But I had fewer problems with the Israelis than with the Jews in France. My books are in Israeli universities.

Q: It surprises me...

It shouldn't.

When I went to Israel, I entered with another name, but once I was there, I was Rajsfus.

Q: But why?

Because otherwise, I wouldn't have obtained a visa, maybe...

Q: Because of your political activities and opinions?

For a time I had two passports. One for Israel and one for the Arabic countries. In Jordan or Algeria, I couldn't have shown a passport with Israeli stamps.

In 1990, with several friends, I founded the "Ras l'front" movement, an anti-Le-Pen movement...[2]

And then in 1994 I started publishing "L'Observatoire des Libertés Publiques" [The Observer of Public Freedom]: basically "Copwatching" [monitoring police activities against people and police brutality].

Q: The magazine was only about that?

The magazine was only about that. I had a connection with Canadians who did the same. So I did that for twenty years. Many were glad to get the

---

2. Ras l'front, an association of far-left-wing organizations, was extremely active in the 1990s against the rise of nationalist parties in France and fascist ideas. They worked together and promoted leftist causes through a monthly publication as well as actions. One of the most famous was a five-hour stand off with police and firemen after the unfurling of an enormous banner "No to fascism, no to racism" on the walls of the Paris Opera on the occasion of a Jean-Marie Le Pen rally in the public square in 1995. Rajsfus was the president of Ras l'front from 1991–1999.

information, but only a few gave me some. So I cut out everything I could find that had been printed in the national press.

Q: *You did everything by yourself?*
Every month, between four to eight pages, with references I could find in the press. I have about thirty thousand examples on index cards at home, compiled before computers existed. It was a pastime like any other.

Q: *What happened to it?*
For fifteen years, it existed on paper. Then, when I put it on the Internet, I realized that the three hundred subscribers I had, paying ten euros a month, changed into a thousand visits a day, [but] it was for free. I didn't know who was watching it, I had no feedback anymore. So I stopped after twenty years.

Q: *And no one carried on?*
No. I offered it to many people.

Q: *Regarding the police, what can we learn from the past, considering the reflection and analysis about the yellow star in your writings?*
Once, the cops arrested some illegal Chinese workers in Paris who were working in fashion. When they arrested them, they put stamps on their wrists. This has nothing to do with the Jewish star, but there's always the temptation to mark people.

Q: *So there has been a continuum of racism in France...*
In 1939, there was strong Catholic anti-Semitism, calling Jews "murderers of Jesus-Christ" and so on... and it went on during the Occupation with a lot of stupid nationalists who had the same ideas as the Nazi anti-Semites.

The Jewish statutes from Vichy in September/October 1940 went further than the laws of Nuremberg from 1935. In Hitler's Germany, Jews were considered as such for religious reasons, whereas in France, it was because of "race." Vichy made the race laws worse. Meanwhile a lot of good French people let out their aggressions. The Jews had suffered so much that they kept their mouths shut.

And racism came back, in two ways—with the asinine behavior of the *pieds-noirs* Jews [colonial French Algerians] who came to France in '62, and with the hatred of the Jews conveyed by Muslim fundamentalists.

There's also this inane competition between the number of anti-Semitic and anti-Arab occurrences. Acts of anti-Semitism are published, but statistics about crimes against halal butchers are rarely published.

Q: We would also like to ask you about the role you played in the trial of collaborator Maurice Papon.

I had written in my newspaper that any prefect could have played the same role that Papon did in Bordeaux, that there were four hundred Papons at the time of the Liberation. So in September 1997, I was surprised to be informed that I was called to be a witness... The lawyer, Alexandre Varaut, must have read my book, where I explain that all the interior administration of the French camps were led by Jews. They were the ones writing the reports, and they were the ones ordered by the Gestapo to organize a convoy of a thousand people. They had to write down a thousand names during the night.

Papon said that the Jews deported the Jews. So I was called as a witness by his lawyer, basing his argument for Papon's innocence on this. And when you are called as a witness you have to go; if you don't, they send policemen. I wrote a letter to the president of the Court in Bordeaux saying that by no means would a son of victims testify for the auxiliary of the hangman. And I didn't go to the trial. I was excused.

Some months later, when Papon was condemned to ten years in prison, [at his age, a life sentence], he said to his lawyer when he came out of the court: " The Jews are striking again..."

Q: And the last question, How have people reacted to your work in English speaking countries?

My books haven't been translated. I do receive some letters from people who read them in French. I wonder if people will be shocked by what I wrote in the Foreword, when I recall that in 1942, when they stuck the Star on us, in the United States, they put all the Japanese families that were there into internment camps, with no exceptions, even though some of them had been there since the end of the 19th century with the construction of the railway system.

Justine Malle interviews Maurice Rajsfus in Paris, April 11, 2016.